GROUND STUDIES FOR PILOTS
Volume 4

GROUND STUDIES FOR PILOTS

Volume 4

METEOROLOGY

R. B. Underdown
FRMetS MRAeS
formerly Director of Ground Training and latterly
Principal, College of Air Training, Hamble

BSP PROFESSIONAL BOOKS

OXFORD LONDON EDINBURGH

BOSTON PALO ALTO MELBOURNE

First published 1988

British Library
Cataloguing in Publication Data

Taylor, S.E.T.
Ground studies for pilots.
Vol. 4: Meteorology
1. Transport planes—Piloting
I. Title   II. Underdown,
R.B.
629.132′5216   TL710

ISBN 0–632–02026–1

BSP Professional Books
A division of Blackwell Scientific
  Publications Ltd
Editorial Offices:
Osney Mead, Oxford OX2 0EL
  (Orders: Tel. 0865 240201)
8 John Street, London WC1N 2ES
23 Ainslie Place, Edinburgh EH3 6AJ
Three Cambridge Center, Suite 208,
  Cambridge, MA 02142, USA
667 Lytton Avenue, Palo Alto
  California 94301, USA
107 Barry Street, Carlton
  Victoria 3053, Australia

Set by DP Photosetting, Aylesbury, Bucks
Printed and bound in Great Britain by
Hollen Street Press, Slough

Contents

Preface

Having revised and updated *Aviation Law for Pilots* and Volumes 1 (Radio Aids), 2 (Plotting and Flight Planning) and 3 (Navigation General) of *Ground Studies for Pilots*, this completely new volume on aviation meteorology has been written to complete the range of 'non-airworthiness subjects' that are in the professional pilots' syllabus.

The text and examples reflect both the professional pilots' licences requirements and aviation practice of the late 1980s. I am grateful to the World Meteorological Organisation for permission to use the cloud descriptions from Chapter II of the 1956 edition of the abridged version of the International Cloud Atlas published by WMO, and to George Philip & Son Limited for authority to use their outline map of the world on which to superimpose the data of figures 15.4, 15.5 and 15.11. My especial thanks are due to my former colleague at the College of Air Training, Mr Max Johnson, for kindly reading the text and for his useful comments.

Civil Aviation Authority examination questions are available by post from the CAA, Printing and Publication Services, Greville House, 37 Gratton Road, Cheltenham, Glos GL50 2BN.

Hamble   Roy Underdown
1987

Introduction

Meteorology is the study of the atmosphere – its composition, structure, properties and behaviour. Travellers down the ages have found their journeys influenced to a greater or lesser degree by the weather. An aircraft flying through the atmosphere is probably the most vulnerable of all of the forms of travel.

The science of meteorology has expanded greatly since the mid-nineteenth century and particularly from World War II on, in parallel with advances in aviation. The field of aviation meteorology to which this volume is devoted may be considered in general terms as:

  (a) What elements are likely to be of significance to aircraft operations, e.g. fog, clouds, winds, storms, etc., and why.
  (b) What information is available to the aviator and how he can interpret the information and apply it.
  (c) What characteristic changes in meteorological conditions can be expected on long flights, i.e. the world's climates.

The syllabus of subject matter that a pilot should know reflects the importance of meteorology to aviators. It is not the intention of the authorities to turn aviators into meteorologists but it is self-evident that a pilot must be able to understand the language and significance of meteorological information given to him and to recognise and correctly interpret the weather conditions about him so that his flight is made with the maximum degree of safety, efficiency and comfort.

Like mariners, experienced aviators are weather-conscious whether they are on duty or not. Early development of a 'weather-eye' is only to be encouraged. Meteorology is a subject where practical exercises are continuously occurring about one!

1: The Atmosphere and Atmospheric Pressure

Meteorology is the science of the atmosphere – the deep gaseous envelope which surrounds the earth – covering both weather and climate. There are various approaches to studying this science but whichever approach is used it will first be necessary to consider the nature of the atmosphere and its basic properties before going on to study their interrelationship.

Composition

Up to the maximum altitudes at which civil and military aircraft are normally operated, the atmosphere is made up of a uniform mixture of gases which we call air. It is an important property of the atmosphere that this mixture of dry air can be assumed to be constant in its composition. With the dry air is mixed a variable amount of water vapour to give moist air. It does not matter whether the aircraft is flying at 2000 feet or 20 000 feet, in east or west longitudes, in the Northern or Southern Hemisphere – the same mixture of gases is affecting the crew, the passengers, the wings, the engines, the pressurisation and air conditioning systems and so on.

Essentially the properties of the air are those of the gases of which it is comprised – invisible, odourless, no taste, etc., so what are the main gases in the mixture? The proportions expressed by volume are:

nitrogen	78%
oxygen	21%
argon	0.93%
carbon dioxide	0.03%

with traces of other gases including ozone, carbon monoxide, the inert gases neon, helium, etc. The dominant gases are therefore nitrogen and oxygen. Incidentally, if you see an analysis of dry air by weight, it will show an approximately 3:1 ratio of nitrogen to oxygen – but you will remember from school that the molecular weight of oxygen (32) is greater than that of nitrogen (28).

Although for the purpose of the mathematical laws which have to be used in considering the behaviour of the atmosphere it is convenient to assume dry air, in reality there is invariably some water vapour present. Water vapour is also a gas which is invisible, odourless, without taste, etc., but only five-eighths the weight of dry air of a comparable temperature and pressure. The evaporation process which adds this water vapour to the atmosphere will be considered as we progress through the following chapters. Even more important to pilots, however, is the reverse process by which the invisible water vapour condenses out to a liquid or solid state. In this way, cloud, fog and mist, precipitation, frost and ice on aircraft are formed, so this process must be considered in detail.

The mix of water vapour with dry air to give moist air is, however, not the end of the story as far as the mix of the atmosphere is concerned. It will be necessary to consider solid pollutants which enter the air and may remain in suspension for long periods. Such pollutants are smoke particles from forest fires or man-made processes of burning fossil fuels, dust blown up by the wind and even, at low level, salt spray blown up off the open water.

Temperature structure

The International Civil Aviation Organisation (ICAO) has specified the conditions which aviation uses for a standard atmosphere of dry air (we will come to the units used shortly). The defined conditions of the International Standard Atmosphere (ISA) are:

1. At mean sea level (msl):

   Pressure   1013.25 millibars (hectopascals)

   Temperature $+15°C$

   Density   1225 grams/cubic metre (0.001225 grams/cubic centimetre)

2. Above mean sea level (amsl):

   (a) Temperature decreases 6.5 C deg/km (1.98 C deg/1000 ft) up to 11 km (36 090 ft) where it is $-56.5°C$.

   (b) From 11 km to 20 km (65 617 ft) temperature remains constant at $-56.5°C$.

   (c) From 20 km to 32 km (104 987 ft) temperature increases by 1 C deg/km (0.3 C deg/1000 ft).

In fact these values are not very far removed from the average conditions of temperate latitudes. As will be shown later, it is only necessary to specify the temperature conditions above mean sea level. Given the standard mean sea level values for pressure and density it is possible, from a knowledge of the temperature structure, to derive the pressure and density at any level in the standard atmosphere.

The lower parts of the atmosphere in which we are interested for aviation purposes are identified by their characteristic distribution of temperatures. On this basis, the lowest part of the atmosphere is known as the *Troposphere* and is distinguished by the decrease of temperature with increase of height. *Tropos* is Greek for turning and because of the temperature structure, this part of the atmosphere is subject to both horizontal and vertical motion. Water vapour is mixed throughout its vertical extent and the troposphere contains all of the cloud and weather in which we are interested. In practice, as well as the ICAO's specifications for ISA, the temperature lapse with height of the troposphere comes to an end at an altitude known as the *Tropopause*. Above the tropopause, one enters the *Stratosphere*. The tropopause thus marks the boundary between the troposphere and the stratosphere.

For basic study, it is convenient to assume a clear-cut transition from the troposphere to the stratosphere although this is not always true. For this reason, an upper air report or forecast may refer to a first and second tropopause where the 'first tropopause' is defined as the lowest level at which the temperature lapse

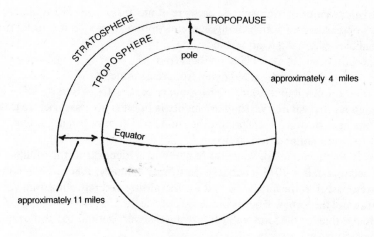

Fig. 1.1   The tropopause

rate decreases to 2 C deg/km (0.6 C deg/1000 ft) or less, provided that the
average lapse rate between this level and 2 km above it does not exceed 2 C deg/
km. Normally, the amount of water vapour in the stratosphere is insignificant.
However (and this is allowed for in ISA), as one climbs up through the
stratosphere it gradually warms in its upper levels due to the presence of ozone.
The amount of ozone and its consequent absorption of ultra-violet radiation is
variable with place and time. Its effect on radio transmissions is dealt with in
some detail in the companion volume, *Ground Studies for Pilots: Volume 1 –
Radio Aids.*

Beyond the stratosphere and aviation's operational altitudes, further 'shells'
of the atmosphere are recognised as one passes through the increasingly rarified
air into deep space. First comes the *mesosphere*, extending from an altitude of
about 50 km to around 80–90 km, and finally the *thermosphere* beyond that
height. Neither the mesosphere nor the thermosphere will concern us further.

Atmospheric pressure

Units

All gases exert pressure and the mixture of gases which comprise the atmosphere
is no exception, either at mean sea level or at altitude. Pressure is the force per
unit area exerted on a surface in contact with the gas. In other connections you
may have already come across p.s.i. (pounds per square inch) or the metric
measure of dynes per square centimetre. You will perhaps remember that 1 dyne
is the force required to produce an acceleration of 1 centimetre per second on a
mass of 1 gram.

As already seen in the definition of ISA, the unit ordinarily used in
meteorology in the UK is the millibar, which is tied into the metric system as
follows.

1 million dynes per square centimetre is called a pressure of 1 bar and is the

approximate value of atmospheric pressure at mean sea level. However, for the ready appreciation of subtle changes in atmospheric pressure, it is usual to use the millibar, where the relationship is:

    1 bar   = 1 000 millibars (mb)

    1 millibar = 1 000 dynes/square centimetre

    1 centibar = 10,000 dynes/square centimetre = 10 mb

Throughout this volume we shall use millibars but it is necessary before leaving the statement of units to mention other units which may be encountered in a meteorological connotation elsewhere.

Firstly the hectopascal, which in magnitude is identical to the millibar (i.e. 1013 hectopascals = 1013 millibars). As from 1 January, 1986, ICAO adopted the hectopascal as the approved unit for measuring and reporting atmospheric pressure and the term will be encountered outside the UK. However, the UK has told ICAO that for the foreseeable future the UK will continue to use the millibar as its pressure unit.

Secondly, pressure may be expressed in terms of the height of a column of mercury. The measurement of pressure by means of a mercury barometer is dealt with in Chapter 16 but the basic principle involved is that the pressure exerted by the atmosphere is balanced against that exerted by a column of mercury. As atmospheric pressure rises, so the mercury rises up the glass. Pressure may then be stated as, say, 29.9 inches mercury (Hg) or, say, 760 mm Hg.

Finally, mean sea level pressure may variously be found referred to as 14.7 lb per square inch or 10 tons to the square metre, but not in this volume.

At mean sea level, our bodies are accustomed to the pressure of the air acting upon us all the time, whether it is 1003, 1013 or 1023 millibars, and subtle changes of pressure which may produce significant weather changes go undetected by our bodily senses. A convenient definition of atmospheric pressure which enables pilots to visualise the situation is:

The atmospheric pressure at any point is equivalent to the weight of the column of air of unit cross-sectional area extending upwards to the top of the atmosphere from that point.

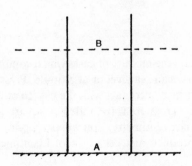

Fig. 1.2   Pressure decrease with height

Thus in fig. 1.2 at A atmospheric pressure is exerted by the whole column above A. At B it is the column above point B that has to be considered and will be less than that at A by the weight of the column AB. From this we have the very important rule, which is the basis of altimetry, that pressure *always* decreases with increase of altitude. The rate of pressure decrease with altitude increase may vary but nevertheless it always decreases as you climb. Pressure also varies horizontally which can also have important implications.

Variation of pressure with height

Although air density has yet to be dealt with in detail, it is common knowledge that warm air is less dense and lighter than a corresponding mass of cold air. Related to the column of air AB in fig. 1.2, this column will be lighter or heavier depending upon its mean temperature. In fig. 1.3, a column of air (MN) with ISA conditions is compared with two other columns, CC_1 which is colder than standard, and WW_1 which is warmer than standard.

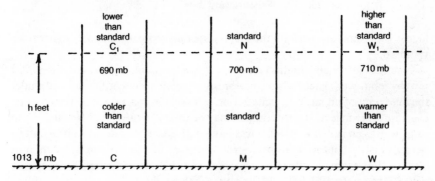

Fig. 1.3   Pressure variation with height

By altitude 'h' in the standard column MN, the upper level pressure has decreased to, say, 700 mb. If we now consider column CC_1, this air is colder than MN so it will be more dense (i.e. heavier) and pressure will decrease more rapidly with increase of altitude than in the standard column MN. Thus by altitude 'h' the upper level pressure will be less at C_1 than at N, say 690 mb. On the other hand, ascending through column WW_1 where upper air mean temperatures are higher than standard, the pressure decrease with altitude is slower than standard and the pressure at W_1 will be greater than that at N, say 710 mb.

The determining factor is the mean temperature of the columns of air MN, CC_1 and WW_1 giving the rule that:

In areas where upper air mean temperatures are relatively high, upper level pressures are relatively high and conversely, above air where upper mean temperatures are relatively low, the upper level pressures are relatively low.

For many purposes later it will be easier for fig. 1.3 to be considered from a different aspect, comparing the altitude to which it is necessary to ascend in order to reach a given upper level pressure.

Figure 1.4 considers the same distribution of upper air mean temperatures as fig. 1.3. The altitude h_c necessary to reach 700 mb is lower than standard because the mean temperatures are lower than standard, while altitude h_w for 700 mb is

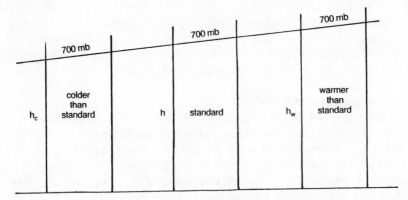

Fig. 1.4   Pressure variation with height

higher than standard because the mean upper air temperatures are higher than standard.

When the upper air situation is depicted on a constant pressure chart (e.g. 700 mb) by joining all places where that pressure value occurs at the same altitude, the lines are not unnaturally called contours and the chart is called the contour chart for xxx mb level. Every contour may be treated as an isobar because in the same way as an isobar joins all places having the same pressure at a given datum (usually msl), a contour joins places where a given pressure occurs at a common altitude. For example, all the places which at 10 000 ft are on the 700 mb isobar will also be on the 10 000 ft contour on the 700 mb chart. Similarly, areas of low contour values are areas of low pressure, and vice versa.

The height interval between lower and upper levels, e.g. between 1000 mb and 700 mb, is referred to as the 'thickness' of the layer. Values of lowest thickness occur where the mean temperature of the layer is lowest and greatest thickness occurs at the greatest mean temperature of the layer. The isopleths of thickness of a layer coincide with the isotherms of mean temperature for that layer.

Formulae
The relationship between altitude, pressure and temperature may be expressed mathematically.
1. The height difference in feet corresponding to 1 millibar change in pressure is given by

$$h = \frac{96T}{p}$$

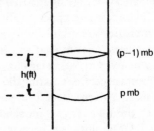

Fig. 1.5

2. The 'pressure-height' formula is:
$$h_2 - h_1 = 221.1\, T\, (\log p_1 - \log p_2)$$
where:
h_1 = lower height in feet
h_2 = upper height in feet
221.1 = constant
T = mean temperature in K
between h_1 and h_2
p_1 = pressure at h_1 in mb
p_2 = pressure at h_2 in mb

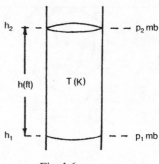

Fig. 1.6

Some useful values to remember, which you may care to check using your pocket calculator and the formulae, are:

(a) The height equivalent to a millibar change in pressure in temperate latitudes is:

At mean sea level	27 ft
At 2000 ft amsl	30 ft
At 20 000 ft amsl	50 ft
At 40 000 ft amsl	100 ft

(b) The following pressure levels for which upper air charts may be seen, occur at these corresponding altitudes (i.e. above mean sea level):

Pressure	Altitude
850 mb level occurs at approximately	5 000 ft amsl
700 mb	10 000 ft
500 mb	18 000 ft
400 mb	24 000 ft
300 mb	30 000 ft
200 mb	40 000 ft
100 mb	53 000 ft
50 mb	68 000 ft

Horizontal variation of pressure

At a given time, different atmospheric pressures are experienced at different places, and for an appreciation of the corresponding meteorological conditions, they are 'reduced' to a common datum (e.g. mean sea level) and maps are drawn of the horizontal pressure distribution. An *isobar* is a line joining all places having the same pressure at a given level (usually mean sea level). Usually isobars are drawn at intervals of 2 mb or 4 mb. 2 millibar isobars are drawn for the even values (e.g. 990, 992, etc., not 991, 993) and 4 millibar isobars' values are divisible by 4 (e.g. 996, 1000 and not 994, 998, 1002). Isobars tend to form characteristic patterns. Some typical shapes are shown in fig. 1.7. Usually mean sea level pressures lie in the range 950 mb to 1050 mb although in December 1986 a centre of low pressure of 916 mb occurred off Iceland followed by a centre of high pressure over Europe of over 1050 mb during the next month!

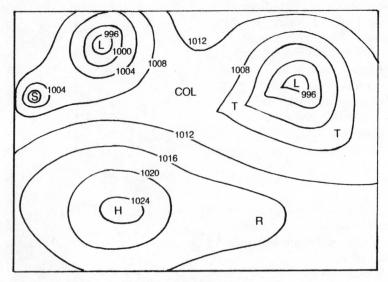

Fig. 1.7   Types of pressure systems

L. Low or depression
An area of closed isobars, usually with a generally circular shape, with the lowest pressure at the centre. The actual central pressure itself is not necessarily important – it is merely relatively lower than the other pressures all around. Forecasters refer to lows as deep or intense, shallow or weak and to whether they are deepening or filling.

S. Secondary depression
An area of low pressure, not necessarily with its own isobar system, within the periphery of a larger depression (then called the primary). The isobars on the side of the secondary away from the primary are often quite close together. Secondaries may also be described as intense or weak, etc.

T. Trough of low pressure
The name given to a pressure system where the isobars around a low become elongated such that the pressure is lower along the axis of the trough than it is on its two sides. Sometimes the isobars at a trough have a pronounced V-shape. Active weather fronts always lie in troughs but not all troughs are frontal.

H. High or anticyclone
An area of closed isobars, usually oval or circular in shape, with the highest pressure at the centre. The isobars are usually wider apart than the isobars of a depression and the anticyclones themselves are slower-moving. Highs are described by forecasters as intensifying or declining. In some parts of the world, highs persist in the same location with little change for quite long periods of time.

R. Ridge or wedge of high pressure

The name given to a pressure system where the isobars around a high become elongated so that the pressure along the axis of the ridge is higher than on its two sides. Unlike the trough, the isobars in a ridge are never V-shaped but are always smoothly rounded.

C. Col

This is an area of almost uniform pressure between two highs and two lows. Sometimes it is referred to as a 'saddle-back' shape. It does not have any one isobar defining its boundary. The two isobars on the two low pressure sides each have the same value, while the isobars on the anticyclonic sides have equal, but one interval (e.g. 2 mb, 4 mb) higher values.

Pressure gradient

It will be seen from these descriptions of the various pressure systems and fig. 1.7 that the spacing apart of isobars is far from constant over the chart. This isobar spacing is significant particularly in the matter of wind strength and weather. The pressure gradient in a particular area is the rate of change of pressure per unit distance measured in the direction in which pressure is decreasing most rapidly, i.e. at right angles to the isobars at that point. Where the isobars are wide apart it would be described as a slack pressure gradient and where the isobars are close together the situation would be described as a steep pressure gradient (fig. 1.8).

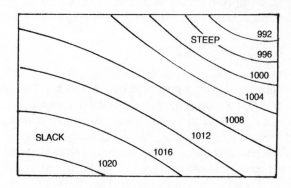

Fig. 1.8   Pressure gradient

Diurnal variation of pressure

If there are no other meteorological factors influencing the situation, a careful study of the pressure record at an observing station shows a semi-diurnal variation in pressure. This is especially so for stations in tropical and sub-tropical regions, but it also occurs in settled weather in the UK. Like the tides of the sea, there are two maxima and two minima per day but in the case of pressure, these always occur at the same local time. From a maximum at 10.00 hrs, pressure falls to a minimum at 16.00 hrs, rises to another maximum at 22.00 hrs and falls again to a second minimum at 04.00 hrs local time. It would seem to be a thermal tide in the atmosphere working steadily around the globe rather than the gravitational basis of the ocean's tides. A knowledge of the existence of this semi-diurnal variation of pressure is important because although in temperate and high latitudes it is usually swamped by pressure variations due to other causes, in low latitudes any interruption to it may indicate an impending tropical storm.

Pressure tendency

Amongst the information included in the routine observations made at meteorological stations is the amount that the pressure has changed in the three hours immediately preceding the observation, and the nature of the change. For example, the overall change may have been by an amount of a rise of 0.5 mb compared with the reading of three hours earlier, but characterised by having risen by more than 0.5 in the first part of the three-hour period but subsequently pressure falling by a smaller amount to produce a net change of 0.5 mb. This 3-hour change of barometric pressure is called pressure tendency and has two components – amount and characteristic. As will be seen from Chapter 12 dealing with synoptic meteorology, identification of areas of falling pressure or rising pressure plays a significant role in understanding what is happening to the weather at a particular place and time, and why. To aid identification the forecaster may draw, or get his computer to draw, lines of equal amount (and sign) of pressure tendency, called isallobars, in addition to the isobaric pattern. These isallobars will then depict 'isallobaric lows' where the pressure falls are greatest and 'isallobaric highs' showing the regions of most rapidly rising pressure.

Pressure settings

When atmospheric pressure is measured by a barometer, the value obtained is that at the level of the measuring element of the barometer. It would be a very rare occurrence if this were to be at mean sea level or even indeed at the official elevation of the aerodrome which the observing station is serving. Amongst other corrections made to the reading of the instrument (considered in Chapter 16) it is convenient therefore to incorporate a further 'artificial' correction to enable pressure comparisons to be made. The practice (except in areas of high level plateaux where the results would be totally unrealistic) is to 'reduce' the pressure reading to mean sea level, although in fact it is usually a case of adding an amount to the instrument reading.

QFF is defined as the barometric pressure at a place, reduced to mean sea level. The 'reduction' is made by using the actual temperature at the time of observation as the mean temperature of a column extending from the barometer level to mean sea level (fig. 1.9).

The values of QFF are used for drawing isobars on meteorological charts but

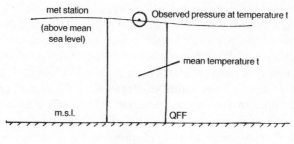

Fig. 1.9

where stations have heights in excess of 500 feet above mean sea level, the values of QFF become increasingly suspect with their altitude.

QFE is defined as the barometric pressure at the level of an aerodrome. If the barometer is not positioned at exactly the same level as the official aerodrome elevation (which is the highest point on the landing area) then, as with QFF, an adjustment to its reading must be made to obtain QFE. In practice, again as with QFF, this correction is read off a card which is entered with the barometer reading and the air temperature, but the correction is normally numerically small. If a pilot sets QFE on the sub-scale of his altimeter, the altimeter will read 0 feet on take-off and on landing. When a runway itself is not level, QFE Touchdown is used by Air Traffic Control (ATC). Also for ATC purposes, a pilot may be passed 'Clutch QFE'. This term is used when military aerodromes are located so close together that their Military Aerodrome Traffic Zones (MATZ) overlap. In this case a pilot will be passed the QFE of the higher aerodrome as 'Clutch QFE'.

There are two other pressure settings and these assume ISA conditions (rather than the actual prevailing aerodrome temperatures which are assumed for QFF and QFE). These additional settings are QNE and QNH.

While it is debatable whether it is an 'altimeter setting', **QNE** strictly is the height indicated on the altimeter on landing at an aerodrome when the altimeter subscale is set to 1013.25 millibars (29.92 inches). It is also called 'standard setting' for obvious reasons. The indicated height from an altimeter whenever its subscale is set to ISA msl conditions is also known as Pressure Altitude. The setting QNE is obsolescent and for aerodrome purposes is the only one which has its value specified in feet. The setting 1013 is, however, standard for flight separation purposes, once the aircraft is operating above the transition altitude.

QNH is the observed barometric pressure reduced to mean sea level assuming ISA conditions. With this pressure setting, the altimeter will read the aircraft's height above mean sea level on landing (because the instrument itself also assumes ISA to prevail from mean sea level). Sometimes this setting is called Spot QNH or Aerodrome QNH to differentiate the value from Forecast Regional QNH.

Regional QNH is the forecast value, valid for one hour, of the lowest pressure expected anywhere in that Altimeter Setting Region (ASR). Its function is to enable an aircraft to maintain terrain clearance when on a cross-country flight.

Airspace is divided into conveniently sized areas (ASRs) and every hour a forecast Regional QNH is issued for each ASR. Pilots can obtain the Regional QNH up to two hours ahead and when making a cross-country flight will normally change one of the altimeter's subscale readings (a) on changing from one ASR to a new ASR, and (b) on the hour if a new value is forecast.

Correct use of the forecast values of Regional QNH should ensure that adequate terrain clearance is always maintained. However it is most important to remember that if an altimeter subscale setting is not changed during the course of a flight then, flying from an area of high pressure to an area of low pressure, the altimeter will read high (over-read). The rule is usually summarised as 'High-Low-High'. The reverse is also true. To give some order of magnitude to the over-reading, the following values would apply to a flight in temperate latitudes. If an aircraft is flying over the UK at 2000 ft with starboard drift from a beam wind of 25–30 knots then the altimeter will over-read by approximately 1 foot for every nautical mile flown. Consider what the altimeter error would be if there was a depression over Northern Ireland and a flight was being made from Southend to the Isle of Man with a strong south-westerly wind. (For altimeter problems, see the companion volume, *Ground Studies for Pilots: Volume 3*, Chapter 11.)

Test questions

Q1.   For a given temperature and pressure, the effect on the density of the atmosphere of an increase in humidity is:
    (a) nil
    (b) to increase the density
    (c) to decrease the density.

Q2.   By weight, the approximate ratio of oxygen to nitrogen in the atmosphere is:
    (a) 1:3
    (b) 1:4
    (c) 1:5

Q3.   By volume, the approximate ratio of oxygen to nitrogen in the atmosphere is:
    (a) 1:3
    (b) 1:4
    (c) 1:5

Q4.   By volume, the proportion of the atmosphere which is carbon dioxide is:
    (a) 3.00%
    (b) 0.30%
    (c) 0.03%

Q5.   In the International Standard Atmosphere, the temperature at mean sea level is:
    (a) 15°C
    (b) 10°C
    (c) 25°C.

Q6.   The temperature in ISA in the lower stratosphere is:
    (a) –56.5°C
    (b) –65.5°C
    (c) –35.5°C

Q7.   What pressure system would be described as an area in which along its axis pressure is lower than on either side:
    (a) ridge
    (b) trough
    (c) col.

Q8.   Values of Regional QNH can be obtained:
    (a) up to one hour ahead
    (b) up to two hours ahead
    (c) up to three hours ahead.

Q9.   When set on the subscale of an altimeter, QNH gives on landing:
    (a) pressure altitude
    (b) 0 feet
    (c) height above sea level.

Q10.   For a flight at 30 000 ft, the contour chart to use is the:
    (a) 700 mb chart
    (b) 500 mb chart
    (c) 300 mb chart.

2: Heat and Temperature

Heat is a form of energy. Temperature, which measures how hot a particular substance is, has been defined as the condition which determines the flow of heat from one substance to another. Before considering the transfer of heat energy, first a revision of the temperature scales in use, based on the temperatures for melting of ice and boiling of pure water at normal pressure as their reference points.

Fahrenheit is a temperature scale invented by a German physicist of that name at the beginning of the 18th century and is now only used in some English-speaking countries, although no longer for aviation purposes in the UK. As shown in fig. 2.1, the scale ranges from freezing at 32°F to boiling at 212°F.

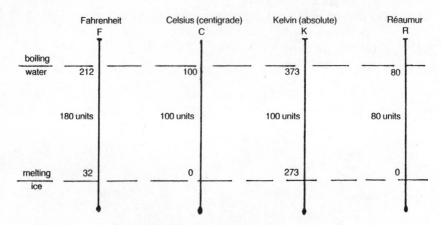

Fig. 2.1   Temperature scales

Celsius, a Swedish physicist, invented the scale which bears his name on the basis of 100 equal units between the freezing point of water at 0 and its boiling at 100, hence the alternative name of centigrade. The Celsius scale is used world-wide in aviation and will be used throughout this volume.

The **Kelvin** or absolute temperature scale is important in gas and meteorological calculations (e.g. the pressure-height formula in Chapter 1). Lord Kelvin deduced that there was a lowest achievable temperature – the absolute zero. This occurs at –273.16°C. The Kelvin scale has the same size degrees as the Celsius scale, it is merely offset 273.16 degrees colder. For aviation meteorological purposes it is usual to omit the decimal part 0.16 (as in fact we shall do) so that 0°C = 273K, 100°C = 373K, 15°C = 288K and so on.

The **Réaumur** scale invented by a French physicist also in the mid-18th century is virtually obsolete and has no relevance in aviation meteorology.

Conversion of units

1. The conversion of °C to K and vice versa is merely a question of adding or subtracting 273 as appropriate.

$$°C = K - 273 \qquad K = °C + 273$$

2. The conversion of °C to °F and vice versa is based upon the fact that there are 180 Fahrenheit degrees (F deg) between freezing and boiling points of water corresponding to 100 Celsius degrees (C deg). To avoid confusion between a specific temperature and a temperature difference, the abbreviations F deg, C deg, etc., will be used for temperature difference throughout this volume.

$$212°F - 32°F = 180 \text{ F deg}$$
$$100°C - 0°C = 100 \text{ C deg}$$
$$180 \text{ F deg} = 100 \text{ C deg}$$
$$9 \text{ F deg} = 5 \text{ C deg}$$

To carry out the conversions, either of two formulae may be used, one using the freezing point of water as its datum, the other using –40° as datum because it is common on both scales, i.e.

$$-40°F = -40°C$$

The alternatives are:

(a) $°C = (°F - 32) \times \dfrac{5}{9}$ and $°F = (°C \times \dfrac{9}{5}) + 32$

or

(b) $°C = (°F + 40) \times \dfrac{5}{9} - 40$ and $°F = (°C + 40) \times \dfrac{9}{5} - 40$

Air and ground temperatures

Before leaving temperatures, let us note the following terms which are commonly used:

Air temperature

This is the temperature taken as representative of the air at or near the earth's surface and in fact is the temperature in the shade at 4 feet (1.25 metres) above the ground (i.e. the meteorological observing office's thermometer screen height, hence also called 'screen temperature').

Air frost

This is the condition when the air temperature is below 0°C.

Ground frost

This is the condition when the temperature of grass-covered ground is below 0°C.

The exposure of thermometers for meteorological observations is dealt with in Chapter 16.

Transfer of heat: radiation

When two bodies have different temperatures, heat flows from the warmer to the colder by one of three ways: radiation, conduction or convection. All three processes are important in the atmosphere. Although the centre of the earth is so hot that it is molten, relatively very little terrestrial heat passes to the earth's atmosphere except when volcanoes erupt. The heat at the earth's surface and in the atmosphere owes its origin to the sun some 93 million miles away, following the sequence radiation then conduction then convection.

Radiation

Radiation is the transfer of heat energy by electro-magnetic waves travelling at 186000 miles per second. The subject is dealt with in companion Volume 1 Chapters 1 and 2, but the basic facts are that all bodies radiate energy, most over a range of wavelengths simultaneously, and the wavelength of the radiation depends upon the nature of the body and its temperature. Students of physics will know that there are several laws governing radiation, the general implications of which are as follows:

Wien's Law (wavelength of most intense radiation is inversely proportional to the absolute temperature) establishes that hot bodies radiate at shorter wavelengths than cold bodies. The sun's radiation is short-wave while radiation from the earth's surface and clouds is long-wave.

Stefan's Law (amount of radiated energy in a given amount of time from a given surface area is proportional to the fourth power of the absolute temperature) establishes that the radiation from hot bodies is far more intense that the rate from cold bodies.

Planck's Law (distribution of radiated energy with absolute temperature and wavelength) may be represented graphically as in fig. 2.2. The distribution curve is the same for all radiators whatever their temperature, and in the figure it is annotated with wavelengths for the sun's surface temperature of 6000K. 1 micron (μ) is 1 millionth of a metre, i.e. 0.001 mm.

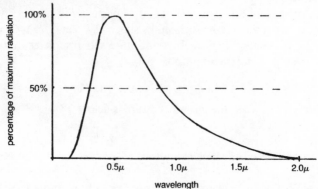

Fig. 2.2   Distribution of radiated energy

At a temperature of 6000K, the solar radiation (0.2μ to 2μ) is primarily short-wave around 0.6 μ , which is visible to the human eye as ordinary light. Within this apparently white light are in fact all the colours of the rainbow which all have slightly different wavelengths, from the longest, red, through orange,

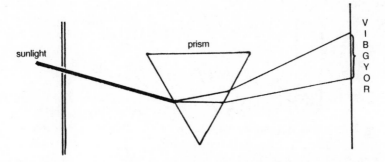

Fig. 2.3   Colours of the spectrum

yellow, green, blue and indigo to violet, the shortest, as can easily be found by passing it through a prism (fig. 2.3)

Solar radiation also encompasses invisible ultra-violet radiation at a shorter wavelength just beyond the violet, and infra-red at a longer wavelength beyond the red. It is this total solar short-wave radiation which is responsible for the heat that the earth and its atmosphere receives from outside.

In contrast to the short-wave solar radiation, the earth's surface and clouds of water droplets or ice crystals, and even water vapour itself, radiate at long-wave because of their much lower temperature. Also, from Stefan's Law, the total terrestrial radiation emitted is proportionately very much less (varies as T^4) with values for the sun of 6000K and for the earth, say, 288K.

In summary, the earth receives short-wave solar radiation on the hemisphere which is day but is continuously radiating on long-wave from its entire surface area.

Insolation

Not all of the solar radiation which is directed towards the earth and reaches the outer parts of the atmosphere ever reaches the earth's surface. Some of the solar radiation is scattered by the individual molecules of the upper air – proportionately more at the shorter wavelengths (blue colours) of the spectrum. The scattered light reaching an observer on the earth is therefore slightly richer in the blue, indigo and violet short-waves, which make the sky look blue while the sun itself looks yellow or red.

The incoming solar radiation is also depleted in other ways. There is absorption in the upper atmosphere mainly by ozone, and nearer the earth by any clouds that are present together with reflection by the earth's surface and by the upper surfaces of clouds. The reflection by the earth and its atmosphere – called its albedo – amounts to about 40% of the incoming radiation, and is the illumination by which astronauts on space flights see the earth. The degree of reflection depends upon latitude, season, time of day and the nature and slope of the surface. For a given amount of solar radiation, typically some 80% is reflected by fresh snow, 50% by thick cloud, 25% by grasslands and only 5% by a dense forest. The solar radiation actually received on a particular area of the

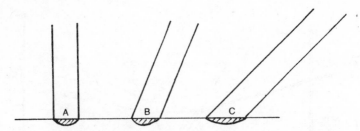

Fig. 2.4   Variation in intensity of solar radiation with angle of incidence

earth's surface is termed **insolation**. Other than the nature of the surface, insolation really depends upon the obliquity of the sun's rays (fig. 2.4).

In low latitudes, in summer and at noon (A), the heating effect of a beam of radiation is greatest because not only does it pass through the atmosphere by the shortest path, so minimising reflection and absorption, but it also illuminates the smallest area of surface. When the sun is nearer the horizon (C) the beam passes through more atmosphere, is spread over a greater surface area and there is greater surface reflection from snow, wet surfaces and sea particularly.

Before considering how various surface materials respond to insolation, two further terms need to be understood.

Specific heat – the heat required to raise the temperature of unit mass of a substance by one degree. Water has a high specific heat, ice one half of that value and most soils about 20% of the specific heat of water.

Latent heat – the heat absorbed or released, without change of temperature, involved in a change of state of a substance. It is absorbed in the process solid to liquid to gas, and is released in the reverse change from gas to liquid to solid.

Taking position B in fig. 2.4 as typical, further consideration can be given to the factors determining the budget of energy at that point.

1. Land or sea surface

If the surface is land, the relatively low specific heat enables it to warm up quickly. This is aided by the fact that the sun's rays do not penetrate the earth's surface anyway and the soil only conducts heat downwards slowly so that in 24 hours only a few inches of topsoil are involved. Bare rock, concrete runways, etc., change temperature most rapidly, while forests and swamps respond most slowly. If the solar radiation is reaching an area of open sea then very different conditions prevail. Firstly, some of the incoming radiation will penetrate to a depth of several metres, so from the outset, a much greater volume of the 'surface layer' is involved in absorbing the heat. Usually the surface layers of the water are in motion, so presenting a constantly changing surface to the sun's rays and also mixing the heat received through a greater volume. Some of the heat received is not used to raise the water temperature at all, but instead it is used as latent heat to evaporate some of the sea water. Compared with land too, when the sun is low in the sky there will be a greater amount of reflection of the solar radiation. Finally, with the far greater specific heat of water, a given amount of incident heat will produce a much smaller rise in temperature of one cubic centimetre of water compared with the temperature rise it would produce in one cubic centimetre of dry soil.

2. Day or night

The preceding paragraph dealt only with incoming radiation but it should not be forgotten that at all times the whole surface of the earth, land and sea, is also continuously radiating heat out to space albeit at a much slower rate than solar radiation. By day the incoming solar radiation is dominant but at night there is only terrestrial radiation to consider. As already noted, the earth, the clouds and the water vapour in the air are all long-wave radiators. Although present throughout the 24 hours, their relationship can most easily be considered in the night-time case with cloudless skies. Under these circumstances, terrestrial radiation is lost to space and the surfaces which have been the most rapid absorbers of radiation by day will be the most rapid coolers at night, e.g. rocky desert areas.

The gases of dry air are, for all practical purposes, 'transparent' to long-wave radiation but water vapour is not completely so. Water vapour absorbs some wavelengths of long-wave radiation whilst radiating in all directions itself. This property of water vapour therefore reduces the amount that the earth's surface will cool on a particular night because the water vapour will absorb some of the terrestrial radiation and radiate some heat downwards to earth. The net cooling is known as 'nocturnal radiation': the warmer the earth's surface, the greater is the nocturnal radiation. Figure 2.5 is a graph showing the nature of the diurnal variation of surface temperatures over land. Over the open sea, the diurnal variation is negligible.

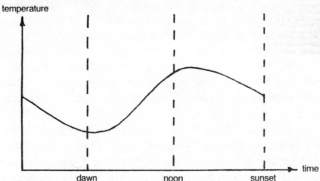

Fig. 2.5   Diurnal variation of surface temperature over land

3. Cloudless or overcast

Everything in paragraphs 1 and 2 has assumed sunny days and cloudless nights, but it has already been mentioned that reflection of solar radiation takes place from the upper surface of clouds, as can readily be seen from satellite photographs. Clouds do also absorb an amount of solar radiation. While a sheet of high cloud will cut off a significant proportion of heat from the sun, when the 'sun goes in' behind a dense cloud the fall in incoming heat is so great that it can be felt bodily immediately. An overcast day with low cloud, or a day with a dense fog, will therefore appreciably diminish the insolation. At night-time, an overcast sky will reduce the cooling to practically zero.

A sheet of high cloud will have least effect but a sheet of dense low cloud will absorb all of the terrestrial radiation while emitting long-wave radiation itself – both towards space and back towards earth. If the low cloud temperature is the same temperature as that of the earth's surface, both will be emitting at the same long wavelength and then the earth will not cool at all. Figure 2.6 shows the diurnal variation with varying degrees of cloudiness.

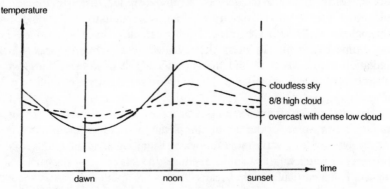

Fig. 2.6   Diurnal variation of surface temperature over land with varying cloud cover

4. Calm or windy

This factor will be dealt with in greater detail in later chapters when considering the formation of cloud and fog. However the preceding paragraphs have assumed a calm day and ignored any air movement. If the air is in motion, apart from adiabatic properties yet to be considered, the air movement will mix the heat, or loss of it, through the layer involved. On a calm, clear night, the terrestrial cooling also may itself initiate an air movement. This will occur with undulating terrain where cold air will collect in valleys, and even shallow 'frost hollows' have significantly colder temperatures than the surrounding country-side (fig. 2.7).

Having mentioned in 3 above that one can physically sense the effect when the sun goes in behind a dense cloud, 'wind chill' effect should also be briefly referred to. If, for example, at an aerodrome in Southern England the forecast air temperature is 0°C with a steady easterly wind of 25 knots, then to passengers walking out to their aircraft the wind chill equivalent temperature will be some 10 C deg colder, e.g. –10°C.

5. Wind direction

This is associated with the source from which the mass of air originated. Air from the interior of a continent will have less water vapour and cloud than air with a long maritime track, and air migrating from polar or tropical latitudes to temperate latitudes will tend to retain its original coldness or warmth for quite a while. Even air movement on a smaller scale can influence the amount of cooling due to nocturnal radiation. For example, a light wind from the English

3: Water in the Atmosphere

Reference was made in Chapter 1 to the presence in the atmosphere of the invisible gas water vapour mixed with the permanent gases of dry air. So far as the troposphere is concerned, water vapour is always present to a greater or lesser extent so tropospheric air is always moist air. It plays its part in the water cycle that takes place in the atmosphere as illustrated in fig. 3.1.

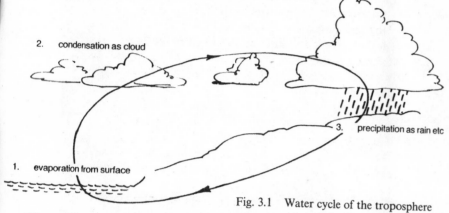

Fig. 3.1   Water cycle of the troposphere

Water evaporates into the air from the surface, particularly from open water such as oceans, seas, lakes, etc. Later it condenses from the invisible vapour form into clouds of water drops or ice or both. From clouds, the precipitation as rain, snow, etc., returns the water to the surface to renew the cycle once again. Several changes of state (gas, liquid, solid) of water are involved in the cycle. The terms used to describe each change are:

Name	Process
Condensation	Water vapour into liquid water drops
Evaporation	Liquid to vapour
Deposition* (or sublimation)	Vapour to solid (e.g. frost from cloudless air)
Sublimation	Solid to vapour
Melting (or fusion of ice)	Solid to liquid
Freezing or crystallisation	Liquid to solid

* Although in chemistry sublimation is only applied to the direct change from solid to vapour, in meteorology the term may be used for either direct change: ice to water vapour or water vapour to ice.

From the pilot's point of view, the condensation of water vapour leading to

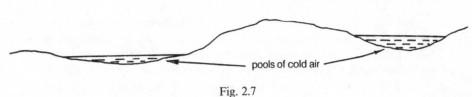

Fig. 2.7

Channel will prevent aerodromes near the coast from cooling as much at night as the cooling taking place at aerodromes well inland.

Transfer of heat: conduction and convection

Conduction is the transfer of heat by bodily contact. At night heat is conducted by the surface layers of air to the earth which is cooling by radiation beneath them. Conversely, by day heat passes from the earth's surface to the lowest layers of the atmosphere by conduction. Because air is a poor conductor of heat energy, this process is limited to only the layer of air nearest the surface. Further transfer of heat energy upwards in the troposphere is by convection. *Convection* is a means of transfer of heat energy within a fluid by which the heat is conveyed by the bodily movement of the fluid – in this case the air movement. Uneven surface heating will give rise to convection currents or 'thermals', and also the vertical component of turbulence due to a wind greater than about 8 to 10 knots will distribute heat upwards. The degree of effect depends upon the state of stability of the lower atmosphere at the time, which is considered in Chapter 5. Where heat is transferred sideways by bodily motion of the air, the process is called *advection*.

Summary of heat processes in the atmosphere

Above the tropopause, the heat balance is brought about by absorption of through-passing radiation. There is no influence from water vapour and no

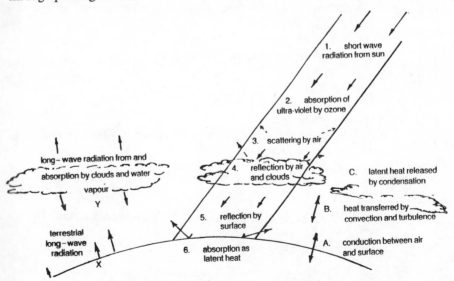

Fig. 2.8   Heat processes in the atmosphere

convection, although there are strong winds in the lower stratosphere.

In the troposphere, the distribution of heat energy may be represented as in fig. 2.8. Taking the short-wave solar radiation (1), some is absorbed by ozone (2) before entering the troposphere and some is scattered by the air molecules (3). In the troposphere, the radiation may be reflected by clouds (4) and the earth's surface (5). When it reaches the earth's surface, the insolation may not all be used to raise surface temperatures as some will be taken up as latent heat in melting and evaporation processes (6). Simultaneously there is outgoing long-wave terrestrial radiation (X), some of which will be absorbed by water vapour or clouds (Y). The clouds themselves and water vapour will also be emitting long-wave radiation – some to earth, some out to space. Depending upon which is the warmer, heat will be conducted between the earth's surface and the lowest layers of the atmosphere (A). These layers of air when in vertical motion will transfer heat upwards through the troposphere by convection (B). Whenever there is water vapour condensing out to form cloud, latent heat will be released (C). The amount of water vapour present in the troposphere at any time is therefore important in its heat balance in addition to the reasons given in the first chapter, so water vapour forms the subject of Chapter 3.

Test questions

Q1.   When latent heat is released, the substance undergoes:
    (a) a fall of temperature
    (b) no change of temperature
    (c) a rise of temperature.

Q2.   Of the surface materials, sea water, forest and desert, the surface with the highest specific heat is:
    (a) sea water
    (b) forest
    (c) desert.

Q3.   The water vapour in the air near to the earth's surface is:
    (a) variable
    (b) 14% of the composition of dry air
    (c) 18% of the composition of dry air.

Q4.   Water vapour is:
    (a) visible as cloud
    (b) visible as cloud, fog and frost
    (c) an invisible gas.

Q5.   In the International Standard Atmosphere (ISA), the tropopause is assumed to occur at an altitude of:
    (a) 11 km
    (b) 20 km
    (c) 32 km

Q6.   In ISA, the mean sea level pressure and temperature are assumed to be:
    (a) 1003.15 mb and 15°C
    (b) 1013.25 mb and 288K
    (c) 1023.35 mb and 273K.

Q7.   Temperatures at the tropopause and lower stratosphere are:
    (a) uniform at all latitudes
    (b) lower at the poles than at the Equator
    (c) higher at the poles than at the Equator.

Q8.   By day, the rise of surface temperature will be:
    (a) greater over wet land surfaces (e.g. swamps) than over dry
    (b) less over wet surfaces (e.g. swamps) than over dry surfac
    (c) the same over wet land surfaces as over dry surfaces.

Q9.   If the temperature at an inland aerodrome is +10°C at sunset a is no wind throughout the night, the temperature at dawn will b if the night has also been:
    (a) overcast
    (b) cloudless but very humid
    (c) cloudless with little water vapour in the air.

Q10.   Complete the table:

	°F	°C	K
(a)	?	15	?
(b)	?	?	273
(c)	23	?	?
(d)	86	?	?

the formation of cloud or fog is obviously of great importance, but in order to be conversant with the terminology, it is necessary to consider the evaporation phase in more detail. The capacity of dry air to mix with water vapour evaporating into it is determined by the air pressure and temperature. The temperature influence is the more significant factor. The terms used to describe the presence of water vapour in the air include the following.

(a) **Dry air:**
Air that contains no water vapour at all. Although as already stated this condition will not be encountered in practice, it is a convenient assumption for some calculations.

(b) **Moist air:**
Air that contains some water vapour.

(c) **Saturated air:**
Air that contains the maximum amount of water vapour at that pressure and temperature. Likening the air to a sponge, it will go on absorbing moisture until it cannot hold any more, i.e. it is saturated.

(d) **Unsaturated air:**
Air that contains less than the maximum amount of water vapour that it could contain at that temperature and pressure.

(e) **Saturation content:**
The maximum amount of water vapour that a given volume of air can contain at a given temperature, expressed in grams per cubic metre.

(f) **Vapour concentration or absolute humidity:**
The actual amount of water vapour contained in a given volume of air expressed in grams per cubic metre.

Working in terms of volume of air, or of any gas, is all very well when laboratory conditions apply and the gas is contained in a gas jar, cylinder or similar container. For practical purposes where the gas is not so constrained within a given volume, say in an aerodrome traffic zone or an altimeter setting region, it is better to express the degree of water vapour's presence in the air either by giving the mass of water vapour which is mixed with a given mass of dry air or by the pressure it is exerting as part of the total atmospheric pressure (Dalton's Laws of Partial Pressures). Thus:

(g) **Humidity mixing ratio (r):**
The actual mass of water vapour that is contained in a given mass of air at a particular time expressed in grams of water vapour per 1 kilogram of dry air (g/kg) but occasionally as grams per gram (g/g).

(h) **Humidity mixing ratio for saturation:**
The maximum mass of water vapour that can be contained in a given mass of air at a particular pressure and temperature, usually expressed in grams per kilogram of dry air. Typical values for 1013 mb are given in Table 1, which in turn is reproduced in graphical form in fig. 3.2.

Table 1

°C	−20	−10	0	5	10	15	20	25	30	35
g/kg	0.75	1.75	3.75	5.8	7.6	10.6	14.8	20	27.1	36.75

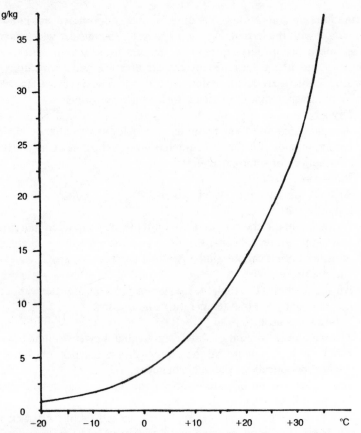

Fig. 3.2   Variation of humidity mixing ratio for saturation with temperature

Two important characteristics of the shape of this graph should be noted:
1. With increase of temperature, the amount of water vapour required to saturate the air increases.
2. With increase of temperature, the rate of increase of saturation value increases.

   (i) **Relative humidity:**
   The ratio, expressed as percentage, of the actual amount of water vapour present in a given sample of air to the maximum amount that the same sample could contain at the same temperature and pressure. Written as a fraction:

$$\frac{\text{Relative humidity } (\%)}{100\%} = \frac{\text{Humidity Mixing Ratio (HMR) (g/kg)}}{\text{HMR for saturation for the same temperature and pressure (g/kg)}}$$

   and

$$\frac{\text{Relative humidity } (\%)}{100\%} = \frac{\text{Vapour concentration (g/m}^3)}{\text{Saturation content for the same temperature and pressure (g/m}^3)}$$

By using the expression Humidity Mixing Ratio, no difficulty arises when considering rising or descending air provided that the air does not become saturated. For example, rising air will experience decreasing pressure and expand but although the mass of water vapour will be spread through a greater volume and there will be an apparent decrease in vapour content (g/m^3) with no change of the actual water vapour present, the Humidity Mixing Ratio will correctly reflect the true state of affairs by retaining the same g/kg value.

On the basis of Dalton's Law of Partial Pressure, all of the gases of the mixture that make up the atmosphere are exerting some of the total atmospheric pressure at any time. Nitrogen and oxygen are the biggest contributors but in the UK up to 40 millibars may be exerted by the water vapour present although the more usual value is around 10 to 20 millibars. Before considering humidity from the pressure aspect, it is necessary to return first to basic principles.

Dealing only briefly with the molecular structure of water, when it is in its solid state of ice the molecules in motion are closely linked together giving the solid its rigid shape. However, they do not all possess the same amount of energy and some with greatest energy escape from the ice surface (sublimation). In water in its mobile liquid form, the molecules have greater energy and a greater number of the fastest moving escape from the water surface (evaporation). In each case latent heat is used. At the same time, unless all water vapour is immediately removed from above, say, the exposed water surface, some molecules of water vapour above the water will return to the liquid surface. The process of molecules of water being evaporated into the air continues exceeding the return of molecules to the water surface until the air becomes saturated, when the flow in and out of the surface is in balance. This applies equally to surfaces of large exposed water areas such as lakes as it does to individual water drops in clouds.

In common experience, e.g. ice cubes in a refrigerator, water freezes at 0°C. However, freely suspended water drops as found in clouds can exist as liquid at temperatures well below 0°C, down to –40°C for some very small droplets. This existence of water in a liquid state below 0°C is called supercooling. The water at –10°C and –20°C in Table 1 will be supercooled water and the table should strictly be annotated 'Saturation HMR over water'. At sub-zero temperatures, the HMR for saturation over ice is lower than that over water at the same temperature because of the slower rate of release of molecules from the ice surface. This is an important fact which will be referred to later in Chapter 6.

(j) **Vapour pressure (water vapour partial pressure) (e):**
    That part of the total atmospheric pressure (p) which is being exerted by the water vapour present at a particular time. It is expressed in millibars. (Hence the pressure of the dry air is ($p - e$) millibars.)

(k) **Saturation vapour pressure (e_s):**
    That part of the total atmospheric pressure of saturated air at a particular temperature which is exerted by the water vapour. It is expressed in millibars (Table 2).

Table 2

Temperature (°C)	–20	–15	–10	–5	0	+5	+10	+15	+20	+25	+30	+35
SVP over water (mb)	–	1.9	2.86	4.22	6.11	8.72	12.28	17.1	23.4	31.7	42.5	56.3
SVP over ice (mb)	1.04	1.67	2.62	4.03	6.11	–	–	–	–	–	–	–

These values when graphed, as fig. 3.3, give the same shape and characteristics as fig. 3.2.

Similarly,

$$\frac{\text{Relative humidity (\%)}}{100\%} = \frac{\text{Vapour pressure } (e)}{\text{Corresponding sat'n vapour pressure } (e_s)}$$

The conditions relating to unsaturated air lie to the right of the curve in figs. 3.2 and 3.3. For example, at point P in fig. 3.3, representing air at +20°C with a vapour pressure of 11.7 mb:

$$\text{Relative humidity} = \frac{11.7}{23.4} \times 100\% = 50\%$$

Another way by which the humidity can be expressed is by means of the dew point temperature.

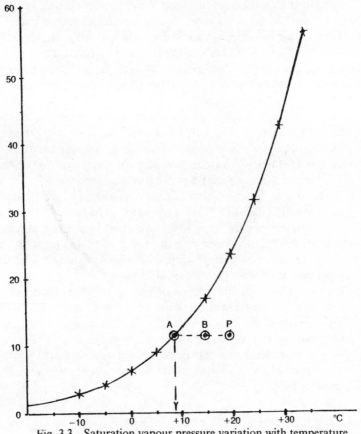

Fig. 3.3   Saturation vapour pressure variation with temperature

(l) **Dew point temperature:**

The temperature to which air must be cooled at constant pressure to become saturated. For example, the air at point P in fig. 3.3 when cooling as represented by the line PBA, will have an increase in relative humidity to 75% at B and to 100% (i.e. it has become saturated) at A, which is the dew point temperature of 9°C. Cooling to below the dew point temperature produces an excess of water vapour which condenses out as dew.

When temperatures fall to below 0°C before the air becomes saturated, then:

(m) **Frost point temperature:**

The temperature to which unsaturated air must be cooled to reach the condition of saturation with respect to an ice surface. Cooling to below the frost point temperature produces an excess of water vapour which is deposited as hoar frost on the ground, grass, parked aircraft, etc.

Finally, the state of humidity may be indicated by referring to the air's wet bulb temperature – a value which must not be confused with the dew point temperature. The wet bulb temperature is an instrument reading which will be dealt with in Chapter 16: Organisation and Observations, etc. For the time being it may be conveniently defined as follows:

(n) **Wet bulb temperature:**

The lowest temperature to which air can be cooled by evaporation into it.

The need to consider the part played by the water vapour in the atmosphere in producing varying types, amounts and densities of clouds and fog will arise repeatedly in the chapters to follow.

Test questions

Q1.   When air is cooled to below its dew point temperature, the amount of water vapour condensed out as water droplets is:

(a) nil because first the air becomes supersaturated

(b) all of its vapour concentration because air cannot be supersaturated

(c) the excess that the original vapour concentration was greater than the prevailing saturation content.

Q2.   With increasing temperature, the saturation humidity mixing ratio of 1 kg of air:

(a) increases

(b) remains constant

(c) decreases.

Q3.   With increasing temperature, the rate of increase of saturation vapour pressure at normal atmospheric temperatures:

(a) increases

(b) remains constant

(c) decreases

Q4.   In unsaturated air, the wet bulb temperature is:

(a) another name for the dew point temperature

(b) colder than the dew point temperature

(c) between the air temperature and the dew point temperature.

Q5.   Supercooled is the term applied to water drops which:

    (a) have formed below the dew point temperature

    (b) are existing as liquid below 0°C

    (c) have formed below the wet bulb temperature.

Q6.   Given that a sample of air has the following properties: 1 000 mb; +21°C; Wet bulb +15°C; Dew point 10.5°C; Saturation vapour pressure 25 mb; Saturation HMR 16 g/kg; Actual HMR 8 g/kg; its relative humidity will be:

    (a) 32%

    (b) 50%

    (c) 64%.

Q7.   The temperature to which air must be cooled at constant pressure to become saturated is:

    (a) cloud base temperature

    (b) dew point temperature

    (c) wet bulb temperature.

Q8.   The lowest temperature to which water droplets can be cooled is, for practical purposes:

    (a) −10°C

    (b) −20°C

    (c) −40°C.

Q9.   In rising, expanding, unsaturated air when there is no addition or removal of water vapour, within the increasing volume of a given sample of air the humidity mixing ratio will:

    (a) decrease

    (b) remain constant

    (c) increase.

Q10.   Of the following statements, it is true to say:

    (a) Unsaturated air is dry air

    (b) Wet bulb temperature is a direct instrumental reading of the dew point temperature

    (c) Dry air is unsaturated air.

4: Air Density

The density of the atmosphere, as with any gas, is defined as its mass per unit volume. Common units used in aviation meteorology are grams per cubic metre or per cubic centimetre, denoted by the Greek letter rho (ρ). The factors which determine the density of a gas are pressure and temperature and it will be remembered that the magnitude of air density at mean sea level in ISA conditions is 0.001225 g/cc. It will also be remembered from the composition of the atmosphere that water vapour density is about five-eighths of that of comparable dry air. For the accurate determination of air density therefore it is necessary to know the prevailing humidity.

Why is a knowledge of air density important enough for ISA to specify the mean sea level value? The answer is simply that every aspect of an aircraft's operation – take-off, climb, turns, descent, landing – depends upon the density of the air through which it is moving. Without going into the formulae in this book, the lift sustaining the aircraft in flight varies directly with the air density. If nothing else changes, an aircraft needs to fly faster to maintain a given altitude if the air density decreases. In turn, an aeroplane's ceiling depends upon the density of the air about. On the runway, a low air density means a reduction in engine thrust coincident with the need for higher take-off and landing speeds, meaning a longer take-off run. Alternatively if there is a limited take-off run available, then a low air density may mean a reduction in payload in order to reduce the take-off weight so that the aircraft can meet the take-off performance criteria. On propeller-driven aircraft it should also be appreciated that, as with lift, the propeller blades will produce less thrust with a reduced air density.

Finally, although we physically can sense when temperatures are high or we can read the temperature value in °C from an instrument in the aircraft, we cannot say the same of air density. There is no instrument on the flight deck panel directly indicating the mass per unit volume of the air through which the aircraft is flying, nor do a pilot's senses alert him when the air density is particularly low as he prepares for take-off. In the absence of visible or bodily warnings, the hazards of low air density must be guarded against at all times and particularly by inexperienced pilots, especially at unfamiliar aerodromes, if they are 'hot and high'.

Formulae

(a) Dry air

The formula for the determination of air density is based upon the Gas Laws which are combined to give the Gas Equation.

Boyle's Law states that, for a constant temperature, the volume of a gas is inversely proportional to its pressure. It may be written in the alternative forms of:

$$V \text{ is proportional to } \frac{1}{p}$$

or

$$pV = \text{constant}$$

or

$$p_1 V_1 = p_2 V_2$$

where:

p = pressure
V = volume
and the suffixes 1 and 2 are the initial and final conditions respectively.

Charles' Law states that, for a constant pressure, the volume of a gas is directly proportional to its absolute temperature. It may be written in the alternative forms of:

$$V \text{ is proportional to } T$$

or

$$\frac{T}{V} = \text{constant}$$

or

$$\frac{T_1}{V_1} = \frac{T_2}{V_2}$$

As the density of a gas is inversely proportional to its volume, these two laws can also be rewritten in terms of density as, respectively:

$$p = \rho \times \text{constant}$$

and

$$\rho \times T = \text{constant}$$

Whether considering a fixed mass of gas in a cylinder or an unrestricted volume of air above an aerodrome, Boyle's Law and Charles' Law may be combined to give the fundamental gas equation of:

$$pV = RT \tag{1}$$

where

p = the gas pressure
V = the gas volume
R = the gas constant
T = the gas temperature

The gas constant value depends upon the gas and the units involved. In the case of the mixture of gases which constitute dry air, the value of R is 2870 when p is in millibars, V in cubic centimetres and T in degrees Kelvin.

However, volume is not a particularly practical term for use in the equation in aviation and it is convenient that for unit mass, air density is its reciprocal, i.e.

$$\frac{1}{V} = \rho \text{ and } V = \frac{1}{\rho} \tag{2}$$

Equation (1) can therefore be rewritten:

$$\frac{p}{\rho} = RT \tag{3}$$

and

$$p = RT\,\rho \tag{4}$$

where $R = 2870$ when ρ is expressed in grams/cubic centimetre Transposing equation (4) for ρ gives:

$$\rho = \frac{p}{RT} \text{ and } \rho = \frac{1}{R} \times \frac{p}{T} \tag{5}$$

and on your pocket calculator:

$$\frac{1}{2870} = 0.0003484$$

so the formula finally becomes:

$$\rho = 0.0003484\,\frac{p}{T} \tag{6}$$

where

$$\rho = \text{dry air density in g/cc}$$
$$0.0003484 = \text{constant}$$
$$p = \text{air pressure in mb}$$
$$T = \text{air temperature in K}$$

When air density is determined in grams per cubic metre, then the constant is one million times greater and the formula is:

$$\rho = \frac{348.4\,p}{T} \tag{7}$$

For almost all practical purposes, it is usually satisfactory to assume the formula for dry air. However, there may be times when this is not the case and allowance has to be made for the presence of less dense water vapour.

(b) Moist air

In the same way that oxygen, nitrogen, dry air, etc., all have their own gas constant, so too does water vapour. If used in equation (1) above for the density of water vapour, the value of R would be 4592 which is 160% or 8/5 times the R value for dry air. The formulae derived for moist air in place of equations (6) and (7) should therefore have a different (but ever-varying) value to 0.0003484 or 348.4, depending upon the prevailing humidity. This would be difficult to say the least, so the problem is approached by considering the vapour pressure (e mb) out of the total pressure (p mb). Then

Dry air: $\qquad \rho_{da} = \dfrac{348.4\,(p - e)}{T}\ \text{g/m}^3 \tag{8}$

Water vapour: $\quad \rho_{wv} = 348.4 \times \dfrac{5}{8} \times \dfrac{e}{T}$

$$= 348.4\ \frac{\tfrac{5}{8}\,e}{T}\ \text{g/m}^3 \tag{9}$$

Adding together (8) and (9) to find the total density (of dry air mixed with water vapour) of a cubic metre of moist air, gives:

$$\rho = \frac{348.4\,(p - e)}{T} + \frac{348.4\,(\tfrac{5}{8}e)}{T}$$

$$\rho = 348.4\,\frac{(p - \tfrac{3}{8}e)}{T}\ \text{g/m}^3 \tag{10}$$

If other factors are such that an air density determined to an accuracy of 1% is sufficient, then assuming pressure of 1013 millibars, the more refined air density Equation (10) need not be invoked until $3e/8$ exceeds approximately 10 millibars.

This in turn means e must be 27 millibars or more which will be seen from fig. 3.3 to correspond to a dew point temperature around 22°C, which does not occur often in the UK. In fact, on summer's days an air temperature of 22°C (72°F) would be appreciated! The type of situation where the humidity is high enough to be significant would be in a moist tropical location, such as an airstrip beside swamps or a river in a jungle clearing.

Variations in air density

(a) At the surface
Apart from the effect of water vapour, the other reasons for the air density to change in value are variations in pressure (p) and temperature (T). It has already been mentioned in respect of fig. 1.7 that mean sea level pressure normally has a value between 950 and 1050 millibars, a range of 100 mb or 10%, so from this cause the surface air density may vary over a range of 10%.

The commonly known property that warm air is light and cold air is heavy (or more dense) can be translated into a more mathematical statement by considering ISA mean sea level conditions of temperature 15°C. This corresponds to 288K so a rise of 2.88 C deg, say 3 C deg in round numbers, is a 1% rise in absolute temperature. Air density varies inversely with the air temperature and a 3 C deg change produces a 1% change in air density.

As regards temperature deviation: pressure altitude is the height in the standard atmosphere at which the aircraft's environmental pressure would be experienced. Aircraft performance is tabulated against pressure altitude (PA) and temperature deviation to allow for variations in air density, where temperature deviation is given by:

Corrected outside air temperature (COAT) – ISA temperature for that PA

For a given pressure altitude, it can therefore be visualised that for every 3 degrees of temperature deviation the air density changes by 1%. There was a time when performance was quoted by reference to density altitude (the height in ISA at which the aircraft's ambient air density would be experienced) but the practice has been superseded and the term Density Altitude is now obsolete.

Generally the values of minimum and average air density at an aerodrome are those likely to be of interest to the pilot. However, the air density itself is not observed and recorded and its value has to be obtained from the records of pressure and temperature. The average air density for practical purposes can be found by substituting average pressure and temperature in the formula. (If a chart is drawn with lines joining places of equal air density, the isopleths are called isopycnics.) Considering formulae (8) and (10), the minimum air density can occur either from extremely low pressure or exceptionally high temperatures or possibly from both occurring simultaneously. In areas which are subject to very low pressure systems, usually temperate latitudes, this will normally be the cause of low density. As very low pressure in these areas seldom coincides with temperatures above average a suitable formula for such areas would be:

$$\text{Minimum air density} = 348.4 \times \frac{\text{Minimum pressure (mb)}}{\text{Average temperature (K)}} \quad (11)$$

In other areas, such as tropical latitudes, the lowest air densities occur with the highest temperatures. In such cases the average pressure experienced at the time of highest temperature will suffice to give a realistic result:

$$\text{Minimum air density} = 348.4 \times \frac{\text{Average pressure (mb)}}{\text{Maximum temperature (K)}} \quad (12)$$

If the maximum temperature occurs when humidities may also be high, then:

$$\text{Minimum } \rho = 348.4 \times \frac{(\text{Average } p - \tfrac{3}{8} \text{ of maximum } e)}{\text{Maximum temperature K}} \quad (13)$$

At the other extreme, it may be of interest but of little practical value to know that in Russia in winter the Siberian anticyclone may have pressures at aerodrome level of 1040 mb and temperatures of –40°C giving an air density of 1555 grams per cubic metre, some 25% to 30% greater than the air density at London on the same day.

Having mentioned the coldness and high pressure of a Siberian winter day, it should be noted that there are of course seasonal variations in air density in most parts of the world. For a particular aerodrome these can be determined by substituting the seasonal values in equation (11) or (12) as appropriate.

Similarly there is a diurnal variation of air density following in step with the changes of air temperature throughout the 24 hours. As a result, lowest air densities occur early in the afternoon and the highest values around dawn.

(b) Variation with height

General references have already been made in earlier chapters to the fact that with increase of height the atmosphere becomes progressively more rarefied. Both the factors determining air density decrease with increase of height and of these, the proportionate decrease of pressure is greater than that of absolute temperature. For example, from mean sea level to 1000 ft amsl:

Height increase of 27 feet = 1 mb decrease
Height increase of 1000 feet = 37 mb decrease
and 37 mb = 3.65% of 1013 mb
In ISA, height increase 1000 ft = 1.98 K deg decrease
and 1.98 K deg = 0.69% of 288K

The overall decrease of density is, per 1000 feet, 3.65% decrease offset by 0.69% = approximately 3%.

The rule is therefore that for practical purposes, air density decreases by approximately 3% per 1000 feet. This rule is reasonably accurate up to 20 000 feet amsl if the loss is compounded, i.e. deduct 3% from the value at a given level to determine the air density 1000 feet higher.

The lowest air densities that will affect aircraft taking off and landing will be found at aerodromes that are high and hot. If conditions at the same time are also humid, this just worsens the situation. Hence in determining aircraft performance into and out of an aerodrome, cognisance must be taken of WAT limitations: W Weight, A Altitude, T Temperature.

In aerodynamics, it may be convenient to work not with the actual air density but its value relative to that at mean sea level in ISA. It is denoted by the Greek letter sigma (σ) and is called Relative Density. It may variously be quoted as a fraction of unity or as a percentage.

$$\text{Relative density} = \frac{\text{Ambient Density (} \rho \text{)}}{\text{ISA msl Density}}$$
$$(\sigma)$$

The following short table of relative densities is useful to know:

Height in ISA	Relative Density
0 feet	1.0
10 000 feet	0.74
20 000 feet	0.53
40 000 feet	0.25
60 000 feet	0.10

It is also true, but there is little practical value in knowing, that the differences in the troposphere tend to smooth out their effects so that by around 26 000 feet above mean sea level the average air density is almost uniform around the world ($\sigma = 0.43$ approximately).

Test questions

Q1.   For a given air temperature, the value of air density:
  (a) varies directly as the air pressure
  (b) varies inversely as the air pressure
  (c) at any time has a value 122.5% greater than the air pressure.

Q2.   For a given air pressure, the value of air density:
  (a) varies directly with the temperature in °C
  (b) varies inversely with the temperature in K
  (c) varies inversely with the temperature in °C.

Q3.   For a given pressure and temperature, water vapour:
  (a) has the same density as dry air
  (b) has a lesser density than dry air
  (c) has a greater density than dry air.

Q4.   Temperature Deviation in C deg at a particular pressure altitude (PA) is given by:
  (a) ISA msl temperature – corrected outside air temperature
  (b) corrected outside air temperature – ISA msl temperature
  (c) corrected outside air temperature – ISA temperature for that PA.

Q5.   On a hot and humid, pre-monsoon day in Asia, the air density will be:
  (a) less than the average for the year for that aerodrome

(b) around the average for the year for that aerodrome

(c) more than the average for the year for that aerodrome.

Q6.   On average, the air density at a particular level may be found by deducting from the air density 1000 feet lower:

    (a) 1%

    (b) 2%

    (c) 3%.

Q7.   Assuming that an error of up to 1% due to ignoring water vapour is acceptable when determining the air density, it is only necessary to know the vapour pressure when the dew point temperature exceeds:

    (a) 17°C

    (b) 22°C

    (c) 27°C.

Q8.   At 40 000 feet in ISA, the relative density is:

    (a) half

    (b) one quarter

    (c) one tenth.

Q9.   A relative density of 74% is likely to be experienced at:

    (a) 10 000 feet

    (b) 15 000 feet

    (c) 20 000 feet.

Q10.   For a diurnal variation of surface temperature through 20 C deg at an airfield where the QFE remains 1000 mb and the dawn temperature is 3°C, the percentage change in air density over 24 hours will be of the order of:

    (a) 11%

    (b) 4%

    (c) 7%.

5: Lapse Rates, Stability and Instability

Before consideration can be given to the formation of clouds and their characteristics, including flying conditions, attention must be paid to the upper air temperature structure and the terminology used to describe it.

Firstly, the term *temperature lapse rate*. A temperature lapse rate is the rate of decrease of temperature per unit increase of height and in aviation in the UK is expressed in C deg per 1 000 feet. Different circumstances of static, ascending and descending air produce different lapse rates which are known by the following names.

(a) Environmental lapse rate (ELR)

Upper air temperatures are observed regularly through the troposphere into the stratosphere and may variously be referred to as the observed, environmental or ambient upper air temperatures. These environment temperatures vary with place and time as well as with altitude.

Environmental lapse rate is the observed rate of decrease of temperature with increase of height at a particular place and time

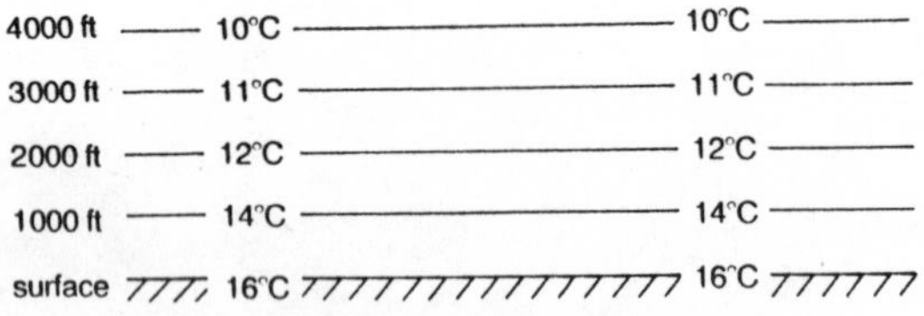

Fig. 5.1 Observed upper air temperatures

With the observed environment temperatures given in fig. 5.1, from the surface to 2000 ft the environmental lapse rate (ELR) is 2 C deg per 1 000 feet while from 2 000 ft to 4 000 ft the ELR is 1 C deg/1 000 ft. In fact where temperatures are decreasing with increase of height, the ELR is positive.

However, the observed upper air temperatures may be as shown in figs 5.2 and 5.3. Where, as in fig. 5.2, the environmental temperatures remain unchanged with increase of height, the ELR is 0 C deg/1 000 ft and the layer from 1 000 ft to 3 000 ft would be called an *isothermal layer*. If, as in fig. 5.3, the environmental temperatures increase with increase of height (i.e. the usual temperature structure is inverted) the ELR is negative and the layer from 1 000 ft to 3 000 ft would be called an *inversion layer* or just 'an inversion'. If the temperature inversion starts at the surface, it is usual to refer to the condition as a *surface inversion*.

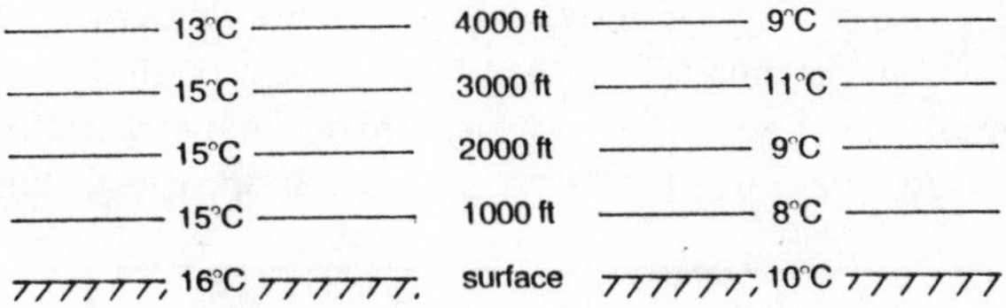

—— 13°C ——   4000 ft   —— 9°C ——

—— 15°C ——   3000 ft   —— 11°C ——

—— 15°C ——   2000 ft   —— 9°C ——

—— 15°C ——   1000 ft   —— 8°C ——

⫻⫻⫻ 16°C ⫻⫻⫻   surface   ⫻⫻⫻ 10°C ⫻⫻⫻

Fig. 5.2   Fig. 5.3

Figures 5.4, 5.5, 5.6 and 5.7 show graphs of observed environment air temperatures plotted against height, called environment curves, which illustrate the various possibilities.

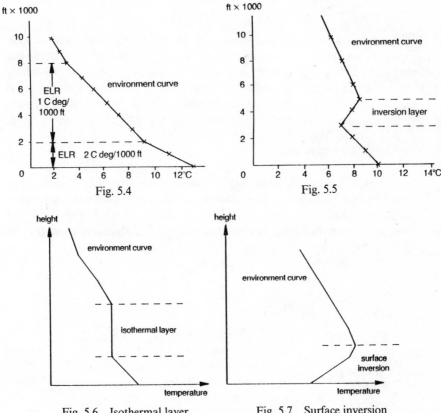

Fig. 5.4

Fig. 5.5

Fig. 5.6   Isothermal layer

Fig. 5.7   Surface inversion

Because it is the practice to forecast both the surface and upper air temperatures for a particular place and time, there will also be a corresponding forecast ELR, the applications of which will be considered later.

(b) Dry adiabatic lapse rate (DALR)

This term is used in relation to vertically-moving unsaturated air. The term adiabatic means that no heat is lost or gained from the system during a particular process. Take the case of a piston moving in a simple cylinder (fig. 5.8). If the piston is moved so that it compresses the gas, work is done on the gas. The energy required for compression passes to the gas leading to an increase of its internal energy, raising its temperature (cf. bicycle hand-pump, diesel engine, etc.).

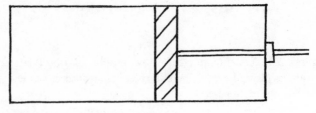

Fig. 5.8

Cooling by expansion of a gas, as in some domestic refrigerators, is the reverse process. In the atmosphere, because air is a poor conductor of heat, any rising bubble of air (called a 'parcel' by met. men) can be considered 'thermally insulated' from its environment as it expands and cools with no loss or gain of heat to or from its environment, i.e. adiabatically. So long as the vertically moving air remains unsaturated it changes its temperature at a predictable, constant rate.

A formal definition would be:

Dry adiabatic lapse rate (DALR) is the rate of cooling with ascent or warming with descent of unsaturated air displaced vertically in which the temperature changes due entirely to dynamical processes and there is no exchange of heat with the environment. Expressed in terms of height, the DALR value is 3 C deg/1000 ft (1 C deg/100 m).

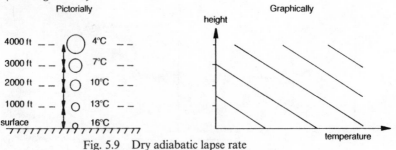

Fig. 5.9   Dry adiabatic lapse rate

(c) Saturated adiabatic lapse rate (SALR)

In rising saturated air, condensation occurs and releases latent heat. This heat partly offsets the expansional cooling so that the saturated adiabatic lapse rate value is less than that of the DALR. The SALR has a variable value although on average at mean sea level in temperate latitudes its value is approximately 1.5 C deg/1000 ft (0.5 C deg/100 m).

At high temperatures the SALR has a low value and at low temperatures its value is greater, approaching the DALR value, and equalling it for all practical purposes at –40°C. Thus the SALR value increases with altitude and also usually with latitude. Remember that the SALR value is derived from the simple sum:

Per 1 000 ft:

Cooling adiabatically due to expansion	3 C deg
Warming due to latent heat of condensation	x C deg
Resultant SALR value per 1 000 feet	3–x C deg

This may be shown graphically (fig. 5.10) for a given amount of cooling ('t' deg).

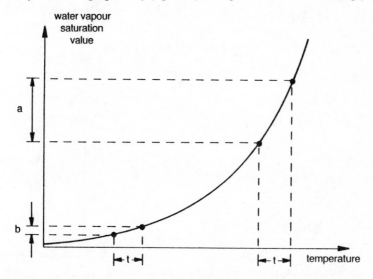

(a) At *High* temperatures, large difference in saturation value, much condensation and latent heat released, hence a *Low* SALR value.
(b) At *Low* temperatures, small difference in saturation values, little condensation and latent heat released, hence a *High* SALR value.

Fig. 5.10   Variation in value of SALR

Typical values of the SALR at mean sea level are:

	0°C	15°C	30°C
Cooling	3	3	3
Warming	0.5	1.5	2
Net cooling = SALR (per 1000')	2.5	1.5	1

Compared with fig. 5.9 for the DALR, the SALR may be represented as in fig. 5.11.

The graph of temperature versus height in a large developing cloud is called an ascent or 'path curve', and would appear as shown in fig. 5.12.

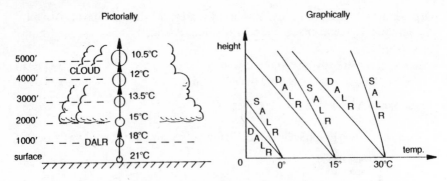

Fig. 5.11   Saturated adiabatic lapse rate

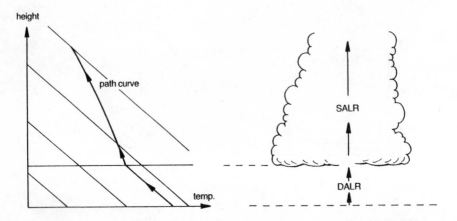

Fig. 5.12   Path curve

Although the DALR applies to both ascending and descending unsaturated air (i.e. is reversible), the SALR strictly should only be applied to ascending saturated air. This is because although in rising air excess water vapour will condense out and latent heat will be released, it cannot be assumed that the same amount of latent heat will be taken up to evaporate all the condensation instantaneously to maintain saturation of descending air. The SALR may be defined as:

Saturated adiabatic lapse rate (SALR) is the rate of cooling with ascent of saturated air in which the expansional cooling is partly offset by the latent heat of condensation, and there is no exchange of heat with the environment. It has a variable value but in temperate latitudes at mean sea level, its value is approximately 1.5 C deg per 1 000 ft.

By comparing the temperatures of rising parcels of air with the environmental temperatures of the air which surrounds them at their new upper levels, the degree of vertical stability (or instability) of the atmosphere at a particular place and time may be assessed. As is true in other applications, a state of stability means that when an object is displaced, it will tend to return to its original position when the displacing force is removed. In an unstable state, the displaced object will continue to become more displaced even though the original displacing force is removed. In the case of atmospheric (in)stability, the object is the mass of air which for some reason has been forced to rise. There are varying degrees of stability which produce different flying conditions.

(d) Absolute (or total) stability

That state of the atmosphere in which air (whether saturated or unsaturated) which is displaced vertically tends to return to its original level when the displacing force is removed.

This state only occurs when the environmental lapse rate (ELR) has a value which is less than that of the SALR. Isothermal layers and temperature inversions are examples of particularly stable conditions.

Absolute stability may be represented pictorially and graphically as in figs 5.13 (a) and (b). Typical weather conditions of totally stable air are haze layers in air of a low relative humidity and sheets of layer cloud in humid air.

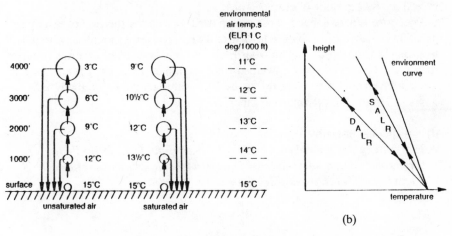

Fig. 5.13   Absolute stability

(e) Absolute (or total) instability

That state of the atmosphere in which air (whether saturated or unsaturated) which is displaced vertically tends to become more displaced even though the original displacing force is removed.

This state only occurs when the ELR has a value which is greater than that of the DALR. Typical weather conditions are dust-devils in dry desert air and violent thunderstorms and possibly tornadoes in very humid air.

It should be noted that when, in an unstable atmosphere, the air becomes disturbed and vertical currents quickly develop, not only is rising unsaturated air cooling at the DALR but also the replacement subsiding air currents are

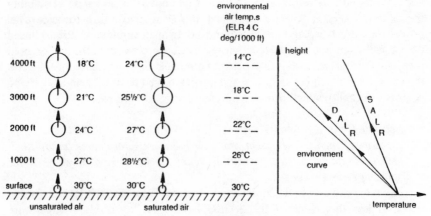

Fig. 5.14   Absolute instability

warming at the DALR. The environmental lapse rate through the whole turbulent layer therefore tends to the DALR value. This means in practice that the ELR can never greatly exceed the DALR value in unsaturated air nor greatly exceed the SALR value in saturated air.

The term 'superadiabatic' lapse rate is used to describe the case of extreme instability occurring in a shallow layer near the surface. If the ground is subjected to strong sunshine, heat may be absorbed by the thin layer of air next to it faster than it can be carried away upwards by convection currents. As a result, for a shallow layer only a few feet thick, the ELR value may then be many times greater than the DALR value i.e. superadiabatic.

(f) Conditional instability

That state of the atmosphere in which air which is displaced vertically tends to become more displaced if saturated, but which tends to return to its original level if unsaturated, when the displacing force is removed.

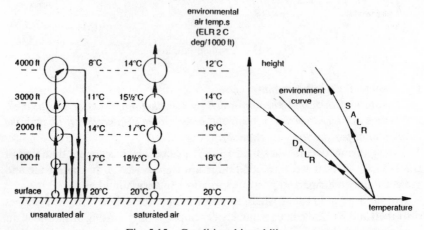

Fig. 5.15   Conditional instability

It only occurs when the ELR has a value between those of the SALR and DALR. In this case, the instability is conditional upon the air being saturated.

Typical weather conditions of concern to the aviator are cumuliform cloud where the disturbed air is saturated but hazy conditions if the air remains unsaturated.

(g) Neutral equilibrium

The three cases of absolute stability, conditional and absolute instability may be summarised as shown in fig. 5.16.

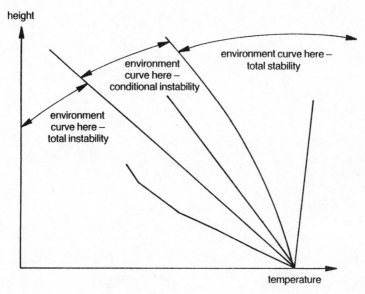

Fig. 5.16

Inevitably, the question must arise – what happens if the ELR happens to coincide with the adiabatic lapse rate value? If in unsaturated air the ELR is the same as the DALR value or in saturated air the ELR is the same as the SALR value for that temperature and pressure, then the condition is described as

a state of neutral equilibrium, because any parcel of air displaced upwards will remain at its new level when the displacing force is removed and will have no tendency to continue rising or to descend to a lower level.

At the risk of stating the obvious, it should be remembered that when the ELR value is greater than adiabatic, upper air environment temperatures will be less than those of air cooling adiabatically, while an ELR less than adiabatic means upper environment temperatures will be greater than those of air cooling adiabatically. The convention is to compare environmental lapse rate against the appropriate adiabatic value.

(h) Latent instability

It has already been seen that in 'latent heat', latent is used to denote hidden. The

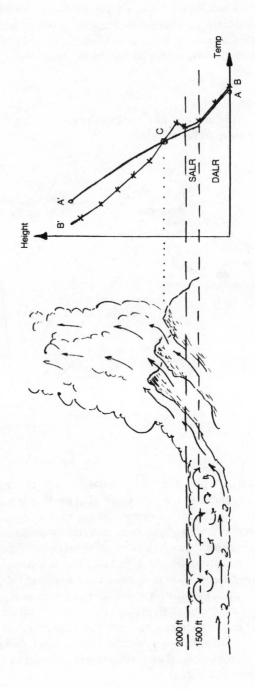

Fig. 5.17   Latent instability

same application is true when the term 'latent instability' is used.

Latent instability is that state of the atmosphere in which there is a small stable layer at low levels with a larger unstable layer above it, such that if air is forced to ascend through the stable layer, instability phenomena will develop.

This may be illustrated as in fig. 5.17, where the condensation level is 1 500 ft and the turbulence layer is 2 000 ft deep. The surface air has to be lifted to above the height at which the path curve A – A' and environment curve B – B' intersect (C). The area between the curves below C is called 'negative area' as it represents the amount of energy to be applied to a parcel of air to make it rise, while the area above C between the curves is called 'positive area'. The positive area similarly gives, proportionately, the kinetic and electrical energy developed in the towering cloud. Simply, from the pilot's point of view, the greater the size of the positive area, the more active the cloud.

Finally, the terms *potential* (or *convective*) *stability and instability* may be met. Whereas all of the cases considered so far have concerned parcels of air rising through the environment, potential (in)stability relates to what would happen if the whole environment were lifted bodily. The simplest case to visualise is of a whole airstream moving from, say, over the ocean or a low-lying plain rising up to a new location over a plateau. Although both terms potential (in)stability and convective (in)stability may be found in meteorological literature, the prefix of potential may be preferred because of its connotations of position. (The case for 'convective' is that the (in)stability arises from the rearrangement of heat due to the bodily movement of the air.)

(i) Potential (or convective) instability

That state of the atmosphere in which there is a high relative humidity at low levels and a low relative humidity at upper levels, such that if a low layer of air is lifted bodily, the ELR value through the layer will gradually increase to attain finally an unstable value. (Figure 5.18.)

This is often a major cause of instability at a cold front (see Chapter 12).

(j) Potential (or convective) stability

That state of the atmosphere in which there is a low relative humidity at low levels and a high relative humidity at upper levels, such that if a layer of air is lifted bodily the ELR value through the layer will gradually decrease to attain finally a stable value. (Figure 5.19.)

When considering the possibility of development of instability and its associated flying conditions of turbulence, etc., due allowance must be made for the modification of the environment curve by any or all of the following:

  (i) diurnal variation of temperature of the underlying surface,
 (ii) inflow of upper air of different temperatures at different levels,
(iii) movement of the whole airstream into an area of different surface temperatures,
 (iv) mixing within the air mass,
  (v) bodily lifting of the whole mass of air,

and also of the increased humidity that will prevail in an airstream that has

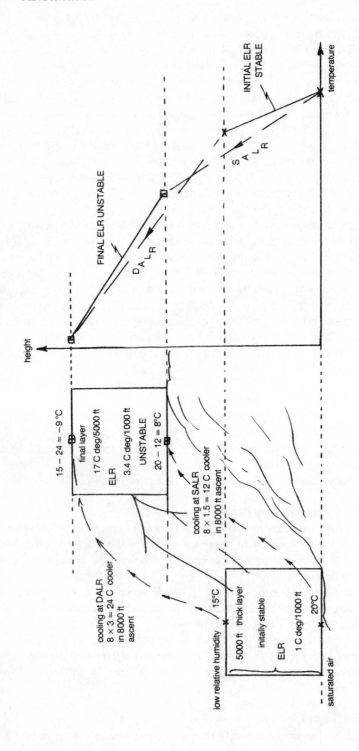

Fig. 5.18   Potential instability

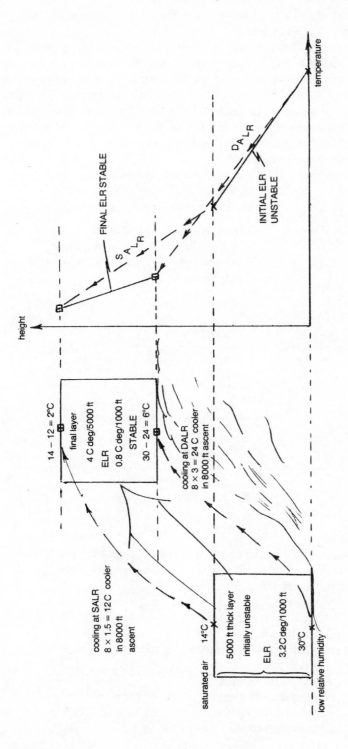

Fig. 5.19   Potential stability

followed a 'maritime' track or decreased humidity downstream of high ground that has acted as a watershed.

Of these considerations, the diurnal variation is regularly significant. As already seen in Chapter 2, different surface materials produce varying ranges of temperature over a 24-hour period. By conduction, this variation is passed to the lowest layers of the atmosphere, with progressively less variation the higher that one goes. As a result in an unchanged airmass, the environmental lapse rate value in the lowest few thousand feet of the atmosphere and the degree of instability vary in step with the surface temperature diurnal variation. For example, as shown in fig. 5.20:

at 2 pm local time (A)   Maximum surface temperature
                          Maximum ELR value near the surface
                          Maximum instability in the lowest layers.

and around dawn (B)   Minimum surface temperature
                          Minimum ELR value near the surface
                          Minimum instability (i.e. maximum stability) in the
                          lowest layers.

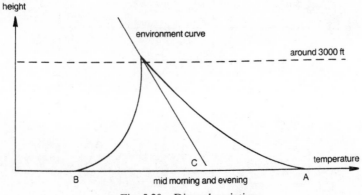

Fig. 5.20   Diurnal variation

Test questions

Q1.   A radio-sonde measures the upper air temperatures on a cloudless day in the UK. When plotted on a temperature-height graph, these temperatures would give:
      (a) the path curve
      (b) the environment curve
      (c) the dry adiabatic curve.

Q2.   A temperature inversion indicates a state of the atmosphere which is:
      (a) absolutely stable
      (b) absolutely unstable
      (c) conditionally unstable.

Q3.   An isothermal layer is a state of the atmosphere which is:
      (a) absolutely stable

    (b) absolutely unstable

    (c) conditionally unstable.

Q4.   An ELR value between those of the SALR and DALR indicates:

    (a) absolute stability

    (b) absolute instability

    (c) conditional instability.

Q5.   On a clear night inland, the stability of the lowest layers of the atmosphere:

    (a) will decrease

    (b) will not change

    (c) will increase.

Q6.   Air moving from the Azores to SW England will:

    (a) become more stable

    (b) become more unstable

    (c) not experience any change in its stability.

Q7.   The DALR value is:

    (a) 1.5 C deg/1000 ft

    (b) 1.98 C deg/1000 ft

    (c) 3.00 C deg/1000 ft.

Q8.   For potential instability, the relative humidity must:

    (a) decrease with increase of altitude

    (b) remain constant with increase of altitude

    (c) increase with increase of altitude.

Q9.   The instability of an airmass moving SE from Iceland to Scotland will normally:

    (a) decrease

    (b) remain unchanged

    (c) increase.

Q10.   It is true to say that:

    (a) at surface levels, greatest instability normally occurs in mid-morning when clouds are forming fastest

    (b) the lapse rate through a layer of cloud is less than the SALR if the conditions are unstable

    (c) generally the ELR can never greatly exceed the DALR value in unsaturated air, nor greatly exceed the SALR value in saturated air.

6: Clouds and Precipitation

To the man in the street, the clouds in the sky are more synonymous with meteorology than any other element and weather lore down the ages has largely been based on clouds; 'Red sky in the morning, shepherd's warning', etc. Even if the licence syllabuses did not spell out the details, private and professional pilots need to know why, how, when and where clouds form and their characteristics. This knowledge is necessary even for 'fair weather fliers' who need to discriminate when to fly and select VMC days! For efficient and safe instrument flying and professional operating, the knowledge is essential.

The nature of clouds

The part played by clouds in the water cycle of the atmosphere has already been shown in fig. 3.1. Clouds consist of water droplets or ice crystals in suspension in the atmosphere, produced when excess water vapour is condensed out of saturated air and present in sufficient quantity to produce a visible mass. When initially formed, the water droplets are very small and the average size cloud droplet is around 0.02 millimetres in diameter. However, within the cloud the droplet may well grow in size so that it eventually becomes big enough to fall from the cloud as precipitation – of which, more anon.

From watching the clouds in the sky it will be seen that as they are carried along by the wind they are constantly changing in their appearance. There is an infinite variety of shapes and of shades of light and dark. Nevertheless, certain general characteristics are sufficiently repetitive for various cloud types to have been given names. It was almost two hundred years ago that the first classification of cloud forms was proposed. The definitive work on cloud names, identifying features, etc. is the *International Cloud Atlas*, abridged version, 1956 edition published by the World Meteorological Organisation (WMO), a specialised agency of the United Nations. The following definitions are taken from the International cloud atlas and assume a ground observer on a day with normal sun's illumination and clear visibility.

1. *Cirrus (Ci)*. Detached clouds in the form of white, delicate filaments, or white or mostly white patches or narrow bands. These clouds have a fibrous (hair-like) appearance or a silky sheen or both.
2. *Cirrocumulus (Cc)*. Thin, white patch, sheet or layer of cloud without shading, composed of very small elements in the form of grains, ripples, etc., merged or separate, and more or less regularly arranged; most of the elements have an apparent width of less than one degree.
3. *Cirrostratus (Cs)*. Transparent whitish cloud veil of fibrous or smooth appearance, totally or partly covering the sky, and generally producing halo phenomena.

4. *Altocumulus (Ac)*. White or grey, or both white and grey, patch, sheet or layer of cloud, generally with shading, composed of laminae, rounded masses, rolls, etc., which are sometimes partly fibrous or diffuse, and which may or may not be merged; most of the regularly arranged small elements usually have an apparent width of between one and five degrees.

5. *Altostratus (As)*. Greyish or bluish cloud sheet or layer of striated, fibrous or uniform appearance, totally or partly covering the sky, and having parts thin enough to reveal the sun at least vaguely, as through ground glass. Altostratus does not show halo phenomena.

6. *Nimbostratus (Ns)*. Grey cloud layer, often dark, the appearance of which is rendered diffuse by more or less continually falling rain or snow which in most cases reaches the ground. It is thick enough throughout to blot out the sun. Low ragged clouds frequently occur below the layer with which they may or may not merge.

7. *Stratocumulus (Sc)*. Grey or whitish, or both grey and whitish, patch, sheet or layer of cloud which almost always has dark parts, composed of tessellations, rounded masses, rolls, etc., which are non-fibrous (except for virga) and which may or may not be merged; most of the regularly arranged small elements have an apparent width of more than five degrees.

8. *Stratus (St)*. Generally grey cloud layer with a fairly uniform base which may give drizzle, ice prisms or snow grains. When the sun is visible through the cloud its outline is clearly discernible. Stratus does not produce halo phenomena except, possibly, at very low temperatures. Sometimes stratus appears in the form of ragged patches.

9. *Cumulus (Cu)*. Detached clouds, generally dense and with sharp outlines, developing vertically in the form of rising mounds, domes or towers, of which the bulging upper part often resembles a cauliflower. The sunlit parts of these clouds are mostly brilliant white; their bases are relatively dark and nearly horizontal. Sometimes cumulus is ragged.

10. *Cumulonimbus (Cb)*. Heavy and dense cloud, with a considerable vertical extent, in the form of a mountain or huge towers. At least part of its upper portion is usually smooth, or fibrous or striated, and nearly always flattened; this part often spreads out in the shape of an anvil or vast plume. Under the base of this cloud which is often very dark, there are frequently low ragged clouds either merged with it or not, and precipitation, sometimes in the form of virga.

General classification of clouds

The first differentiation between clouds may be made on their general appearance in the sky, to describe the clouds as either stratiform or cumuliform. Stratiform clouds are in the form of a layer of cloud as in fig. 6.1, while

Fig. 6.1   Stratiform or layer cloud

cumuliform clouds are characterised by vertical development in the form of heaps or lumps, as in fig. 6.2.

Secondly, although it is sometimes difficult to determine the cloud base height when rain, drizzle, or snow particularly, is falling from clouds, clouds are also classified by their base height. (If cloud is 'on the deck', it is really fog.) On this basis, clouds may be categorised as being 'high cloud', 'medium cloud' or 'low cloud'. This categorisation may be further refined by making a sub-group of the low clouds which are of such great vertical extent that they extend into the medium and high levels of the troposphere.

Fig. 6.2   Cumuliform or heap cloud

Table 3 classifies the ten fundamental cloud types. The heights and cloud base temperatures tend to be higher than average in summer and lower in winter. As they vary too with latitude, comparative base height figures are given for low (tropical) and high (polar) latitudes, as well as approximate values for the UK (temperate latitudes).

Table 3

Cloud	Latitude		
	Temperate	Polar	Tropical
High			
Cirrus (Ci)	16 000 to 45 000 ft	10 000 to 25 000 ft	20 000 to 60 000 ft
Cirrocumulus(Cc)			
Cirrostratus(Cs)	$-20°$ to $-60°C$		
Medium			
Altocumulus (Ac)	6500 to 23 000 ft	6500 to 13 000 ft	6500 to 25 000 ft
Altostratus (As)	$+10°$ to $-20°C$		
Low (stratiform)			
Nimbostratus(Ns)	500 to 6500 ft $+10°$ to $-10°C$	500 to 6500 ft	1000 to 6500 ft
Stratocumulus(Sc)	1000 to 6500 ft $+15°$ to $-10°C$	1000 to 6500 ft	1000 to 6500 ft
Stratus(St)	Surface to 1500 ft $+20°$ to $-5°C$	Surface to 1500 ft	Surface to 1500 ft
Great vertical extent			
Cumulus (Cu)	1500 to 6500 ft $+20$ to $-5°C$	1500 to 6500 ft	1500 to 6500 ft
Cumulonimbus (Cb)	1000 to 6500 ft	1000 to 6500 ft	1000 to 6500 ft

Cumulus clouds on fine sunny days with a stable atmosphere may be very limited in their vertical extent and are then referred to as 'fair weather cumulus' – to the meteorologist, 'cumulus humilis'. However, in unstable atmospheric conditions when the cumulus build upwards through the troposphere, the clouds are then called 'towering cumulus' (cumulus congestus).

Apart from these rather self-evident prefixes to the basic cloud name 'cumulus', there are a number of other terms used to amplify the descriptions of clouds and of these a practising pilot should know the following:

Calvus (cal). Cumulonimbus is described as calvus (from the Latin for bald) when although there is no visible cirriform part, some of the 'cauliflower' cloud top is starting to change to a fibrous structure.

Capillatus (cap). This suffix is added to the name by meteorologists observing cumulonimbus to indicate that the cloud(s) have a definite cirriform top – usually anvil-shaped. The cloud is probably associated with a thunderstorm with squalls and showers, possibly of hail, and virga beneath it. It has been said that if the aircraft is near Cb cap then the aircraft captain should be the pilot handling the controls.

Castellanus (cast). A term applied to Ci, Cc, Ac and Sc (and previously termed 'castellatus') when the cloud takes on a turreted or crenellated appearance. This appearance is most noticeable when a line of the cloud is seen from one side. It is indicative of instability at the cloud level.

Fractus (frs). This suffix is applied only to cumulus and stratus. It indicates that the cloud is broken or ragged in appearance. *Lenticularis (len)*. Clouds such as Cc, Ac, Sc which are described as lenticular are in the form of lens or almond shapes. They are good indicators of standing waves (Chapter 10).

Virga. This is a term used in relation to clouds and not as suffix to a particular cloud name. It is the name to describe precipitation descending from the base of a cloud but not reaching the surface. The precipitation may be falling vertically or slantwise and is also described as 'fallstreaks'.

Cloud formation

Clouds form in what previously was clear sky because the air is cooled so that it becomes saturated and then cooled further so that there is an excess of water vapour over and above the amount required to saturate at that temperature and pressure. This excess water vapour then condenses out onto condensation nuclei as visible water drops or ice crystals.

The necessary cooling can take place by:

(a) long-wave radiation from the air itself, although there is little evidence that on its own it is likely to produce condensation. Long-wave radiation from the upper surfaces of pre-existing cloud may however lead to enough cooling to produce further cloud.

(b) contact with a cold surface, so losing heat from the air by conduction, but this process too is unlikely to be significant in producing cloud. In calm or very light winds, the condensation is deposited as dew or frost. In slightly stronger winds, the condensation will be as mist or fog. In winds exceeding 8 knots the vertical motion within the turbulence then generated will produce adiabatic cooling and conductional cooling is not then the significant factor.

(c) mixing two nearly saturated masses of air at markedly different temperatures. There is again little evidence that this process is a reason for clouds to form. However, the process can contribute to additional condensation in certain circumstances. It will be considered later in the context of fog formation.

The basic reason why clouds form is adiabatic cooling, as was described in Chapter 5. The sequence is:

1. For some reason, air is caused to rise. The four different reasons for this are often used to categorise the resulting clouds:

   (a) Orographic cloud – formed due to the ascent of air over high (or rising) ground.

   (b) Convection cloud – formed due to surface heating of the air producing thermal up-currents.

   (c) Turbulence cloud – formed due to the air flow producing a frictional turbulence layer caused either by the underlying earth's surface or, at upper levels, another airflow associated with a rapid wind change with height.

   (d) Frontal cloud – formed when there is a general ascent of air over a wide area. This situation is typical of low pressure systems where large air masses of different characteristics are in juxtaposition. Frontal cloud will be considered in Chapter 12.

2. The rising air is subjected to a steady decrease of pressure as it ascends.

3. The decreasing pressure causes the air to expand.

4. The expanding air cools adiabatically.

5. If stages 1, 2, 3, and 4 are continued sufficiently, the originally unsaturated air will become saturated. The height at which this saturation occurs is called the 'condensation level'. It should be noted however that the temperature of the air at the condensation level is not the original surface air's dew point temperature. Remember the definition from Chapter 3 is 'Dew point temperature is the temperature to which air must be cooled at constant pressure to become saturated by the water vapour it contains'. In the case of ascending air, while it is unsaturated the temperature will decrease at the DALR while the dew point temperature will decrease at 0.5 C deg per 1000 ft. This latter decrease is due to the fact that as the pressure on air is reduced, so its capacity to hold water vapour at a given temperature increases. For example, the saturation humidity mixing ratio at 20°C and 1000 mb is 15 g/kg but at 20°C and 900 mb is 16.5 g/kg. In fact at 900 mb, 15 g/kg will saturate the air at 18.5°C. Thus in 100 mb (approximately 3000 ft) the dew point corresponding to 15 g/kg has decreased by 1.5 C deg, i.e. 0.5 C deg per 1000 feet.

6. Further ascent and expansional cooling will produce the excess invisible water vapour which condenses out as the visible water droplets (or ice crystals) of cloud.

Cloud characteristics

Generally, the mode of uplift of the air which will be explored in more detail in later paragraphs tends to determine the cloud characteristics of:

(a) the time of the occurrence of the cloud
(b) the location of the clouds and their horizontal distribution
(c) the persistence of the cloud and often their dispersal
(d) the location and nature of any precipitation associated with the cloud.

The degree of stability or instability of the environment in which the air is forced to ascend determines:

(a) the vertical extent of the cloud
(b) turbulence within the cloud and other flight conditions.

Cloud dispersal

The ultimate dispersal of cloud involves a reversal of the formation process – the visible water drops or ice crystals disappear either due to evaporation or by just falling out of the air that had previously sustained them. In the former case, the cloud evaporates either because the air becomes warmer (and as its capacity to contain water vapour increases so the relative humidity falls to below 100%) or because the cloud, especially if it is isolated as in the case of cumulus, is surrounded by drier air with which it mixes. In the latter case, precipitation physically removes the water from the air by returning it to the surface. Further reflection on fig. 3.1 will substantiate that this is indeed a significant factor.

Orographic cloud

When an airstream meets a range of hills or mountains or even just generally rising terrain, it too ascends and, due to the decreasing pressure, cools adiabatically. The effect is also true with individual hills or peaks although some of the airflow will, in this case, be diverted around the hill or peak. Provided that the basic parameters are satisfied, orographic cloud forms irrespective of the time of day or season of the year. Depending upon the stability of the airstream and the humidity at different levels, there are variations in the orographic cloud that results which are as follows.

Stable air

Consider first an airstream which has moved from over the sea and is moist through a deep layer, say 10 000 feet or more. The air ascends to beyond the condensation level and cloud is formed, perhaps at a base height of only a few hundred feet if the initial humidity is very high. Each of the moist layers above the surface will also rise, as shown in fig. 6.3, producing a thick layer of stratiform cloud. Because of the stable lapse rate, when the air is no longer physically being forced to rise by the shape of the terrain it will descend on the leeside to warm adiabatically. The high ground will be enveloped in cloud (hill fog), there will probably be continuous precipitation ranging from drizzle to rain or snow on the windward side and a rain shadow on the leeside.

The loss by precipitation on the windward side means that there is less water to be re-evaporated on the leeward side so the cloud base is correspondingly

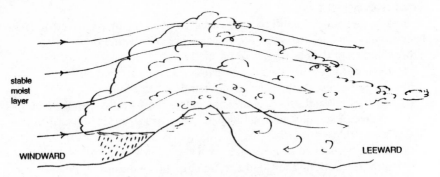

Fig. 6.3   Orographic cloud in moist stable airstream

higher. It also means that where the rising air in the cloud has cooled relatively slowly at the SALR (say 1.5 C deg per 1000 ft), on the lee side for much of its descent it will be warming at the greater rate of the DALR (3 C deg per 1000 ft), and an aerodrome here will experience a warm dry wind. This is generally known as 'föhn effect' after the Alpine name 'Föhn wind', but there are various local names where the effect occurs elsewhere, e.g. Chinook in Canada, Bohorok in Indonesia, etc. Apart from the hazards arising from the orographic cloud obscuring the high ground and the effects of precipitation, such cloud is also associated with airframe icing problems and turbulent flight conditions in 'mountain waves' which are considered in later pages.

If the lifted moist air is not very deep, as may happen when air from the North Sea moves over the eastern coast of the UK, then the cloud may produce no precipitation, even as drizzle, and the rather flat cloud base is effectively the same on the lee side as on the windward, as shown in fig. 6.4. The cloud is commonly stratus, its base may be as low as 200 to 300 feet and in some favoured valleys amongst the moors, may disperse locally.

The other characteristic orographic cloud of stable air is lenticular cloud, as shown in fig. 6.5. This cloud is often a significant indicator to the mountain waves mentioned earlier and it may occur as low, medium or high cloud. All that is required in this case is a low enough relative humidity at low levels so that the surface air is still unsaturated by the time that it reaches the summit of the high ground and starts descending again, while above it there is a moist layer which is also diverted upwards and which produces the cloud.

The outline of the lenticular cloud is quite sharp. The cloud appears stationary

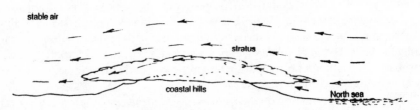

Fig. 6.4   Orographic stratus over low hills

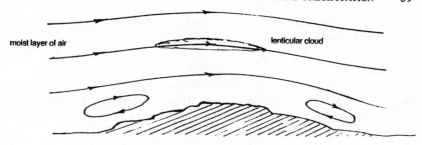

Fig. 6.5   Lenticular cloud over high ground

in the sky, although in fact the cloud droplets of which it is composed are streaming along with the upper wind, forming on the windward side and dispersing on the leeward, the one contradiction to the general comment made on shapes of clouds and their movement with the wind, in the opening paragraphs of this chapter!

Other hazards associated with stratiform orographic cloud

Apart from the eddy turbulence that occurs whenever an airflow crosses high ground, the danger from downdraughts found on the downwind side of the hills and the ever-present risk for unwary pilots of colliding with the high ground through failing to maintain safety altitude, two other hazards arise when pre-existing cloud sheets move into hilly or mountainous areas.

Firstly, it may well be possible to fly a cross-country beneath a cloud sheet in VMC. However, the air beneath the cloud may well also have become nearly saturated, even though this will not be discernible from the flight-deck. In this event, when the cloudy airstream meets high ground the ascent and adiabatic cooling quickly produces cloud. The cloud base then lowers appreciably so that it may prove impossible to maintain VMC.

Secondly, if committed to flying through orographic cloud, beware of an increase in severity of airframe icing where a front rises over high ground. It should not be assumed that, because crossing a belt of frontal cloud produced no problems when encountered over flat terrain on an outward journey, on the return flight crossing the same front in a mountainous area will produce the same weather: it may be much worse. This is because the orographic updraughts will

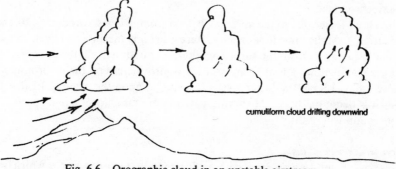

Fig. 6.6   Orographic cloud in an unstable airstream

supplement the frontal uplift so supporting bigger and more water drops than earlier in the day.

Unstable air

The airstream may be unstable for a number of reasons including potential instability which develops as the airstream rises over the high ground. Depending upon the relative humidity and the degree of instability, so either of the possibilities shown in figs. 6.6 and 6.7 may occur.

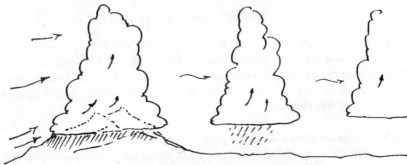

Fig. 6.7   Shower cloud of orographic origin

If the airstream is not very humid at low levels, there may well be a clear space between the hill-tops and the cumuliform cloud base (fig. 6.6). However, once the air is forced to rise, the instability will permit it to continue to rise even after the parcel of air has moved away from the 'source hill' which has triggered off the initial upward movement. This often results in the individual cumulus clouds lining up in distinct 'cloud streets' which are readily seen from the air and even better from satellite cloud photographs.

If the airstream is very humid, the cloud base will obscure the high ground and towering cumulus or cumulonimbus and showery precipitation will be triggered off, as well as the clouds again drifting off downwind. Not only do these produce difficult conditions for aircraft operations (especially for light aircraft) but also the rapid deteriorations cause the annual crop of accidents to unwary mountaineers and hill-walkers.

Convection cloud

This cloud forms due to the air being heated from below so producing thermal upcurrents. At the same time as the surface is heating the air irregularly, causing some to rise away from the surface in a series of convective bubbles or parcels, so the conduction of heat from beneath is also increasing the environmental lapse rate (ELR) in the lower levels. Depending upon the original ELR value which is being modified, so varying patterns of cumuliform cloud formed by convection will result.

Fair weather cumulus

This type of cloud is associated with predominantly stable conditions which limit

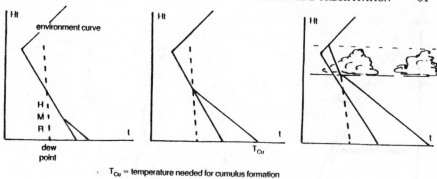

T_{Cu} = temperature needed for cumulus formation

Fig. 6.8   Formation of fair weather cumulus

the vertical extent of the convection. Figure 6.8 illustrates a series of ELRs such as would prevail.

Initially, the convection currents start over the terrain which warms most rapidly, as already discussed in Chapter 2. For a while however, because of the stable lapse rate, they do not reach the condensation level. Nevertheless the absence of cloud enables the surface temperatures to increase steadily in the continuing sunshine, producing stronger convection currents and deepening the surface unstable layer. Provided that there is no marked wind shear which will sever the rising currents, and also that the general humidity is not so low that mixing with their surroundings, called entrainment, will keep them unsaturated, the upcurrents will eventually reach and rise above the condensation level. However, because of the basic stability of the initial ELR, vertical development of the cloud is inhibited and generally each small cumulus will last less than half an hour before dispersing. If the surface temperatures continue to rise there will be a corresponding rise in the height of the cloud base and top. Sometimes if there is a marked stable layer such as an inversion above the condensation level, the rising bubbles of air having initially formed the small cumulus spread out sideways to form a layer of stratocumulus (fig. 6.9).

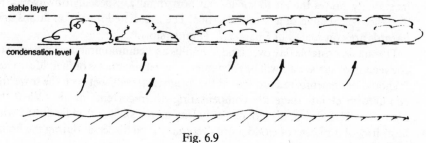

Fig. 6.9

Towering cumulus

In this case the environment is unstable through a deeper layer, usually in excess of 10000 feet. The surface heating of the moist air may either be due to the normal overland daytime heating by the sun or to advection of cool air to over

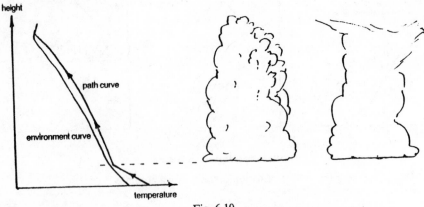

Fig. 6.10

a warmer surface at any time during the 24 hours. The surface air continues to ascend because while cooling at the saturated adiabatic lapse rate it remains warmer than the environment (fig. 6.10).

The rising currents produce condensation and despite the entrainment of unsaturated air around, this condensation continues to great heights. The ultimate cloud tops are limited by the tropopause so although convection clouds extend to 20 000 feet in polar regions, they commonly develop to over 50 000 feet in low latitudes. Similarly their vertical extent is greater in summer than in winter.

Assuming the dawn of a fine day when, through a deep layer, the air is humid and the environmental lapse rate exceeds the saturated adiabatic value, surface heating starts bubbles of air rising. Typically the initial cloud base may be around 1500 to 2000 feet. While the cloud is developing, the top is rounded and cauliflower-like as it reaches upper levels. When it reaches temperatures of –10°C and colder, ice starts to become a feature of the upper parts of the cloud which then take on a fibrous appearance. When ultimately the tropopause is reached, its stability causes the air to spread out horizontally, especially downwind, to give the typical anvil of a cumulonimbus. The associated flight conditions and hazards are considered in Chapter 7: Thunderstorms.

During an unstable day over land, cumulus and cumulonimbus clouds due to convection of surface air will be encountered in varying stages of their life cycles. It should be remembered too that in the 'bright intervals' between the towering cumuliform clouds there are compensating down-currents of air. When the convection dies down, the clouds decay leaving the sky for a while dotted with large irregular masses of cloud, until eventually it all disperses during the hours of darkness.

Turbulence cloud
Turbulence may occur at any level due to the friction between two differing airflows where there is a marked windshear. It is even more common near to the earth's surface due to friction between the lower atmosphere and the terrain

below, together with small-scale, localised orographic and convection effects.

Stable air

The simplest case to consider is the formation of a sheet of stratocumulus cloud due to turbulence, for which the basic requirements are:

(a) air of a sufficiently high humidity for it to become saturated within the turbulence layer,

(b) a sufficiently strong wind speed (8 knots or more for all practical purposes) so that air rising in the up-currents of the turbulence layer will cool adiabatically, rather than have its temperature determined by conduction to/from the underlying surface,

(c) a sufficiently strong wind for the underlying surface to produce a deep enough turbulence layer to reach up to beyond the condensation level,

(d) a stable lapse rate so the cloud is restricted to the height to which the turbulence lifts the air.

Sheets of stratocumulus (or stratus where the cloud base is below 1000 feet) commonly occur due to surface frictional turbulence.

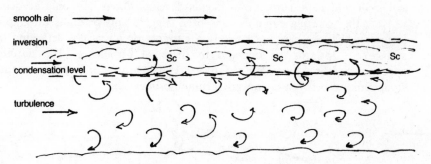

Fig. 6.11   Formation of stratocumulus by turbulence

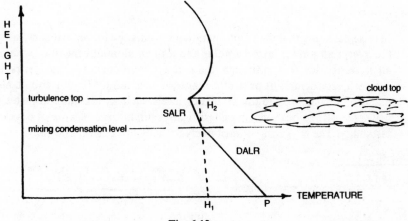

Fig. 6.12

Taking factors (a) to (d) in sequence, (a) determines the distribution of humidity through the layer. The effect of the turbulent mixing is to produce a uniform humidity mixing ratio through the layer (H_1H_2 in fig. 6.12).

Provided that the wind speed is strong enough, (b), the lapse rate through the layer will tend towards the adiabatic lapse rate – warmer at the bottom of the layer, colder at its upper parts. Then if (c) also applies, the adiabatic cooling will cause the air to become saturated when the path curve from P intersects H_1H_2 at 'the mixing condensation level' and produce cloud above this level.

Finally, given condition (d) the stable atmosphere will prevent air rising (and producing cloud) beyond the height to which it is forced to rise by the turbulence. This produces the sheet of cloud with very smooth flying conditions and a temperature inversion above it.

The corresponding clouds formed at medium and high levels are altocumulus and cirrocumulus respectively.

Unstable air
In an unstable airstream, the turbulence layer is of greater vertical extent than in stable air and large cumuliform clouds develop. Often it is only academic whether the towering cumulus have been triggered off by some orographic features which are causing convection currents or physically deflecting the surface air upwards, as opposed to frictional turbulence. The resulting appearance of the sky is as depicted in fig. 6.13 with broken or ragged stratus and stratocumulus between the towering cumuliform clouds.

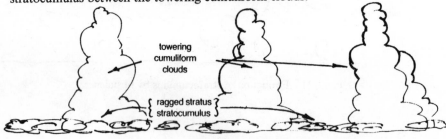

Fig. 6.13

It is interesting that in the international system used for reporting cloud types, the interpretation for large cumulus and for cumulonimbus with or without an anvil recognises that although these are the dominant cloud types being reported, stratocumulus or stratus may also be present. Mention should also be made of turbulence clouds at higher levels such as altocumulus which are 'triggered off' to become characteristically cumuliform because of developing instability. The triggering is most likely to be by the general uplift of air near to

Fig. 6.14   Altocumulus castellanus and virga

a depression but may be by orographic uplift. The resulting cloud is altocumulus castellanus, as shown in fig. 6.14.

The sprouting turret-like tops of the altocumulus, and possibly virga below, if seen ahead of the aircraft, are good indicators to pilots of a bumpy ride ahead and the possibility of development in that area of cumulonimbus and thunderstorms. Cirrus castellanus does also occur for similar reasons, but only rarely.

Frontal cloud

This is dealt with fully in Chapter 12: Low Pressure Systems and Fronts. For completeness of this chapter it will be noted that in the UK, where the terms are in common use on radio and TV by the weather forecasters, the following generalisations apply.

Stable

When a large warm moist air mass overtakes a large cold air mass at a warm front, the structure is usually stable so producing widespread stratiform cloud as shown in fig. 6.15.

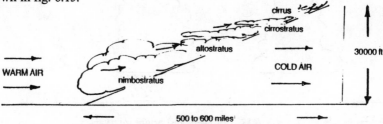

Fig. 6.15   Stable: warm front – layered cloud

Unstable

Conversely, when a cold air mass overtakes a warm air mass at a cold front, instability may well develop giving cumuliform cloud as shown in fig. 6.16.

Precipitation

Although precipitation is a common topic of conversation in the British Isles, it is probably as well to establish the meaning of terms associated with precipitation in aviation meteorology, to avoid misunderstanding.

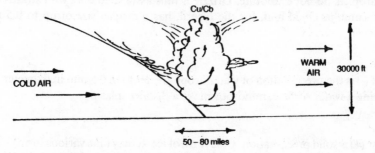

Fig. 6.16   Unstable: cold front – cumuliform cloud

Continuity of precipitation

Three terms are used: *continuous*, *intermittent*, and *showers*. 'Continuous' is self-evident. Intermittent is applied to the state in which precipitation is discontinuous when it is falling from a layer of cloud, as in fig. 6.17. Showers fall from the individual cumuliform clouds with which they are associated, as in fig. 6.18.

Fig. 6.17   Overcast with intermittent precipitation

Fig. 6.18   Showers and bright intervals

Types of precipitation

Drizzle

Drizzle (,) is liquid precipitation in the form of very small water drops, normally very close together, indeed so small that their impact on an exposed water surface is imperceptible. The droplets are so small that the up-currents against which they are falling must be very weak and the air below the cloud very humid so that the droplets do not evaporate. Drizzle is thus associated only with stratus and stratocumulus cloud and, for the record, has a droplet size of up to 0.5 mm diameter.

Rain

Rain (·) is the precipitation of water drops greater than 0.5 mm in diameter. On striking a water surface, raindrops make a distinct splash.

Snow

Snow (✳) is solid precipitation in the form of ice. It may take various forms In the UK, snow mostly occurs as snowflakes which are white, opaque, ice crystals. At lower temperatures the flakes have an individual, six-pointed, crystalline structure but at surface temperatures around 0°C crystals amalgamate to give large snowflakes. Snowflakes can occur at surface temperatures up to 4°C and a foot of freshly fallen snow is approximately equal to an inch of rainfall. In very cold temperatures, the precipated ice may fall as 'granular snow' consisting of small (less than 1 mm in diameter) white opaque grains or as ice needles, the latter giving a scintillating fog – often nicknamed 'diamond dust' by the hardy souls inhabiting such cold climes.

Sleet

Sleet (⁂) in the UK means either snow that is melting as it falls to earth or a mixture of snow and rain (or even drizzle) falling together because the surface air temperature is just above 0°C. However, although the international symbol (⁂) reflects the state of affairs on this side of the Atlantic, beware, because the term sleet may be used in general parlance in the USA to indicate frozen or freezing precipitation.

Hail

Hail (△) comprises precipitation in the form of small balls or chunks of ice which may vary in size from 2 to 5 mm in soft hail (or graupel) (△) to golf ball or tennis ball size in the hail (▲) associated with violent thunderstorms, of which more later.

Because they are also means by which water is deposited from the atmosphere, dew and frost are included in precipitation totals recorded for a meteorological station.

Formation of precipitation

Precipitation in general can be quite a significant weather factor to a pilot, especially during the take-off and initial climb and then later in the approach and landing phase. Not only is it usually associated with a rapid lowering of the cloud base but there is also a reduction in visibility at the same time as there may be turbulence, downdraughts and gusty winds or squalls. In the cases of hailstones or rain which is freezing as it falls, these bring their own additional hazards. Just when and why a cloud system may be expected to produce precipitation is therefore a matter of some importance to the pilot.

It has already been stated that a cloud water droplet will probably have a diameter of 0.02 mm and that raindrops have a diameter of greater than 0.5 mm (in fact, up to a maximum of 5.5 mm diameter). Whatever its size, the water drop has mass and so will fall through the air around it at a speed called its terminal velocity. The heavier the drop, the greater its terminal velocity. Of course, if the air current in the cloud is travelling upwards as fast as or faster than the terminal velocity downwards, then the water drop will not leave the cloud base. There are two mechanisms by which cloud particles can grow large enough to fall as precipitation:

(a) Ice-particle (Bergeron Process) growth
(b) Coalescence/collision growth.

Ice particle theory of growth

Although it had been suggested soon after World War I that there needed to be both ice crystals (i.e. temperatures below 0°C) and water drops in cloud for rain to form, it was not until the mid-1930s that the Norwegian scientist Bergeron put forward the basis of this theory. Recall Table 2 in Chapter 3 for saturation vapour pressure following the discussion on relative humidity. When cloud temperatures fall below 0°C and ice nuclei are present, ice crystals form amongst the supercooled water droplets. However, in these circumstances, although the air is saturated in respect of water it is supersaturated in respect of the ice crystals. Consequently the ice crystals will grow rapidly by condensation upon them. By rapid growth they become large enough to fall through the up-currents (possibly growing further by the coalescence/collision process), enter a part of the cloud with temperatures over 0°C where they melt, and fall from the cloud as rain.

Coalescence/collision theory of growth

Despite Bergeron's theory, sometimes rain falls from clouds which are warmer at all levels than 0°C. In this case the precipitation occurs because within the cloud not all of the droplets are of the same size nor are all of the up-currents of equal strength. Large water droplets rise more slowly in up-currents than small droplets and grow in size at the expense of the small drops by collisions and coalescence. When they fall back through the cloud they then grow rapidly from more collisions with rising cloud droplets, so that after a minimum period of about half an hour, the water drops are big enough to fall as rain.

In the UK, precipitation is usually caused by both processes acting together. Of course, once the precipitation leaves the cloud base, it will be falling through unsaturated air, albeit probably of a high humidity, so the droplets or particles will diminish by evaporation. In fact, rain or snow originating from altostratus may be encountered by an aircraft in flight but evaporate entirely before reaching the runways of an aerodrome below. On the debit side, the evaporation may itself saturate the air below the cloud and ultimately produce condensation as very low stratus (known as pannus) which can easily obscure the upper parts of even small hills.

What other problems should a pilot guard himself against in precipitation? First, and perhaps most obvious, is the effect on visibility. In snow, sleet and drizzle it will be extremely poor indeed, with no time to manoeuvre if something solid looms up ahead, so a re-check of altitude and safety altitude is called for. In rain the visibility may be no worse than 1 kilometre unless you are in a tropical downpour. The rain on the windscreen does not help either and, at night, judgement of the distance of lights requires great care.

Although the worst conditions are experienced with the thunderstorms considered in the next chapter, precipitation causes static interference on the aircraft's radio systems.

Precipitation also 'contaminates' runway surfaces. The associated hazards are so serious that the United Kingdom Civil Aviation Authority normally has one or more of its pink 'Safety' Aeronautical Information Circulars (AICs) currently valid on this topic at any one time. Runways which are wet during or after precipitation can produce handling or braking problems so pilots are told the runway surface state in the following terms.

Damp – the runway surface shows a change of colour due to moisture.

Wet – the runway surface is soaked but no significant patches of standing water are visible.

In each of these two cases, pilots can assume an acceptable degree of braking action is possible.

Water patches – significant patches of standing water are visible.

Flooded – extensive standing water patches are visible.

In these two latter categories there is a distinct possibility of aquaplaning, and the procedures laid down in the aircraft's flight manual and the company's operations manual must be followed. In fact, together with runways contaminated with snow and slush, the CAA warn that operations from such runways involve a significant amount of risk.

During cold weather, aerodrome authorities do their best to keep runways, taxiways, etc., clear of snow and slush. Particulars are given in the Air Pilot of the UK Snow Plan and SNOTAMs give current situations at aerodromes during wintry conditions. Depending upon the specific gravity (SG) of the contaminant, the subjective assessment is made as:

Dry snow	less than 0.35 SG
Wet snow	0.35 to 0.5 SG
Compacted snow	over 0.5 SG
Slush	0.5 to 0.8 SG
Standing water	1.00 SG

The risks high-lighted by CAA are:

1. additional drag
2. possible power loss due to ingestion or impingement
3. reduced braking or risk of aquaplaning
4. reduced directional control
5. possible structural damage

So pilots are cautioned by CAA:

(a) not to attempt to take off in depths greater than
    60 mm of dry snow
    15 mm of wet snow, slush or water
(b) ensure the good condition of tyres and all retardation and anti-skid devices
(c) to operate as advised in the Flight Manual
(d) not to carry unnecessary fuel
(e) to check all de-icing has left the aircraft completely 'clean' for take-off

(f) not to take off in a tail wind or in more than a slight cross-wind

(g) to avoid snow/slush adhering to the aircraft while taxying, especially not to use reverse thrust

(h) to use maximum runway distance and maximum take-off power available together with the normal rotation and take-off safety speeds.

The same guidelines are applicable to landing on heavily contaminated runways, with the extra problem that if aquaplaning starts, it may well continue in much lower depths of water and slush than would normally be expected.

For completeness of information, the following relevant information is reproduced from the companion volume *Aviation Law for Pilots* concerning the measurement and reporting of runway braking action:

'Measurements are taken of runway braking action and snow/slush depth as follows:

Runway braking action is assessed by the use of a continuous recording runway friction measuring trailer (Mu-meter) and the brake testing decelerometer (Tapley meter). Assessment of ice, snow and slush is reported as GOOD, MEDIUM-GOOD, MEDIUM, MEDIUM-POOR, POOR when the braking action is passed to the pilot. Wet runway condition is reported as GOOD, MEDIUM or POOR. The Tapley meter is used on ice and dry snow. The Mu-meter indicates the possibility of slush-planing when it gives a low value of coefficient of friction, but braking action is not assessed in slush-planing conditions.' (See also Chapter 16: METAR.)

Test questions

Q1.   Most cloud in the UK is formed due to air cooling:

    (a) by conduction

    (b) by convection

    (c) adiabatically.

Q2.   Clouds with 'strat' in their names are:

    (a) rain bearing

    (b) layer type

    (c) composed only of water drops.

Q3.   Of the following clouds, the one with the lowest base height is:

    (a) altostratus

    (b) stratocumulus

    (c) stratus.

Q4.   If altocumulus castellanus is seen ahead of the aircraft, this indicates:

    (a) increasing stability

    (b) increasing instability

    (c) improving weather to probably cloudless skies.

Q5.   Heights at which clouds are found in the UK:

    (a) do not vary with the seasons

    (b) are generally higher in summer than in winter

    (c) are generally lower in summer than in winter.

Q6.   A sheet of cloud which is producing a halo round the sun is:

    (a) cirrostratus

(b) altostratus

(c) nimbostratus.

Q7.   When cumulonimbus cloud is reported in a meteorological observation:

(a) stratus may also be present

(b) stratus will not be present

(c) stratus and nimbostratus will also be present.

Q8.   In a stable airstream producing orographic cloud and precipitation, the cloud base on the windward side of the high ground will be:

(a) lower than the cloud base on the leeward side

(b) higher than the cloud base on the leeward side

(c) the same height as the cloud base on the leeward side.

Q9.   Convection clouds over the UK in spring:

(a) tend to show no diurnal variation

(b) form by night and disperse by day

(c) form by day and disperse during the night.

Q10.   Of the following statements, it is true to say:

(a) drizzle never falls in showers

(b) hail is rain that has frozen as it falls from cloud

(c) rain always leaves the cloudbase as snowflakes.

7: Thunderstorms

In some parts of the world thunderstorms are a frequent occurrence; for example, Indonesia has over 200 thunderstorm days per annum. Other aerodromes, in countries mainly situated on coasts which are washed by cold sea currents, experience thunderstorms very rarely if ever at all. Whether rare or common, thunderstorms are synonymous with cumulonimbus clouds so their causes can be restated as:

    (a) something has caused the air to rise – 'trigger action'
    (b) a high humidity through a deep layer
    (c) instability through a deep layer.

Depending upon the cause of initial uplift of the air, thunderstorms may variously be categorised as:

    air mass: orographic thunderstorms
                 heat thunderstorms
    frontal: particularly cold front storms.

By so referring to the thunderstorm type, the pilot can infer the timing, location and track of the storm.

Orographic thunderstorms may be encountered at any time in the 24 hours and often hang about in the mountainous areas that first generated them.

Heat thunderstorms are what are generally understood when the term 'air mass thunderstorm' is used. In this case, the surface heating 'triggers off' convection cloud development. In light winds such as occur in cols inland in summer, convection currents are not sheared off and strong solar heating soon builds up cumuliform cloud so that storms can start breaking out in mid-afternoon and continue till after nightfall. The movement of such storms is often slow and irregular.

Other heat thunderstorms occur when a moist air mass, perhaps already unstable, moves over a much warmer surface. This would apply over land in spring and summer, and over sea areas in autumn and winter. The heating of the lower layers increases the instability of the environmental lapse rate and at the same time triggers off the convection currents. These thunderstorms move along with the air mass in which they have developed and may well be quite widespread. Although over land such heat storms have a diurnal variation, over the sea which has a fairly equable temperature they may be met at any time in the 24 hours. Where cool land air moves over an inland sea or lake to produce thunderstorms, it is found that such storms often develop in the late evening or during the night.

In contrast, frontal thunderstorms which are usually associated with cold fronts are arranged along a line in a trough of low pressure and they move with this trough in a direction perpendicular to the trough line. The line of cumulonimbus will be shown on the meteorological station's radar so its future movement can be reasonably forecast and when airborne, a pilot can check progress on the aircraft's weather radar. Because of the greater frequency of cold fronts in winter, this is the season when frontal thunderstorms are most likely to be encountered in NW Europe. However, whether the storms will be met by day or by night, over land or over the sea, is merely a matter of chance of timing of the flight and the passage of the frontal trough across the flight path.

Although many storms follow the 700 mb (10 000 ft) airflow the movement of others, especially heat thunderstorms in cols and slack pressure gradients, is more erratic.

Development

Although it involves some repetition of explanations made in Chapters 5 and 6 on instability and cloud formation, the serious hazards presented by the development of cumulonimbus to pilots, particularly the inexperienced, more than justify a restatement of the sequence of the formation process.

Observations show that the development of a cumulonimbus cloud can be conveniently considered as having three phases:
1. Developing or cumulus phase (fig. 7.1)
2. Mature phase (fig. 7.2)
3. Dissipating phase (fig. 7.3)
For simplicity of visualising the sequence of events, assume the thunderstorm to be developing inland on a hot and humid summer's day in a col.

Fig. 7.1   Developing or cumulus phase

Phase 1
Convection bubbles rise from the surface to produce small cumulus clouds which, because of the instability, then merge to grow into a larger cumulus. This is the start of a thunderstorm cell – probably of a diameter of one to five miles and composed at this time only of up-currents. The ultimate cumulonimbus will be composed of a number of such cells in different phases of development, each cell having a life-span of two to three hours. This developing or cumulus phase may last for up to half an hour, with the original bubbles of rising air being supplemented by entrainment of air from the environment around them. Flight through the cumulus can be quite turbulent even at this stage as the speed of ascent of the air in the individual cells will vary.

Fig. 7.2   Mature phase

Phase 2

Enough growth has now occurred so that droplets start to fall from the cloud. In this mature phase, while the upper parts of the cloud are still developing well above the 0°C level, the precipitation is producing down-draughts in the cloud warming at approximately the SALR value. The instability not only permits the cloud tops to build upwards but also encourages the down-draught of the relatively cold cloudy air to burst out of the cloud as a cool squall, often called the 'first gust'. There is still entrainment to supplement the vertical movement of air.

Phase 3

By this time, the original cells have spent most of their energy – in fact, most was generated in the first $\frac{1}{2}$ to $\frac{3}{4}$ hour. Visually, the ice crystal part of the cloud will be seen spreading out as the anvil of the cumulonimbus while at low levels the precipitation has become sporadic. Because a state of balance between the cloudy air and its environment is being effected, the vertical currents weaken.

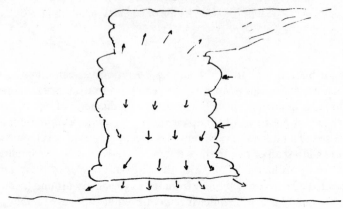

Fig. 7.3   Dissipating phase

There are still slight up-currents in the upper parts of the cloud but much of the body and lower part of the cloud consists of subsiding air.

Because of the cellular nature of thunderstorms, there may well be new cells forming while the older cells are decaying and the associated cloud is dissipating, so it is not uncommon to see groups of clouds arranged as shown in fig. 7.4.

Fig. 7.4

Self-propagating storms

For ascending air currents to travel approximately vertically, ideally there should be a flat calm at all heights and certainly no marked wind shear which would sever them. Sometimes the wind does change with increase of height so that, assuming that the instability over the area is great enough for a thunderstorm still to develop, the axis of the cumulonimbus is tilted. In this case, the vertical motion in and around the cloud will produce a strong forward down-draught. This down-draught then in turn will cause the whole cellular process to be repeated, i.e. the storms are self-propagating (fig. 7.5). Accidents have occurred where pilots have kept a wary eye on an old anvilled cumulonimbus only to commit themselves to a long final approach path through a newly forming large cumulus with its activity at its peak, between phases 1 and 2.

Lightning

Once the developing cloud contains ice crystals, a risk of lightning exists. As the cumulonimbus matures, charges as shown in fig. 7.6 are distributed throughout the cloud. When the potential difference between the charges has built up to a critical strength so that it can overcome the resistance of the air separating them,

Fig. 7.5   Self-propagating storms

a discharge (the flash of lightning) occurs and neutralises the electrical field for the time being. However, if the cumulonimbus cells are still active, the charges immediately start to build up again. The discharge may be entirely within the cloud, from cloud to cloud or from cloud to earth. Because the heat of the lightning stroke causes the air through which it is passing to expand explosively, we hear the clap of thunder. Dividing by five the time interval in seconds between a ground observer seeing a flash and hearing the thunder gives the distance away in miles of the lightning, because although the light is seen instantaneously (or at strictly 186000 miles per second), the sound will travel from the flash at approximately one-fifth of a mile per second.

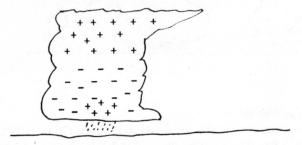

Fig. 7.6   Distribution of electrical charges

If the non-aviating pundit in the airport restaurant declares 'Forked lightning is dangerous, sheet lightning is not', this is perfectly correct as far as risk to a ground observer is concerned. Forked lightning means the directly sighted flash and describes the irregular path adopted by the discharge. Sheet lightning is the name given colloquially to the general illumination of the sky as seen by a ground observer because the lightning flash has taken place either within the cloud or on its other side so that the actual flash is obscured from view.

Hazards
From time to time, the CAA has thought it appropriate to issue a pink 'Safety' Aeronautical Information Circular to remind pilots of the care required when flying in the presence of thunderstorms. The carriage of weather radar on the flight deck has enabled pilots to have early recognition of thunderstorms near the flight path. It is prudent, and always appreciated by the passengers, to avoid thunderstorms rather than to fly in or close to them if it is operationally feasible to do so. All thunderstorms are potentially dangerous and their external appearance is no guide to the severity of the hazards that may be expected. The hazards, not in any order of priority, may be summarised as:

1. Base height. Many large cumuliform clouds have a base height of some 1500 feet or more above ground level so there is space for light aircraft to operate beneath them if necessary. Once thundery precipitation starts, the cloud base lowers and terrain clearance beneath the clouds becomes difficult to maintain. Inside the thunderstorm the visibility may be down to 20 metres.

2. Hail. Despite the mass of information which has been gathered since World War II, there is still no means by which hail can be forecast to fall from particular cumulonimbus clouds with 100% certainty. The forecaster can only provide a pilot with a percentage probability at the best.

Soft hail or graupel are insignificant. Large hailstones, however, are a problem and form when the up-currents prevent small, soft hail from falling out of the cloud. These small stones are carried upwards, striking water drops which freeze around them as a sheet of clear ice. Successive journeys up and down give alternate layers of soft and clear ice as well as the possibility of hailstones fusing together. With the great vertical extent and strong up-currents of thunderstorms in low latitudes, hailstones can build up to golf-ball or tennis-ball size. Although the period involved in transiting the hail area of a thunderstorm may be relatively short, damage from large hailstones can be considerable especially to radomes, transparencies, upper and leading surfaces (including de-icer equipment). The greater the aircraft's speed, the greater the damage and hail can be met anywhere in or under the storm – even under an overhanging anvil.

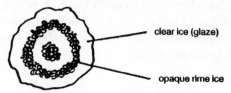

Fig. 7.7   Section through a hailstone

3. Icing. The subject of icing is dealt with as a topic in its own right in Chapter 9. Nevertheless, it should be noted that thunderstorm clouds give icing problems both in the engine(s) and on the airframe. In a piston engine even at temperatures above 0°C there can be a serious loss of power while a turbine engine may suffer a flame-out. On the airframe, the large supercooled water drops freeze to give a rapid build-up of clear ice with its attendant problems of increased weight, disturbed relative airflow decreasing lift and increasing drag, risk of control surfaces becoming less effective, etc. Check the operation of all anti-icing and de-icing equipment and that the pitot heaters are switched on.

4. Instrument errors. Turbulent airflow around the aircraft and the localised variations in pressure can produce rapid and serious errors in the readings of the altimeter, airspeed indicator and vertical speed indicator. If the pressure head suffers serious rain ingress or, worse still, ices up, the pressure instrument readings are useless. Remember too that a lightning strike on the aircraft will probably rearrange the aircraft's magnetism so the compass heading will be suspect.

5. Lightning. This can be used, especially at night, to supplement the aircraft's weather radar for pinpointing the most active storm areas. Because of metal-to-metal bonding and screening of vulnerable equipment, an aircraft struck by lightning is unlikely to suffer more than a scorch mark on the aircraft's skin. Nevertheless the sudden brilliance of the flash, the noise, and sometimes the burning smell, can be distracting to say the least. In a thunderstorm, lightning may occur at any level but has been observed most frequently on test flights between +10°C and –10°C, that is, in a 10000 feet band about the freezing level. To avoid the distraction and blinding effect, wind up the cockpit lighting to full. At least one of the operating pilots on the flight deck should wear dark glasses.

6. Squalls, windshear and micro-bursts. Squalls from thunderstorms wrecked mariners for centuries before aviation commenced. Flying has led to a continuing study of such airflow and yet its pattern cannot be precisely forecast or measured despite an intense study set up by ICAO in 1977. Major airports issue windshear alerting messages and pilots are expected to report any windshear experienced. Figures 7.8, 7.9, and 7.10 depict three possible circumstances which present problems to aircraft taking off or landing.

Sometimes the normal variation of wind speed with height becomes greatly accentuated, perhaps decreasing from 40 knots or more at 1000–2000 feet to less than 10 knots near the surface. If the pilot does not intervene, the actual flight path will divert progressively from that intended (fig. 7.8). A varying crosswind component complicates the matter.

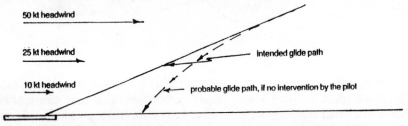

Fig. 7.8   Effect of decreasing headwind when on the approach

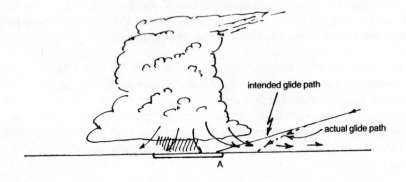

Fig. 7.9   Effect of a gust front ahead of a thunderstorm of an aircraft on the approach

The gust front already referred to in the paragraph on self-propagating storms may be 15 to 20 miles ahead of the storm which generated it. It may be marked by newly-forming cumuliform cloud or by a line of duststorms in desert countries, but equally it may be quite invisible. A typical airflow structure could then take the form shown in fig. 7.9 and take-offs and landings at aerodrome A should be delayed.

Microbursts are particularly intense and localised – probably not more than half a mile across – and especially hazardous when they are overhead or near the runway in use, as in fig. 7.10. Again, if on the approach in thunderstorm conditions it is found that abnormal levels of power are necessary to maintain the airspeed, attitude and glideslope, then a windshear go-around should be initiated.

intended glide path

localised micro–burst from base of storm

actual glide path

Fig. 7.10   Change in flight path due to micro-burst

7. Precipitation. Apart from problems from virga under the cloud base and from the possible ingestion of precipitation into the pitot head, forward visibility is always seriously reduced in heavy precipitation. For departing and arriving aircraft there are the hazards of wet runways to contend with.

8. Static. This is often more of a nuisance than a hazard, as it builds up noise on the radio and can affect communications. It can be an infuriating distraction just when it is least wanted. It is as well to take care when using non-directional radio beacons (NDBs) near their maximum range under these conditions and if in doubt, disregard radio navigation information from ADF and OMEGA.

9. Turbulence. Although last in this alphabetical list, turbulence is by no means the least of the hazards. It makes the aircraft difficult to handle and indeed, incorrect handling can lead to loss of control. If the aircraft is flown at a higher speed than that specified as its 'rough air' or 'thunderstorm penetration speed' in the flight manual then there is a risk of structural failure. On the other hand, speeds lower than that recommended may lead to the aircraft stalling.

Because of the handling problems in rough air, pilots should make sure before entering the turbulence that the 'Fasten seat belts' sign is switched on, the aircraft positioned at the correct safe altitude, power set and the aircraft trimmed to fly at the recommended penetration speed and at the correct attitude. The temptation to chase the small-scale fluctuations of the instrument readings must be resisted and instead, pilots should observe the basic instrument flying principles of maintaining power and attitude.

Test questions

Q1.   Thunderstorms are caused by:
    (a) thunder and lightning
    (b) anvil cumulonimbus
    (c) instability, high humidity, trigger action

Q2.   Frontal thunderstorms are mainly associated with:
    (a) warm fronts
    (b) cold fronts
    (c) ridges of high pressure.

Q3.   Orographic thunderstorms occur:
    (a) at any time during the 24 hours
    (b) almost exclusively during the daylight hours
    (c) mostly after dark, between sunset and 2 am.

Q4.   Heat thunderstorms occur over land in cols because:
    (a) the humidity and ELR may be high and the wind speed low
    (b) the land will be warmer than the sea
    (c) warm fronts frequently occur.

Q5.   With a cumulonimbus cloud over the approach end of the runway a microburst may be experienced:
    (a) over or near the runway in use
    (b) 15–20 km away, at the edge of the downward 'first gust'
    (c) under the nearest self-propagated cumulus.

Q6.   If a cumulonimbus has developed a large anvil:
    (a) it has reached the beginning of the most active (mature) stage
    (b) it is in the most active (mature) stage
    (c) it has reached the third or dissipating stage.

Q7.   If a thunderstorm 10 miles ahead is assessed as still being in the mature phase, the pilot of a light aircraft:
    (a) still has time to climb above the storm
    (b) still has enough visibility and terrain clearance to pass beneath the storm
    (c) should alter heading to circumnavigate the storm.

Q8.   When flying through a turbulent thunderstorm cloud, increasing up to maximum speed (V_{NE}):
    (a) will enable the storm to be penetrated safely in the shortest time
    (b) will probably cause the aircraft to suffer a high speed stall
    (c) will greatly increase the risk of structural failure.

Q9.   To minimise the effect of lightning striking an aircraft in flight, the pilot should:
    (a) wear dark glasses and turn the cockpit lighting to maximum
    (b) turn off all the radios and unnecessary electrics
    (c) engage the autopilot and relax.

Q10. The general rule relating to the probable direction of movement of a
thunderstorm observed to be 20 nm ahead of your aircraft is:
(a) it will follow the direction of the surface wind
(b) it will follow the direction of the 2000 ft wind
(c) that its motion is not reliably predictable.

8: Visibility and Fog

Visibility is of major importance to the pilot and is one of the parameters which determine whether he can fly under Visual Flight Rules (VFR) on the basis of 'see and be seen'. Legally flight visibility is defined as 'visibility forward from the flight deck of an aircraft in flight'. When the meteorologist uses the term 'visibility' in discussions with a pilot he is referring to surface conditions and means the maximum horizontal distance at which an object can be clearly recognised by the naked eye. The object has to be of a size commensurate with its distance away from the observer and ideally of a dark colour, on the horizon. If there is a marked variation in the visibility observed in different directions, then the visibility in the poorest direction is that reported. Particularly, a pilot is interested in the visibility prevailing along the runway in use in the take-off and landing direction and this requirement is catered for in poor visibility conditions by the provision of Runway Visual Range (RVR). This is a measurement service (not forecast) provided by Air Traffic Control. If the RVR is measured by instruments called transmissometers (and there may be three down the length of the runway) then the system is called IRVR – Instrumented Runway Visual Range. The RVR and IRVR are properly Air Traffic Services and as such are dealt with in the latest edition of the companion volume, *Aviation Law for Pilots*.

The basic gases which constitute the atmosphere are all invisible. Pilots', and other travellers', problems stem from the fact that the atmosphere is polluted by matter which comes between the observer's eye and the object which he is trying to identify. For the following pages, the non-meteorological factors such as the effect of a pitch-dark, overcast, moonless night, or an observer with less than perfect vision will be ignored. The pollutant between the eye and the object may be:
(a) falling – mainly as precipitation,
(b) rising – dust, sand, snow in a blizzard, etc.,
(c) held in suspension – fog, mist or haze.

Sometimes the pollution can be quite localised. At other times it is very widespread. Whatever the distribution, pilots should be aware of the circumstances when the visibility may be expected to deteriorate and those under which it will improve. Consider each of the cases in turn.

Poor visibility due to falling matter

(a) Precipitation
Already mentioned in Chapter 6, visibility may fall to below 50 metres in thickly falling snow, especially where flakes are large. Visibility is better in sleet and in the UK it is better still in rain where, unless the rain is extremely heavy, visibility is usually 800 to 1000 metres. In torrential tropical downpours, visibility of 50 to

100 metres has been reported. Visibility can also be very poor in drizzle when it becomes a matter of fine judgement distinguishing between fog and drizzle droplets. From a pilot's point of view, continuous heavy drizzle may be associated with visibilities of 400 to 500 metres.

(b) Solid particles

Usually this is a problem in the lowest layers of the atmosphere and associated with rising matter or particles subsequently held in suspension which are considered later. There is one case that should be noted – volcanic eruptions. No-one in his senses would knowingly fly through the clouds above an erupting volcano. Although not frequent, volcano dust is ejected high into the sky at times and sometimes persists over quite a long period of time. This dust sinks only slowly downwards from the upper parts of the troposphere and for some days there will be poor visibility where the dust is still settling.

Poor visibility due to rising matter

(a) Wind-blown matter

(i) Sea spray. In winds of gale force or stronger, spray is whipped off the waves and tends to reduce the visibility. This situation is of somewhat academic interest to the pilot as in these sea conditions, a flying boat or seaplane take-off or landing would be hazardous to say the least.

(ii) Snow. Strong winds are capable of lifting snow, especially if it is dry and powdery, and carrying it along in its surface turbulence layer. This is a problem largely associated with aerodromes in high latitudes particularly in continental winters. There is then virtually a white-out with no discernible horizon in any blizzard.

(iii) Dust and sand. Although primarily associated with desert or semi-desert countries, even eastern Britain has had wind-blown dust from finely tilled soil after a period of dry weather. In the main, places with an annual rainfall of less than 10 inches are most vulnerable. Helicopters of course have their own problems and accentuate already dusty atmospheric conditions. The colour of, and the terminology used with, such storms varies from place to place and many storms have local names. Some are described in Chapter 15. In general, sand may be considered as the heavier, grittier particles which are not raised to such great heights as lighter dust particles. If the windspeed exceeds 15 to 20 knots in a desert area, dust and sand are blown up from the surface and are borne along by the surface turbulence. Although the sand is confined to a shallow layer, the dust may well be spread through a turbulence layer 3000 feet thick. As long as the wind speed remains strong enough, the duststorm will continue and the dust may be carried a considerable distance downwind; for example, from time to time, Saharan dust reaches the UK. Near their source, visibility in duststorms may be less than 100 metres. If the storm is associated with a freshening wind as part of the diurnal variation, as the wind speed drops down again in the evening so the duststorm abates. If the storm is caused by strong winds associated with depressions or troughs of low pressure, then its arrival in a particular area can usually be anticipated, but its effect may be widespread.

(b) Convective storms

(i) Dust-devils. On a normal hot, sunny day in a desert or semi-desert area, the development of strong convection may be followed by small local whirlwinds of dust. Usually called dust-devils, they are also sometimes known as dust or sand pillars because the dust is carried up in a column to 1000 feet or more. They can be relatively easily avoided but add to the general dust haze of the area.

(ii) Haboobs. These are much larger-scale storms of the Sudan and are described in Chapter 15.

Poor visibility due to matter in suspension

Before considering the various possibilities, first some definitions.

Fog: a state of visibility less than 1 kilometre (symbol $\equiv$).

Mist: a state of reduced visibility caused by water drops in suspension, but where the visibility is one kilometre or more (=). Thus when visibility is deteriorating mist precedes fog and when the fog is dispersing it is followed by mist as the visibility improves.

Haze: a state of reduced visibility due to solid particles in suspension; it has no upper or lower visibility limit.

Next an interesting fact concerning relative humidity in fog and mist. Until now, it has been stated that as air becomes more humid the relative humidity approaches 100%. At 100% the air is saturated and if, say, it is subjected to cooling, it produces excess water vapour which condenses out. This is true for pure water but with hygroscopic nuclei present fog may form at relative humidities of 90 to 100% and sometimes mist has occurred down to 80%.

Air may become saturated close to the earth's surface to produce water droplet fog due to:

(a) addition of water vapour into the air – 'evaporation' fogs: steaming fog; arctic sea smoke; frontal fog.

(b) cooling either by conduction of heat to the underlying surfaces – radiation fog; advection fog – or adiabatically – hill or upslope fog.

(c) mixing with other almost saturated air at a markedly different temperature: mixing fog.

Steaming fog or Arctic sea smoke

On a small scale we have all no doubt seen a road or roof 'steaming' into the cool clear air after a rain shower. The 'steaming' or 'smoking' condensation re-evaporates after some inches ascent from the surface. The evaporation fogs form by the same principle but on a grander scale.

Referring back to Chapter 3 and the discussion on relative humidity, it will be remembered that evaporation from an exposed water surface depends upon its vapour pressure, whether it be open sea or a rain drop (fig. 8.1). If the water temperature (and hence its vapour pressure) is greater than that of the nearby air, the evaporation continues faster than the air can absorb the water vapour, even

Fig. 8.1   Evaporation into cool air

though the cool air's relative humidity is 100%. This further evaporation immediately re-condenses as visible fog which rises up in convection currents. If the wind blows across cold icy areas to over fjords or breaks in the arctic ice sheet where clear water is exposed, the water surface 'steams' into the air producing fog. The fog is usually shallow but may be as much as 500 feet deep in a Scandinavian fjord (fig. 8.2). The conditions for such fog formation require not only low surface temperatures but also a pre-existing surface inversion of temperature to inhibit the rapid development of instability.

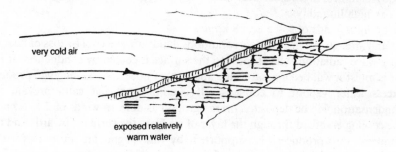

Fig. 8.2   Arctic sea smoke

Frontal fog
The accumulative evaporation from the raindrops falling through the cold air ahead of a warm front for a matter of hours also produces a potential supersaturation condition. In the main, the evaporation is re-condensed out as stratus 'of bad weather' under the main nimbostratus cloud sheet but at times the condensation will occur at surface levels (fig. 8.3). In this case a belt of fog, perhaps over 100 nm wide, will be formed along the length of the front and will move along with the front, immediately ahead of its surface position.

Radiation fog
Although auto-land has enabled enterprising airlines using major airports to continue their operations, radiation fog regularly prevents small aircraft from taking off or landing. This fog may well form irregularly over a part of the countryside so some aerodromes may have a total clamp while others are still

SIDE ELEVATION   PLAN

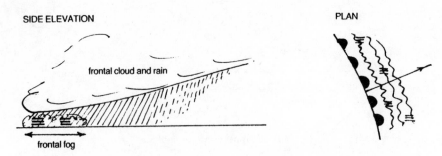

frontal cloud and rain

frontal fog

Fig. 8.3   Belt of frontal fog

clear, a circumstance in which unwary pilots on a cross-country flight can be caught out with nowhere in their destination area available for landing.

In the name radiation fog, the 'radiation' refers to the process by which the surface underlying the fog loses its heat. The air producing the fog cools by conduction of its heat downwards to the ground beneath. The basic requirements for the fog to form are:

    (a) cloudless night skies over land
    (b) high humidity
    (c) light winds of some 2 to 8 knots.

At and after sunset in cloudless conditions, land surfaces cool by loss of heat by long-wave radiation. The air next to the surface is cooled by conduction. If the air is moist it will become saturated and further nocturnal cooling will produce excess water vapour to condense. If conditions of flat calm prevail, the condensation will be deposited on the ground as dew. In winds of 2 to 8 knots the cooling is spread through the layer of air from the surface upwards and the condensation produced is supported by the slight air motion in this approximately isothermal layer as fog droplets. (If the wind speed exceeds 8 to 10 knots, the turbulence would set up an adiabatic lapse rate through the surface layer and a sheet of stratus or stratocumulus cloud would be formed as already described in Chapter 6.) The environmental lapse rate at dawn in the three cases

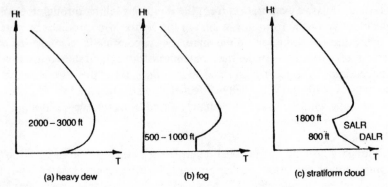

Fig. 8.4   Effects of surface cooling

would be as shown in fig. 8.4. The inversions shown in each case results from the cooling process and are not prerequisites for the fog to form. If the vertical thickness of the radiation fog is less than about 250 to 300 feet, the sky will probably still be discernible.

The formation process gives the clue to the circumstances when radiation fog will disperse. In winter when the nights are long, the absence of such circumstances will mean that although the radiation fog may thin out a little around lunch-time, it will thicken again in the late afternoon and evening and the fog persists for some days. If there is enough daylight and the sun shines warmly enough, then the fog will be evaporated away. First the fog may temporarily thicken with the start of turbulence but then it will thin to mist and probably lift to patches of thin wispy stratus (called 'lifted fog') before disappearing. Alternatively, if the wind speed freshens the visibility will improve. Either the fog is lifted to low cloud (as in fig. 8.4(c)) or it is mixed with sufficiently dry air above it for the fog to disperse and give clear skies.

Variations in radiation fog formation

1. *Diurnal.* Although caused by cooling, radiation fog is most likely just after sunrise rather than at dawn itself. This is really due to requirement (c) above. A calm night with only a heavy dew may be followed by barely perceptible turbulence as the sun rises. Even so, this extremely slight turbulence can be sufficient for fog suddenly to form or thin mist patches which have formed during the night to thicken rapidly into fog. Many a pilot has gone into the flight planning room around dawn on a late autumn morning to prepare his flight and emerged less than an hour later to find the visibility too bad for immediate departure. If there are no changes in the synoptic situation which would affect the cloud cover or wind speed, fog formed in the evening thickens throughout the hours of darkness and on till about an hour after sunrise. Then it will gradually disperse with 1 to 2 hours after midday likely to be the clearest times.

2. *Seasonal.* The coincidence of requirements (a), (b) and (c) together with nights of sufficient length to enable adequate radiational cooling is most likely in the UK in autumn and early winter. The sea around the British Isles is still relatively warm so the air then has ample moisture content. The land is gradually becoming cooler at this time of the year, making the dew point temperature easier to be reached, and the long nights give the best cooling period.

3. *Locations.* Radiation fog does not form over the sea. Inland it forms first in valleys and in low-lying areas (fig. 8.5). Several factors combine to give this characteristic. Firstly (as will be considered in detail in Chapter 10 – katabatic

Fig. 8.5   Radiation fog forming in low-lying areas

winds), air cooled at night tends to drain down into and collect in low-lying areas – some are known locally as 'frost hollows' – so these are the locations most likely to be cooled enough to give radiation fog. Secondly, sheltered valleys experience cooling of the air both from below and from the sides which are also cooling by radiation, which produces lower temperatures when compared with flat terrain cooling the air only from below (fig. 8.6).

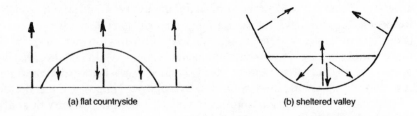

(a) flat countryside   (b) sheltered valley

Fig. 8.6   Cooling of surface air by conduction to terrain cooling by radiation

Thirdly, valleys and low-lying regions tend to be the site of water courses so that there are often locally higher relative humidities.

Although nothing like as bad as conditions were before the Clean Air Acts were introduced, radiation fog will be worsened and more persistent if polluted by domestic and industrial smoke in highly urbanised areas. The other areas prone to radiation fog are marshes, fens and waterlogged ground generally. The local relative humidities in light winds are so high in such localities that this more than offsets any slight effect there might be of the moist ground cooling more slowly than drier areas.

4. Pressure systems. For reasons to be dealt with in later chapters, anticyclones, ridges of high pressure and cols bring light winds. Frequently too, they have little or no cloud. These pressure systems are therefore the synoptic situations in which the fog should be expected and as anticyclones are usually slow-moving, they give the most persistent radiation fog.

Advection fog
In this case the air is cooled by conduction from below because it has moved horizontally to a colder surface area (fig. 8.7). The surface temperature 'B' has to be colder than the dew point temperature of the incoming air 'A', but wind speeds can be much stronger than with radiation fog, up to 20 to 25 knots.

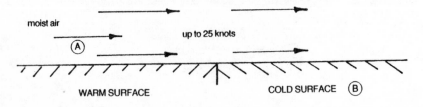

Fig. 8.7   Formation of advection fog

Although the same remarks apply about the turbulence causing adiabatic cooling, a strengthening of wind speeds in advection fog from say 5 to 15 knots merely brings in the moist air faster for cooling by the underlying surface. Typical situations for advection fog to form are as follows (figs 8.8 to 8.11) and in each case, for the fog to disperse, either the wind direction must change markedly – the most likely cause – or it must freshen up towards gale force (when the fog will lift into very low cloud), while over land (fig. 8.8) the fog may also

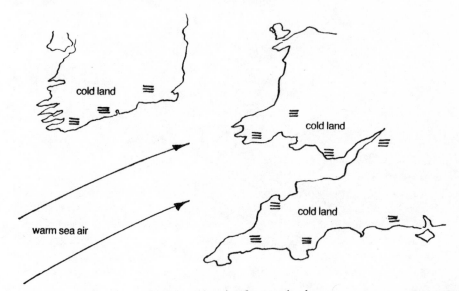

Fig. 8.8   Advection fog over land

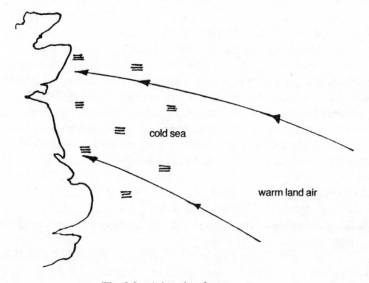

Fig. 8.9   Advection fog over sea

be dispersed by solar heating. In the cases shown in figs 8.9, 8.10 and 8.11 there is no diurnal variation in the fog, which is just as likely to be encountered out at sea (say when operating to an off-shore oil rig) by day as at night. In all cases, provided the basic airflow is maintained over the cold surface, advection fog will form irrespective of the cloud cover or pressure system.

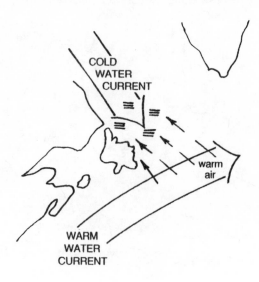

Fig. 8.10   Advection fog over cold sea current

1. *Advection fog over land.* This is most likely in the autumn and winter when the sea is still relatively warm and the land is cooling or already cold.

2. *Advection fog over the sea with air moving from the land.* This is most likely to occur in the spring and summer when land temperatures have warmed up while the sea has remained cool. In order for the land air to become sufficiently humid, the air may pass for some distance over open sea before the fog forms. The haar blown in from the North Sea to the east coast of Britain is typical of such fog.

3. *Advection fog over a cold sea current.* In some parts of the ocean, some sea currents are much colder than nearby areas which may even contain warm water currents. Such situations occur off Japan and Newfoundland. Warm moist air blown over the cold current will produce advection fog. Figure 8.10 depicts air blown from the Gulf Stream to the Labrador Current. It may occur at any season but in summer, land air from the North American continent can also give fog over the Labrador Current.

4. *Advection fog in air moving over the ocean to higher latitudes.* Except for localities where there are warm or cold sea currents, sea temperatures decrease gradually with latitude from the equator to the poles. In some synoptic

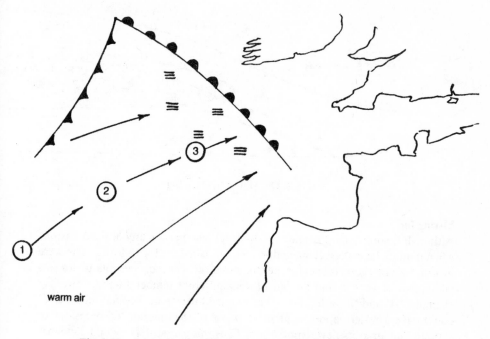

Fig. 8.11   Advection fog forming in air moving into colder latitudes

situations, as for example that shown in fig. 8.11, air can be moved appreciable distances over sea of steadily decreasing temperature.

The gradual decrease in sea temperature from '1' to '2' to '3' reduces the air temperature to below the original dew point temperature and widespread advection fog results. Fog often forms in the south-western approaches to the English Channel for this reason and depending upon whether the wind direction is more westerly or more southerly so the fog spreads either up the Channel or into the Celtic Sea, often hampering operations from coastal aerodromes as well as from offshore rigs.

Hill or upslope fog
This is nothing more than orographic cloud of which the base is obscuring high ground. Unfortunately not all pilots in the past have realised that it is not necessary to have steep cliffs or precipitous mountain sides to produce adiabatic cooling. Air that is moving over ground which is gradually sloping upwards also cools adiabatically. Depending upon whether or not the observer is within any cloud that forms as a result of the adiabatic cooling, so the observer will call it cloud (low stratus) or hill fog (fig. 8.12). Gradually rising land near coasts is a most favourable locality for upslope fog but any cloud, whether orographic or not, of which the base is obscuring high ground is a state of hill fog for an observer on the high ground.

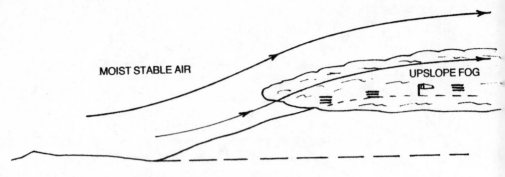

MOIST STABLE AIR

UPSLOPE FOG

Fig. 8.12   Hill or upslope fog

Mixing fog

Although theoretically possible, it is doubtful whether, on any of the occasions when it might have been claimed that mixing caused the fog to form, there were no other equally good causes for the condensation. The requirements are for two air masses of very humid air but of very different temperatures to mix (for example, 'A' and 'B' in fig. 8.13). When mixed together, the final mixture 'C' could have a water vapour content in excess of the amount 'D' necessary to saturate the air at its new temperature. Thus this excess 'CD' would condense and be suspended (in the turbulence associated with the mixing) as fog. No doubt the mixing process may aid the thickening of fogs formed due to other causes, on which it would probably be better for pilots to focus their attention.

Smoke haze

As already mentioned in the description of radiation fog, the Clean Air Acts have improved the visibility generally over the UK in recent years. Smoke may nevertheless be a problem when operating, particularly internationally. It arises from two main sources: urban areas and burning vegetation. In the former, the

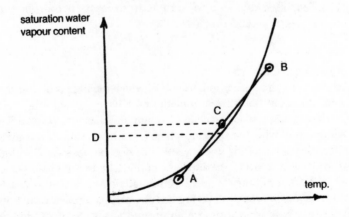

Fig. 8.13   Mixing as a fog-producing process

smoke arises from both industrial and domestic buildings. In stable air conditions, e.g. a surface inversion, the particles of soot, etc., are neither dispersed vertically nor washed from the air by precipitation. In calm conditions a general haze develops, trapped below the inversion, while in a light wind the pollution moves slowly to the downwind side of the urban area. The haze is worst at night. Strong winds and/or precipitation will clear the smoke. In the case of burning vegetation, heath and gorse fires occur in the open countryside, especially in hot dry weather. In some parts of the world, widespread grass, bush or forest fires can occur and cover a large area. With these sorts of fires, whether caused accidentally or as a feature of the local cultivation practice, the opposite is true (compared to urban smoke) as regards wind speed. A freshening wind brings more oxygen to make the fires burn faster and blows sparks downwind to ignite new material. Because of the strong convection, such smoke rises to great heights over and downwind of the fire. Visibility is reduced, flying is bumpy and you may well smell the smoke through the air conditioning system.

Visibility from the air

One of the first facets of visibility noted by a student pilot on his early map-reading exercises is that from the flight-deck the visibility is not the same in all directions, nor necessarily the same as he observed before take-off. Even in a given direction, vertical, oblique (slant) and horizontal visibility may well differ, as is shown if fig. 8.14, where there is a layer of fog or surface haze. For

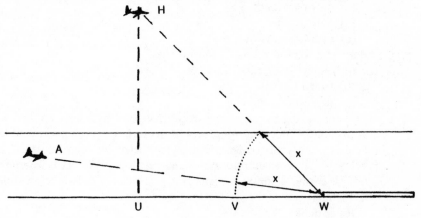

Fig. 8.14   Visibility from the air

simplicity, it is assumed that fog or haze is of uniform density in all directions and that the maximum visibility through it is x metres. An aircraft 'H' flying above the fog or haze layer can see the point 'U' vertically beneath the aircraft because there are less than the limiting amount of particles (x) in his sight line. In fact, the pilot can see up to a distance UW from the aircraft's geographical position, this distance being called the *oblique visibility*. As the aircraft's altitude decreases so proportionately (on the principle of similar triangles) does the oblique visibility. Ultimately, when the aircraft is on the approach within the haze layer or fog, the visibility will be poorest with the end of the runway 'W' coming into view overhead 'V' at a slant range of x.

Away from a given direction, the distance at which ground objects can be recognised from the air may well vary with the relative position of the sun or even a fairly full moon. Because of the minimum glare that a pilot will experience when looking down-sun ground features directly away from the direction of the sun will be seen to greater ranges than when looking towards the sun. On the other hand, in bright moonlight when glare is no problem, objects can be most easily identified when looking towards the moon when reflection can help in their recognition.

Test questions

Q1.   For radiation fog to form, the requirements are:
       (a) light winds up to 10 knots, high humidity, instability
       (b) cloudless inland night, high humidity, wind 2 to 8 knots
       (c) clear skies, calm to 2 knots wind, high humidity.

Q2.   Prerequisites for the formation of steaming fogs are:
       (a) unstable lapse rate, high humidity, water warmer than the air
       (b) inversion, low air temperature, water much warmer than the air
       (c) high humidity, lapse rate approximately ISA, water warmer than the air.

Q3.   Advection fog forms:
       (a) only over land
       (b) only over sea
       (c) over land and over sea.

Q4.   Radiation fog forms most frequently in:
       (a) anticyclones, ridges and cols
       (b) troughs of low pressure
       (c) depressions and cols.

Q5.   You are making an early winter night cross-country flight over land and at the time of collecting your forecast the surface conditions at your last landing point were cloudless, calm and the dewpoint temperature 2 C deg below the air temperature. Assuming that it is $2\frac{1}{2}$ hours before dawn and no change of air mass occurs, the possibility of radiation fog at that last landing point:
       (a) is unlikely
       (b) is most likely between midnight and dawn
       (c) is greatest just after dawn.

Q6.   Flying in the circuit on a cloudless winter day in the UK with a surface haze layer, visibility will be poorest when landing:
       (a) on runway 31 at 1400 hours local time
       (b) on runway 25 at 1000 hours local time
       (c) on runway 25 at 1500 hours local time.

Q7.   Advection fog does not form when:
       (a) skies are overcast or nearly so
       (b) wind speeds exceed 8 to 10 knots

(c) it has been, and remains, calm.

Q8. A 'thaw fog' over melting snow will be a case of:

(a) advection fog

(b) evaporation fog

(c) radiation fog.

Q9. Flying over a desert area:

(a) dust is encountered at greater heights than sand

(b) sand is encountered at greater heights than dust

(c) dust and sand haze are experienced up to the same heights.

Q10. Dust storms in semi-desert regions:

(a) only occur during daylight hours

(b) do not affect the visibility when they reach the coast

(c) can occur along troughs of low pressure instead of dense frontal cloud.

9: Icing

Icing is a hazard which the aviator shares with the mariner but unfortunately on a wider global scale. However, whereas a mariner may find icing conditions developing over an area of ocean faster than he can move clear of the area, in the case of the aviator keeping clear of airframe icing conditions should normally be entirely within his control. Although most of this chapter is devoted to airframe ice accretion, it is concluded with a discussion of power plant icing which also could significantly affect the aircraft's performance by, for example, causing total engine failure in a light aircraft flying in a cloudless sky.

A quick revision first of terms already introduced in earlier chapters which must be borne in mind.

Latent heat – heat involved in a change of state of a substance without change of temperature. It is released in the change from liquid to solid.

Supercooling – water remaining in its liquid state despite its temperature being below 0°C. This is an unstable state of affairs with the water turning to solid (ice) when disturbed.

Because of its relevance to the type of icing formed when supercooled drops freeze, also be reminded of the value learnt at school that the figure for the latent heat of fusion of ice is 80 calories per gram, i.e. when 1 gram freezes it releases 80 calories. (In turn, of course, 1 calorie is the amount of heat required to raise the temperature of 1 gram of water through 1 C deg.)

In aviation forecasts, two other terms are used in connection with icing:

Freezing level or *0°C isotherm*. This is the height at which the environmental temperature is 0°C. In fact there may be more than one such height, if there is an inversion present. Usually the temperatures are sub-zero at greater heights than the 0°C isotherm but also this is not true if there is an inversion.

Icing index or *intensity*. This relates to the rate of accumulation and may be classified as light (Ψ), moderate (ΨΨ) or heavy (ΨΨΨ). The terms mean, respectively – light: no problem if de-icing/anti-icing equipment is used; moderate: use of de-icing/anti-icing equipment, or diversion, is necessary otherwise potentially dangerous even over a short period; severe: de-icing/anti-icing equipment will not reduce or control the hazard and diversion is essential.

Hazards of airframe ice accretion

The effects are cumulative but are treated separately below to simplify the explanations. Do not ever assume that, whether in level flight or about to taxi out for take-off, increasing speed will cause the ice or snow to blow off your aeroplane's surfaces. In a series of pink 'safety' Aeronautical Information Circulars, the CAA repeatedly issues warnings to pilots, backed up by examples of accidents and incidents.

(a) Lift and drag

The icing, particularly when forming on leading edges of mainplanes and other surfaces, soon alters the profile so that the relative airflow is disturbed. Not only is there an increase in drag but it is accompanied with a reduction in lift so the lift/drag ratio is quickly eroded. Because all surfaces (including propellers) exposed to the relative airflow are affected, ice accretion on the tailplane, fin and all control surfaces will impair their efficiency and can ultimately lead to loss of control. For example, this can happen due to icing on the tailplane when flaps are lowered on the approach. Flutter set up by quite thin layers of ice on control surfaces can lead subsequently to structural damage.

(b) Hinges, locks and seals

Moving on from iced-up control surfaces, serious problems occur when other moving parts are covered, even partially, by ice. For example, on selecting 'undercarriage down' the doors may be impossible to open if they have an external coat of ice, ice in the locking mechanisms, in hinges and seals or moisture freezes in pressure lock systems.

(c) Weight

The increase in all-up weight due to icing is not negligible, so requiring more lift and hence more power to maintain level flight. If the ice accumulates unevenly there may be a change in the aircraft's centre of gravity and hence its 'weight and balance'.

(d) Vibration

Apart from the flutter mentioned in (a) above, serious vibration can also result from an unbalanced distribution of icing, not so much due to irregular formation but more due to an unequal breaking away of ice.

(e) Aerials

On older aircraft, ice on aerials can impair communications and in the case of 'whip' aerials may lead to their vibration and eventual fracture.

(f) Instrument readings

If, despite use of the pitot heater, ice blocks the pressure head or static vent then the pressure instruments – machmeter, airspeed indicator, altimeter and vertical speed indicator – will give false readings (or even no reading!).

(g) Transparencies

Often ice can first be detected visually by its appearance in flight in the corners of windshields. Allowed to develop, vision will quickly become obstructed.

Icing on parked aircraft

The ice may occur in one of three ways: deposited as ice already formed (i.e. from snowflakes), sublimation direct from water vapour, or freezing of water.

(a) Packed snow

Dry snow does not adhere readily to a dry aircraft but will be blown into intakes, apertures, corners, etc. If the aircraft surface is wet or the snow is wet (i.e. contains some liquid water) then the snow will 'pack' down onto all exposed areas and to some depth, requiring careful removal.

(b) Hoar frost

The white winter equivalent of dew, hoar frost forms when the air temperature falls below 0°C and then to below the hoar frost point temperature to give direct sublimation of the excess water vapour into the white crystalline frost deposit. While not particularly heavy, it must be removed before take-off not only to give a clear view through the transparencies but also because it disturbs the boundary layer airflow, so seriously reducing total lift while increasing drag.

(c) Rime

Rime is the result of freezing fog and forms when the temperature falls to below the dew point temperature to produce fog and then falls further to below 0°C. The fog droplets then become supercooled. As they drift gently along and come into contact with objects with surface temperatures below 0°C such as parked aircraft, the disturbed droplets turn to ice. The ice is therefore found on the windward side and builds out into the wind. It is a rough, white, opaque, porous deposit (and often used by photographers to produce picturesque Christmas cards using frosted trees and shrubs as their subjects). It is the form of ice around the lining of the domestic refrigerator or deep-freeze.

(d) Glazed frost

Unlike the three preceding cases, glazed frost is fortunately relatively rare in the UK, but when it does occur it poses serious problems for all forms of transport and, because of its weight, brings down overhead wires, power cables, etc. It is sometimes called clear ice or rain ice and is a sheet of transparent or translucent ice with a glasslike appearance which forms over all exposed surfaces. It forms when the temperature is below 0°C and rain falls from an inversion above. The raindrops form a sheet of water which then freezes, excluding any air, so giving a solid, heavy sheet of ice everywhere that the rain has fallen and run. Going back to the domestic refrigerator or deep-freeze for comparison, the same sort of ice is formed when ice cubes are made in the tray.

Although all ice must be removed before take-off, there are therefore various forms of frost and it must be clearly understood which type is being forecast when assessing whether operations at the planned time will be possible and if so, what will be involved in the clearing of the aircraft and possibly the airport facilities. In fact, eight different frost terms may be met in the UK:

1. *Ground frost* – temperature of 0°C or colder measured by a horizontal thermometer lying touching grass 1 to 2 inches in length.
2. *Air frost* – air temperature below 0°C in a thermometer screen 4 feet above ground level.

3. *Radiation frost* – a particular case of 2 caused by the air being cooled by the underlying ground which itself is cooling by radiation.

4. *Wind frost* – a particular case of 2 caused by the sub-zero air condition developing elsewhere and being brought in by the wind.

5. *Black frost* – an air frost but no hoar frost on the ground.

6. *White frost* – hoar frost as described in (b) above.

7. *Glazed frost* – as described in (d) above.

8. *Silver frost* – a surface deposit of frozen dew (which may co-exist with hoar frost.)

If the motoring organisations are issuing warnings of 'black ice' for the roads to the airport, they are referring to glazed frost.

Action pre-flight

1. If it is your responsibility for safeguarding the aircraft between flights, heed frost warnings for the period prior to your flight so that the aircraft can be best protected against the elements so minimising the de-icing required to prepare the aircraft for service. Ideally, keep it in a heated hangar!

2. Fit all orifice guards, covers, engine blanks before starting to de-ice. Although some loose snow can be brushed off, de-icing fluid of the correct strength will really be needed to clear it all off together with any frost and ice.

3. Surfaces which remain wet from under-strength de-icing fluid will in fact enhance re-formation of icing or packing snow especially if there is any delay between de-icing and taking off. In fact, it is not bad practice to tend to finish the de-icing with some over-strength fluid on leading edges of all surfaces to give some anti-icing protection.

4. Remove all the covers, guards, blanks, etc., and check that all orifices are clear of ice, snow or slush. At the same time, double check that all inlets and outlets, vents, hinges, exposed operating mechanisms, seals and gaps between surfaces are completely clear of contamination.

5. Check that the de-icing fluid has not cleaned away grease from vital areas.

6. Do not taxy if there is likely to be a hold which will negate all the de-icing procedures that have been carried out.

7. When taxying, remember the advice already given in Chapter 6 for operating on contaminated runways and use engine anti-icing, carburettor heat and propeller de-icing as appropriate.

8. Keep well clear of the other aircraft taxying ahead. It is *not* a clever idea to put your aircraft in the wake of the hot engine exhaust of the aircraft in front of you to keep your aircraft de-iced.

9. Immediately prior to take-off re-check that all the visible surfaces are still uncontaminated by snow or ice and that all anti-icing devices available have been set. Once airborne, be ready to operate the de-icing equipment as appropriate.

Ice accretion in flight

In flight, although the same forms of icing are experienced as occur on the ground, there is a wide range of variations due to differing degrees of the contributory factors of:

the temperature and the degree of supercooling of the water drops being
    encountered by the aircraft
kinetic heating
cloud density and/or concentration of liquid water
airspeed
size of supercooled drops
cloud base temperature
effect of high ground
which are now considered in turn.

Temperature

For all practical purposes, supercooled water drops may be encountered down
to –40°C. Only the smallest drops can be supercooled to –40°C, larger drops
being supercooled to a lesser extent. As each drop is struck by an aircraft it starts
to change from liquid to solid, i.e. ice. Because the latent heat of fusion of ice is
80 calories per gram, one-eightieth of a supercooled drop freezes on impact for
each C deg of supercooling (fig. 9.1).

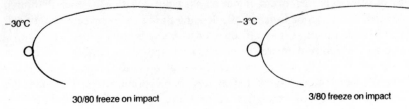

Fig. 9.1   Supercooled water drops freeze partially on impact

The freezing process releases latent heat which warms up the remaining part
of the drop to 0°C. This liquid part of the drop then flows over the aircraft
structure to freeze fractionally later by conduction. The ice formation is
therefore a two-stage process (fig. 9.2).

The nearer the sub-zero temperature is to 0°C, the greater will be the flowback
and the worse will be the resultant icing.

Kinetic heating

Although fig. 9.2 shows an aircraft which has acquired the same temperature

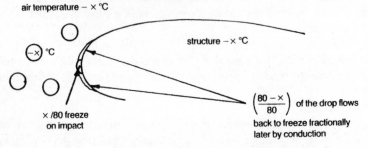

Fig. 9.2   The freezing process of a supercooled water drop

(–x°C) as its environment, this may not be true for fast aircraft. However, for relatively slow aircraft cruising in level flight at speeds up to, say, 250 knots, this is a realistic approximation.

Kinetic heating arises from the airflow around the aircraft from two sources – compressibility and frictional effects. Compressibility at the stagnation points in the relative airflow heats the air adiabatically. Where the relative airflow is greatest (and the compressibility heating least) there is maximum heating due to friction between the air and the aircraft surface. The temperature rise in C deg due to kinetic heating on and near leading edges is given by:

$$\text{Temperature rise (C deg)} = \left(\frac{\text{TAS knots}}{100} \right)^2$$

e.g. for 500 knots, the temperature rise will be 25 C deg.

Sometimes the kinetic heating may be offset to some degree. This occurs when the aircraft surface has become wet, say by flying through cloud. The wet surface then evaporates its moisture away using latent heat of vaporisation (which is around 600 calories per gram). In practice, the rule is to use the indicated air temperature in assessing the icing risk as the thermometer element itself will be subject to both the kinetic heating and the cooling due to latent heat of vaporisation.

Concentration of liquid water (cloud density)
As the ice accumulated by an aircraft originates from the water it encounters, the greater the concentration of liquid, the faster and more severe will be the ice accretion. There will be more latent heat to be dissipated before the freezing is completed, more water spreading over the aircraft surface and merging with adjoining drops, all tending towards producing clear ice.

Airspeed
Increasing air speed serves to increase the rate of catch of water drops in the aircraft's flight path so acting in the same way as an increase of cloud density.

Size of supercooled water drops
It has already been mentioned that the smallest drops can be supercooled to a greater degree than the largest water drops. They also tend to be sufficiently spaced from neighbouring small drops so that they freeze on impact. This means that air is trapped between the separately frozen drops, giving a soft white opaque deposit of rime. At the other extreme, large water drops (which may be associated with a high cloud density and only a small amount of supercooling) will have a large spread-back of water over the aircraft while the freezing is occurring. Merging with the liquid portion of adjoining drops gives a sheet of freezing water excluding air and becoming clear ice. The two contrasting conditions are depicted in fig. 9.3.

Often the situation is not so clear-cut as depicted in fig. 9.3, with drops of an intermediate size or a mixture of sizes and this produces an ice formation intermediate between rime and clear ice (see below – cloudy or mixed ice).

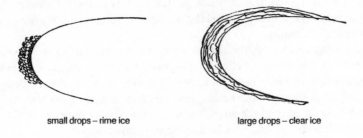

small drops – rime ice   large drops – clear ice

Fig. 9.3   Effect of supercooled water drop size

Cloud base temperature

When flying at levels well above the cloud base, cloud base temperature may seem to be totally unconnected with any assessment of icing risk at cruising level. The reason why it is very significant as far as towering cumuliform clouds are concerned is because the warmer the cloud base temperature, the greater the concentration of liquid water, of which the effects have been described above. The base height of cumuliform cloud is much the same everywhere but at the warmer temperatures of summer or tropical latitudes there is more condensation in the lower parts of the cloud than in the cooler temperatures of winter or higher latitudes. The vigorous convection carries the condensed droplets upwards so the warmer clouds contain more free water than the clouds with lower base temperatures. Because of their warmer base temperatures, towering cumulus and cumulonimbus in summer will have a greater liquid water concentration than those in winter in temperate latitudes.

Effect of high ground

This is in some ways a rather insidious effect which must be guarded against. Suppose that the flight has been in cloud for some time and the aircraft's de-icing system is coping with the ice that has been forming because the supercooled drops have been small and the liquid water concentration relatively low (fig. 9.4(a)). When the aircraft moves into a mountainous region the up-currents in the cloud will be reinforced by the upward deflection of lower level winds (fig. 9.4(b)) supporting larger drops in denser cloud and probably with a lowered freezing level. The consequent increase in severity and rapidity of ice accretion

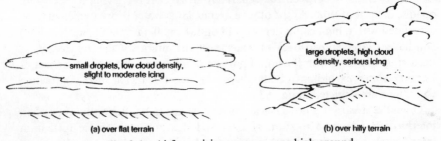

small droplets, low cloud density,
slight to moderate icing

large droplets, high cloud
density, serious icing

(a) over flat terrain   (b) over hilly terrain

Fig. 9.4   Airframe icing worsens over high ground

while flying in apparently unchanged IMC can quickly lead to a serious situation.

Forms of in-flight ice accretion

Hoar frost
Hoar frost occurs in moist cloudless air which is cooled by a cold aircraft moving from a colder layer, so that the air in contact with the aircraft surface is cooled to below 0°C and to below its frost point. This could occur either following a rapid descent or after taking off into a marked surface inversion such as on a winter's night in a cold country (fig. 9.5(a) and (b)).

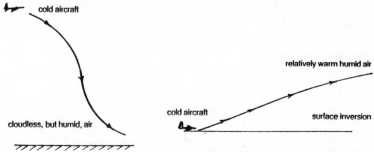

Fig. 9.5   Hoar frost in flight in clear air

Rime ice
Rime ice occurs under flight conditions which are the equivalent of freezing fog, i.e. small supercooled water drops in cloud with a relatively low rate of catch. When these water drops freeze almost instantaneously, small ice particles are produced along leading edges with air entrapped between them to give a rough white opaque deposit, with little spread-back over the mainplanes etc. Typical conditions to give rime ice are illustrated in fig. 9.6.

Clear ice
Clear ice occurs when the aircraft encounters large, slightly supercooled water drops giving a high rate of catch. This may occur in dense cloud or in rain. The freezing of the supercooled water drops is relatively slow so that while some ice is formed on impact, most of the water spreads back while freezing to give a heavy, adhesive, clear or translucent deposit of ice with a glassy surface. The dense cloud conditions are usually as depicted in fig. 9.7.

Cloudy (mixed) ice
Cloudy (mixed) ice occurs when conditions are intermediate between those quoted for rime and for clear ice, arising from the wide range of supercooled water drop sizes between 0°C and –40°C, varying cloud density, etc.

The smaller the drop size and the lower the temperature, the more rough and rime-like will be the cloudy ice that is formed. Conversely, the larger the drop size, the nearer the temperature to 0°C and the higher the rate of catch, the

(a) clouds of limited vertical extent, in temperatures between 0°C and − 40°C, such as

stratus, stratocumulus, altocumulus, 'fair-weather' cumulus

(b) upper parts of dense clouds, *either*

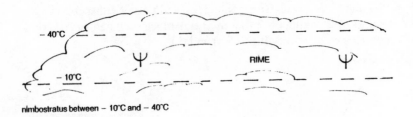

nimbostratus between − 10°C and − 40°C

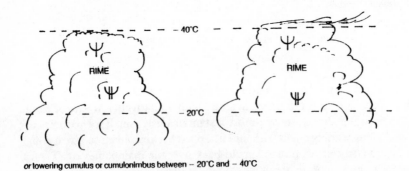

or towering cumulus or cumulonimbus between − 20°C and − 40°C

Fig. 9.6   Flight conditions for rime ice

smoother and glassier will the ice become. Also if the cloud contains ice crystals as well as the freezing water drops they will become frozen in the ice accretion, giving a rougher cloudier form.

Cloudy (mixed) ice is unlikely in stratocumulus, altocumulus or altostratus unless the cloud has been formed orographically. It is most likely in towering cumulus, cumulonimbus and orographic cloud at temperatures around –20°C and in nimbostratus around –5°C to –10°C depending upon the degree of frontal activity.

Packed snow
If snowflakes are met while flying in icing conditions they will become embedded on the airframe ice accretion making the deposit opaque, which may be referred to as 'packed snow' as on the ground. It may not be particularly dense compared

(a) towering cumulus or cumulonimbus between 0°C and −20°C

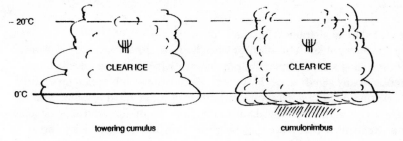

or (b) dense nimbostratus between 0°C and −10°C

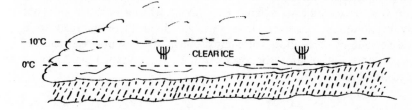

or (c) orographic cloud, particularly altostratus, nimbostratus and stratocumulus between 0°C and −20°C

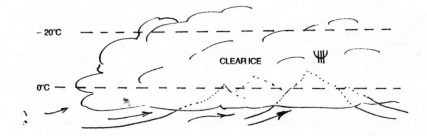

(d) clear ice in rain at temperatures below 0°C is most likely ahead of a warm front, especially if the aircraft has expedited a rapid descent from a much colder upper region

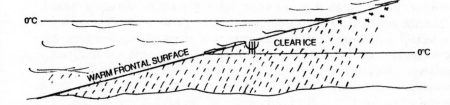

Fig. 9.7   Flight conditions for clear ice

with clear or cloudy ice but it can be very effective in blocking intakes and apertures.

Flight procedure in airframe icing conditions
At temperatures colder than –40°C or when flying in cirriform cloud the chances of airframe icing are very small indeed and any rime that may be encountered will not be of any significance. However, when flying at sub-zero temperatures in other cloud or in precipitation, airframe icing must be anticipated and the appropriate procedure followed, including the use of the aircraft's de-icing systems. Remember that there may be power loss due to engine icing too.

Icing in scattered or broken cloud
In these circumstances it is important to remember that when an aircraft emerges from cloud with ice on the mainplanes, etc., this ice, whatever its type, does not quickly evaporate. Successive passes through cloud therefore lead to a progressive build-up of ice and a worsening problem. The best practice therefore (within the constraints of air traffic control) is to fly around rather than through detached cloud masses (fig. 9.8).

Fig. 9.8   Avoid detached clouds giving severe icing

Icing in continuous cloud or precipitation
In freezing rain a decision is required urgently as the ice reaches dangerous proportions in a matter of minutes. The choice of how to get clear of the freezing rain is simply:

1. Descend to an icing-free layer where the temperatures are definitely warmer than 0°C, provided that there is sufficient terrain clearance. The pilot must know his position and the safety height.

2. Climb to an icing-free layer (ideally an inversion where temperatures are warmer than 0°C). In this case there are also provisos. Firstly it must be remembered that the aircraft will continue to collect ice while it is climbing, so reducing the performance if there is no reserve of power in hand. Secondly, in the climbing attitude there will be a change in the wetted area of the aircraft's surface and hence where the airframe will ice over. Finally, except for the ice that can be removed by the de-icing system, at the new cruising level the aircraft will be committed to continued flight carrying the ice already formed.

3. Turn back while the aircraft still has full manoeuvrability. Certainly this is the safest option in freezing rain, subject to air traffic control. It may then be possible to obtain ATC clearance for another altitude or route clear of the icing region.

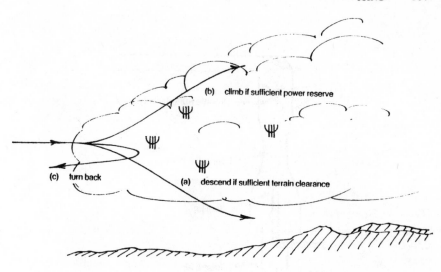

Fig. 9.9   Avoiding icing in continuous cloud or precipitation

If not, it will be necessary to divert to the specified alternate and to wait for conditions to improve (fig. 9.9).

Power plant icing

This is a matter which is best considered in conjunction with the specific flight manual and operations manual as constructors strive to design engines with minimum susceptibility to power loss due to icing. Starting with the most straightforward case, both piston and turbine engines suffer from impact icing. This icing forms where supercooled water drops strike the intake or induction system surfaces and is merely airframe ice accretion occurring in a locality where it chokes the air supply to the power plant. The icing occurs in all of the situations where the aircraft is experiencing airframe ice accretion and is also worst at temperatures just below 0°C.

Within an engine, pressure is reduced in the induction process causing expansion and adiabatic cooling and may be sufficient to give both condensation and supercooling and hence icing on adjoining surfaces. Depending upon the turbine engine, this can occur at particular rpm and airspeeds. In a piston engine the throttle effect together with fuel evaporation icing (jointly called carburettor icing) may cause a temperature fall of 20 to 30°C and has caused so many incidents and accidents resulting from partial or total power failure that it led to the CAA issuing a pink 'safety' Aeronautical Information Circular drawing pilots' attention to the hazard. Light aircraft with direct injection engines are not prone to such engine icing.

Figure 9.10 represents schematically the induction airflow of a conventional float-type carburettor. Air from the intake (A) passes through the venturi (choke) where the pressure drop and expansional cooling can cause the temperature fall to produce throttle ice and the vaporising of the fuel from the

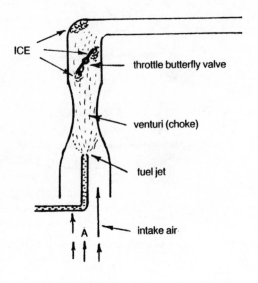

ICE

throttle butterfly valve

venturi (choke)

fuel jet

A

intake air

Fig. 9.10   Carburettor ice

jet will require latent heat so producing a further temperature fall. Depending upon the throttle butterfly setting, this may amount to 25°C and this is where the trouble lies.

On a quite warm, cloudless, but humid day, it is very easy, especially at small throttle openings such as on a glide approach, to experience serious carburettor icing and if the engine fails it may not restart. Incidentally, tests show that MOGAS is more likely to produce carburettor icing than AVGAS. It is important to be guided by the relevant flight manual and operations manual, including the use of the carburettor heat control. The carburettor heat when selected, heats the intake air by an exhaust heat exchanger but unless selecting 'hot air' actually produces temperatures over 0°C in the carburettor, the situation may be worsened by its use. This situation occurs if the initial intake air temperature was so low that even applying heat does not prevent sub-zero conditions occurring around the throttle butterfly.

Advice on recognition and avoidance of carburettor icing may be summarised as:
1. Check with the Flight and Operations Manuals for start-up, taxy, in-flight drills.
2. Be prepared for the icing in precipitation, cloud or clear humid air (relative humidity over 60%) even at +°C temperatures, especially at small throttle settings. The extreme temperature range is probably +25°C to –10°C and some authorities consider that the most serious icing occurs at outside air temperatures of around +13°C, but it all depends upon the particular engine.

3. Suspect its onset in level flight if the aircraft has:
   (a) a fixed pitch propeller and there is a slight drop in rpm and airspeed (preceding rough running, by which time action should have been taken)
   (b) a constant speed propeller and there is a drop in manifold pressure and airspeed
   (c) an exhaust gas temperature (EGT) indicator which shows a drop in temperature.
4. Use carburettor heat. Normally it will need to be fully ON, for the reasons given in the preceding paragraph. Because ice in the induction system cannot be melted and cleared instantaneously, CAA's advice is to allow up to 15 seconds for the process to be completed. Except for take-off, the continuous use of hot air is not normally permitted for an engine – again follow the manual.
5. Finally remember that, like carbon monoxide poisoning from exhaust leaks, carburettor icing can sneak up on the pilot and failure to deal with it will have dire results.

Test questions
Q1.   When fog freezes on a parked aircraft it produces:
      (a) hoar frost
      (b) rime
      (c) glazed frost.
Q2.   Frost point temperature is:
      (a) 0°C
      (b) the temperature at which fog freezes
      (c) the sub-zero temperature at which air becomes saturated at the surface.
Q3.   Glazed frost forms on a parked aircraft when:
      (a) there is a cold cloudless night with no wind
      (b) rain freezes
      (c) fog and dew freeze.
Q4.   One of the ways in which packed snow may be removed from a parked aircraft is by:
      (a) brushing it off
      (b) taxying quickly down a perimeter track to blow it off
      (c) storing it in a heated hangar.
Q5.   When using de-icing fluid to remove ice from a parked aircraft, air intakes:
      (a) should be kept clear of, as they will de-ice when the engine starts
      (b) should be blanked off and carefully cleared separately
      (c) should be cleared last using diluted fluid to which detergent has been added.
Q6.   In flight, rime ice would be expected when:
      (a) in rain at temperatures below 0°C

(b) in small supercooled water droplets and the aircraft surface temperatures are 0°C or colder

(c) in towering cumuliform cloud over NW Europe in temperatures 0°C to –10°C.

Q7. Flying in altostratus giving slight icing, the next part of your flight will take you over mountainous terrain. If the cruising level and IMC remain unchanged, the airframe ice accretion may be expected to:

(a) remain unchanged

(b) increase in severity

(c) decrease in severity.

Q8. Under which of the following conditions should carburettor icing be expected?:

(a) clear of cloud, high humidity, +13°C, aircraft gliding with throttle nearly closed

(b) in cloud, low relative humidity, –23°C, full throttle

(c) clear of cloud, low humidity, –13°C, full throttle.

Q9. If carburettor icing is suspected when operating at cruising power:

(a) select full power and fully rich mixture

(b) select partial carburettor heat first to see if this is sufficient to clear the ice

(c) select full carburettor heat.

Q10. If you are flying just above your safety altitude and at 1000 feet below the aircraft's ceiling when you encounter clear ice in freezing rain, you should:

(a) fly through the rain as quickly as possible to clear the icing zone

(b) climb or descend for up to 15 minutes to see if the icing will stop

(c) turn on to a reciprocal heading and seek ATC clearance for a change of route.

10: Winds

Although the last of the individual elements to be considered, wind speed has had to be mentioned in earlier chapters in connection with weather conditions as diverse as fog and thunderstorms. It is therefore not the least significant property of the atmosphere and indeed, as already mentioned under squalls and microbursts, it may well present a hazard of its own.

The convention when a forecaster presents information on horizontal motion of the atmosphere to a pilot is that he states wind velocity (w/v) i.e. both wind direction in °True and wind speed in knots. For example, 'surface wind 180°T/20 kt' means a wind blowing from 180°T (south to north) at an average speed of 20 knots (because the wind speed is not constant).

Changes of wind direction are described as 'veering' and 'backing'. A veer of wind is a change of wind direction in a clockwise manner, e.g. from 090°T to 180°T. The wind backs where there is a change of direction in an anticlockwise manner e.g. from 315°T to 270°T. (fig. 10.1). The terms veer and back apply in the same manner in both the northern and southern hemispheres.

Terms used in describing windspeed include:

Gust – a temporary increase in windspeed above its mean value lasting for a few seconds.

Lull – a decrease in windspeed.

Squall – a marked increase in the mean value of the windspeed lasting for some minutes and usually associated with a meteorological feature (e.g. as with a thunderstorm – Chapter 7.)

Gustiness factor – the degree of gustiness prevailing in relation to the mean windspeed, determined from the equation:

$$\frac{\text{Gustiness factor (\%)}}{100\%} = \frac{\text{Range of widespeed from lull to gust}}{\text{Mean wind speed}}$$

e.g. A mean windspeed of 30 knots dropping to 20 knots in lulls but gusting to 40 knots would have a gustiness factor of 66.67%.

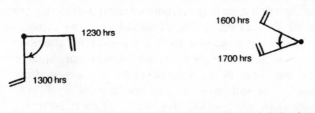

(a) VEER   clockwise change   (b) BACKING   anti-clockwise change

Fig. 10.1   Veering and backing

Gale – a surface windspeed of either a mean value of 34 knots or more, or gusting to 43 knots or more. (It is force 8 on the Beaufort scale.)

Hurricane force – a surface windspeed of 64 knots or more (Beaufort force 12). Hurricanes as tropical storms are described in Chapter 15.

Effective wind component – a flight planning rather than a meteorological term, being equal to the aircraft's ground speed less its true air speed. Effective and true wind components and their applications are described in Volume 2 of this series.

The nature of horizontal airflow

Generally, and for the purpose of this chapter, the horizontal motion of the atmosphere may be considered as comprising 'the lower atmosphere' of a layer of turbulent air near to the earth's surface containing many eddies, and above it, the 'free atmosphere' in which the airflow is reasonably horizontal (fig. 10.2). The height of the top of the surface turbulence layer is very variable but 2000 feet is a convenient, practical assumption for the terrain of NW Europe.

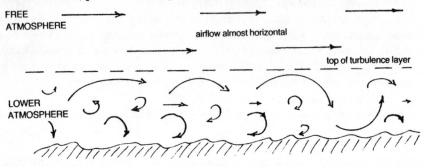

Fig. 10.2   Free and lower atmosphere

As was mentioned in Chapter 6 when describing the formation of turbulence cloud, the disturbances in the flow of the lower atmosphere arise from surface friction and from small-scale physical deflections and convection currents. The former vary with the terrain, its vegetation and man-made structures, together with the direction from which the wind strikes them. The latter depend upon the surface temperatures and the lapse rate. Although the uniformity of surface temperatures throughout the 24 hours over the sea mean that there is also no diurnal variation there in the turbulence layer, over the land thermal turbulence variations do produce a diurnal variation of the turbulence layer from a minimum around dawn to a maximum in the early afternoon.

The actual surface airflow itself arises from the horizontal pressure gradient in the area but is not in the direction of the pressure gradient. The correlation between winds and pressure was first defined by C.H.D. Buys-Ballot, a professor at Utrecht, in 1857. Buys-Ballot's Law states that:

If an observer stands with his back to the wind, the lower pressure is on his left in the northern hemisphere and on his right in the southern hemisphere.

Pressure gradient is not therefore the only force which acts horizontally on the air – it may also be affected by geostrophic and cyclostrophic forces. In figs 10.3

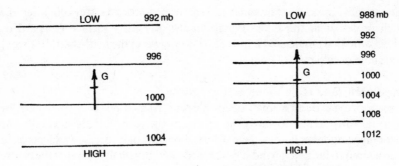

Fig. 10.3   Variation of pressure gradient force

to 10.9 the forces will be represented vectorially, but first the rules governing their magnitude and direction.

Pressure gradient force (G)

The primary cause of the wind acting perpendicularly to the isobars from high to low pressure, irrespective of latitude (north or south). Its magnitude is inversely proportional to the distance apart of the isobars (dp/ds).

Geostrophic force (F)

Once the air starts moving over the surface of the rotating earth it will be held to the earth's surface by gravity but tends to follow a straight path in space. The air appears to be acted upon by an earth's turning (geo-strophic) force which acts at right angles to the path of the moving air. It acts to the right in the northern hemisphere and to the left in the southern hemisphere. Mathematically its value may be expressed as:

$$2V \rho\omega \sin \varphi$$

where V = wind speed
          ρ = air density
          ω = earth's rotational rate in radians per second
          φ = latitude

It is represented graphically in fig. 10.4.

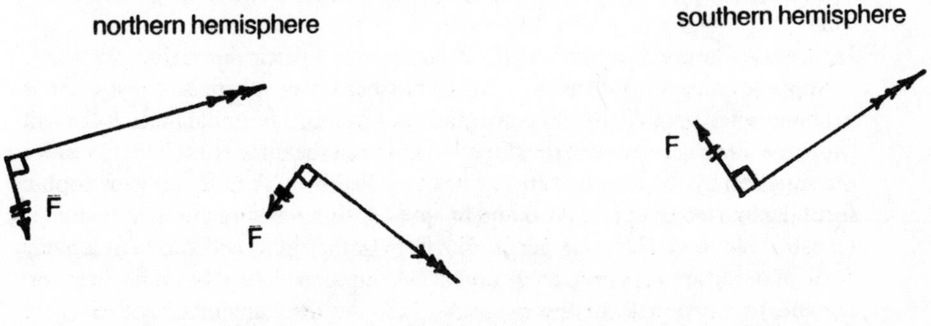

northern hemisphere   **southern hemisphere**

Fig. 10.4   Geostrophic force

Geostrophic effect is sometimes alternatively known as Coriolis after the French professor at the Ecole Polytechnique in Paris, Gustave Gaspard de Coriolis, who first enunciated it in 1835. (He also wrote the mathematical theory of the game of billiards!)

Cyclostrophic force (C)

If air is moving around a small circle, it is constrained on its circular path by centripetal force acting towards the centre of the turn. Strictly it is only the horizontal component of centripetal force – cyclostrophic force – which needs to be considered so far as the wind is concerned. Acting radially towards the centre of curvature, whatever the latitude or hemisphere, cyclostrophic force has a magnitude of:

$$\frac{\rho \, V^2 \cot \theta}{E}$$

where:

ρ = air density
V = wind speed
θ = angular radius of the isobar along which the wind is blowing
E = earth's radius

This is represented graphically in fig. 10.5.

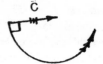

Fig. 10.5   Cyclostrophic force

Winds at 2000 feet

This height is at the top of the lower atmosphere where the airstream may be considered to be unaffected by the influence of the earth's surface. At the same time, the pressure gradient at 2000 feet may be assumed to be accurately represented by the mean sea level isobars. Consider various isobar patterns.

(a) Straight, equidistant isobars which are not changing with time: geostrophic wind

In this case, the pressure gradient (G) is constant in a particular region (fig. 10.6).

Suppose some air of density ρ in the northern hemisphere is at rest when it becomes acted upon by the pressure gradient force G. The unbalanced force will cause the air to accelerate in the direction in which the force is applied. Consider the situation by the time that the air has travelled from A to B and geostrophic force has started to apply. At B and at speed V_1 the pressure gradient is still G. Geostrophic force F (acting perpendicularly to the right) will still be relatively small at the speed V_1. The acceleration at B from speed V_1 will be in the direction of, and proportionate to the magnitude of, the resultant of G and F (BP). Subsequently at points C and D, while pressure gradient force G remains

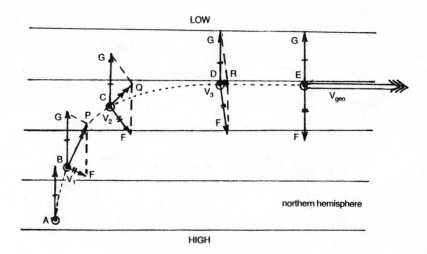

Fig. 10.6   Geostrophic wind

unchanged, geostrophic force F is progressively increasing at speeds V_2 and V_3 and turning further to the right to remain at right angles to the direction of motion. At C its acceleration is proportionate to resultant CQ while at D, although it has increased its speed to V_3, the acceleration proportional to resultant DR will be small. Finally the state will be reached eventually (E) at a speed V_{geo} when the air is travelling parallel to the isobars with forces G and F equal and opposite so that there is no resultant and hence no further acceleration (or deceleration). The flow is then said to be 'geostrophic'.

Geostrophic wind may thus be defined as the wind blowing along straight, equidistant isobars not changing with time, with lower pressure on the left in the northern hemisphere, under the balance of pressure gradient and geostrophic forces only.

The geostrophic wind equation is:

$$dp/ds = 2V\rho\omega\sin\varphi \tag{2}$$

If it is wished to solve the equation, it must be remembered to use cgs or MKS

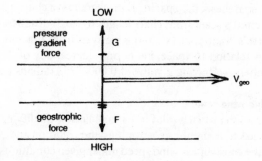

Fig. 10.7   Balance of forces in geostrophic flow

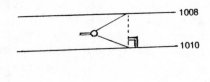

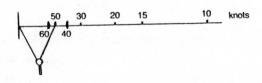

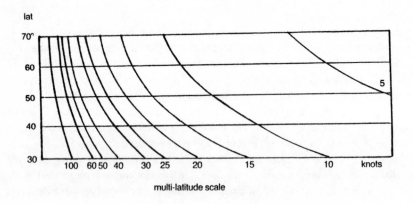

multi-latitude scale

Fig. 10.8   Geostrophic wind scales

units throughout and that the isobar spacing relates to their distance apart on the earth (ds), so if the isobar spacing is measured on a chart it needs to be converted using the chart's scale from chart length to earth distance.

The earth's rotational rate (ω) is derived from one complete rotation (2π) radians) in relation to space, i.e. in one sidereal day of 23 hr 56 min 04.09 sec approximately, so having a value of 0.00007292 radians per second.

Geostrophic wind scale
There was a time when a pilot in his civil licence qualifying examinations could have been asked to use the geostrophic wind equation and 5-figure logarithms to calculate the geostrophic wind speed under given conditions, but this is no longer so. Meteorological charts do, however, carry not only graduated scale lines but

also geostrophic wind scales from which wind speeds can be readily determined, corresponding to various isobar spacings. As shown in fig. 10.8, they may be applicable to one particular latitude or they may be multi-latitude scales.

To construct a geostrophic wind scale, constant values are assumed for all the terms in the geostrophic equation (except for the isobar distance apart and the wind speed). The distances (ds) are then evaluated for different wind speeds (V). If the circumstances warrant and the accuracy of the isobar drawing is sufficiently precise, then the scale reading of the wind speed can be adjusted for the amount that the prevailing conditions depart from those assumed in calibrating the scale.

(b) Regularly curved, equidistant isobars which are not changing with time: gradient wind

In this case, although the magnitude of the pressure gradient force is constant over the region, its direction is variable (fig. 10.9). In the case of isobars around a depression (cyclonic curvature) the force is directed radially inwards and

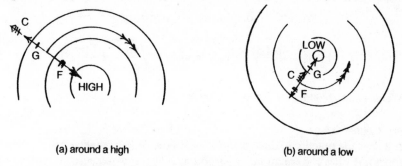

(a) around a high   (b) around a low

Fig. 10.9   Gradient wind around curved isobars

around an anticyclone the pressure gradient force is radially outwards from the centre of curvature of the isobars. It will be remembered that cyclostrophic force also acts radially on air moving on a curved path so it will either augment or reduce the pressure gradient force. On the other hand, using a geostrophic wind scale will give the geostrophic wind speed corresponding to the pressure gradient.

Around an anticyclone, the cyclostrophic force is additional to the pressure gradient force and the actual wind (called the *gradient wind*) is stronger than the geostrophic wind scale value by an amount which produces a proportionately greater geostrophic force to balance the other two forces.

Pressure gradient force + Cyclostrophic force = Geostrophic force   (3)

Around a depression, the pressure gradient supplies the cyclostrophic force and there is less to be balanced by geostrophic force which is achieved at a gradient wind speed less than the geostrophic wind scale value.

Pressure gradient force − Cyclostrophic force = Geostrophic force   (4)

The rule is therefore that with curved isobars the wind speed (gradient wind) around a LOW is LOWER than the value obtained from a geostrophic wind scale for that isobar spacing, while around a HIGH the actual wind speed is HIGHER than the scale value.

For this reason, winds around a depression may not be as strong as might be expected from a first glance and the winds around a small anticyclone may be appreciably (proportionately) greater than expected.

(c) Regularly curved isobars around an intense depression: cyclostrophic wind

The assumptions in this case give the best approximation to the actual wind speed. In low latitudes in violent tropical low pressure systems, although there is enough geostrophic force to deflect the initial air motion so that it conforms to Buys-Ballot's Law, the magnitude of the force is insignificant when compared to the pressure gradient force. In such circumstances, the geostrophic force term in equation (4) above may be considered negligible for all practical purposes and the wind speed determined from the cyclostrophic wind equation of:

$$\text{Pressure gradient force} = \text{Cyclostrophic force}$$

or:

$$dp/ds = \frac{\rho\,V^2\cot\theta}{E} \quad \text{and} \quad V = \sqrt{\frac{dp}{ds}\cdot\frac{E\tan\theta}{\rho}} \tag{5}$$

Winds above 2000 feet

(a) Contour charts

If it were the practice to draw isobars for 10 000, 20 000, 30 000 feet, etc., then the foregoing rules and equations applicable at 2000 feet would also be applicable to these higher levels. As explained in Chapter 1, however, this is not the practice and the procedure is to have contour charts of specified pressure levels e.g. 700 mb, 500 mb, 300 mb, etc. Instead of wind speed being proportional to pressure

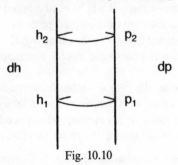

Fig. 10.10

gradient (expressed as dp/ds) it is proportional to the contour slope (dh/ds) and this in fact simplifies the geostrophic wind equation by eliminating the variable air density term.

For a small section of a column of air (say 200 feet) as in fig. 10.10, the decrease of pressure (dp) corresponding to an increase of altitude (dh) is given by the fundamental hydrostatic equation of:

$$dp = dh \times \rho \times g \tag{6}$$

where ρ is air density and g is gravity,

So if Equation (6) is substituted in Equation (2), the geostrophic equation becomes:

$$\frac{dh}{ds} \times \rho\, g = 2V\rho\omega \sin \varphi$$

and

$$\frac{dh}{ds} = \frac{2V\omega\sin \varphi}{g} \tag{7}$$

As air density is no longer a factor, a gestrophic scale based on Equation (7) can be used on contour charts for any upper level when transposed to:

$$V = \frac{dh}{ds} \times \frac{g}{2\,\omega \sin \varphi} \tag{8}$$

Again depending upon the curvature of the contours, the scale value will underestimate the actual gradient wind speed with anticyclonic curvature and overestimate the gradient wind speed with cyclonic curvature.

(b) Thermal wind

In the absence of contour charts, pilots can make use of a vector method of determining the upper wind which has been in use since the early days of aviation. It is usually called the 'thermal wind' method although it should be more correctly entitled the 'thermal component of the upper wind' method.

Consider fig. 10.11. The required upper wind is considered as the resultant of two components, the 2000 ft wind and a thermal component. The rules for the direction and magnitude of the thermal component are:

Direction – parallel to the isotherms of mean temperature for the layer between the known lower level wind (usually 2000 ft wind) and the required upper wind, with the lower temperature on the left in the northern hemisphere, on the right in southern hemisphere (i.e. similar to Buys-Ballot's Law).

Speed – proportional to the temperature gradient given by the isotherms of mean temperature. For mental calculations, the modified geostrophic equation can be simplified for UK use to:

$$1\ \text{knot} \times \frac{\text{gradient of mean temperature in C deg/100 nm}}{} \times \frac{\text{height interval in 1000s feet between lower and upper wind}}{}$$

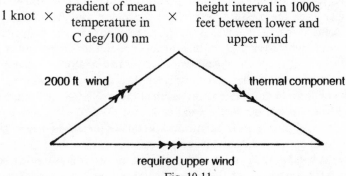

Fig. 10.11

For example, the strength of the thermal wind component between 2000 ft and 20 000 ft when the gradient of mean temperature is 4 C deg/100 nm will be:

$1 \times 4 \times (20–2) = 4 \times 18 = 72$ knots

The one knot constant strictly applies at latitude 50° so if the formula is used at a much different latitude, multiply the answer by sin 50°/sin correct latitude.

The reasoning for the rules for the direction and speed of the thermal component of the upper wind is as follows.

Case 1. When upper wind = 2000 ft wind i.e. there is no thermal component. This situation arises when the pressure distribution is the same at both lower and upper levels. Because everywhere pressure has decreased with height by the same amount, everywhere must have had the same mean temperature between the two levels. Hence the first relationship: where there is no horizontal gradient of mean temperature, there is no thermal component.

Case 2. When there is no lower wind and the upper wind is composed entirely of the thermal component (fig. 10.12).

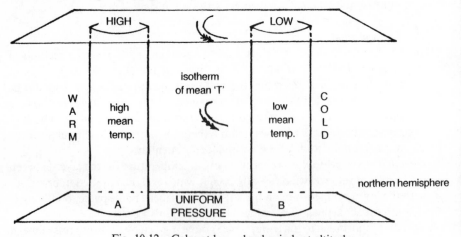

Fig. 10.12   Calm at lower level, winds at altitude

At the lower level, the uniform pressure gives no pressure gradient and no wind. At the upper level, the pressure distribution consists of low pressure (i.e. low contour height) over areas of low mean temperature, and relatively high pressure (high contour height) over areas of high mean temperature. Every upper level contour then corresponds to an isotherm of mean temperature. If column 'A' has a mean temperature that is 1°C warmer than column 'B' which is 100 nautical miles away in temperate latitudes, then the resulting pressure gradient 1000 feet higher up will produce a wind of 1 knot. A 10°C difference over a 10 000 feet interval for the two columns will produce a pressure gradient giving a $10 \times 10 = 100$ knot wind (thermal component).

Because the wind blows parallel to the upper contours, which are themselves coincident with the isotherms of mean temperature, the wind (thermal component) is parallel to the isotherms, with low values on the left in the northern hemisphere, right in the southern hemisphere.

Case 3. General case, when there is a lower wind and an overlying gradient of upper air mean temperatures, producing a different upper wind (fig. 10.13).
In fig. 10.13, column AA is warmer than column BB but both are on the same 1 016 mb isobar. Between mean sea level and 10 000 ft, in column AA pressure decreases by 304 mb while in the colder and denser column BB the pressure fall is greater – in this case 316 mb. In consequence, at 10 000 ft 'A' and 'B' are no longer on the same isobar and there is a new pressure gradient and upper wind.

The correlation between the isobar pattern and winds at the lower and upper levels and the thermal component method of determining the upper wind is shown in the plan view of fig. 10.13. In this case, the 2000 ft wind is assumed to be 240°T/20 kt, 'B' is 350 nm away from 'A' in the direction of 030°T, with a mean temperature (2000 to 10 000 ft) difference of 8.75°C which gives a thermal component of 300°T/20 kt, so that the resultant 10 000 ft w/v is 270°T/35 kt.

Although for simplicity of illustration fig. 10.13 uses an isobaric chart for

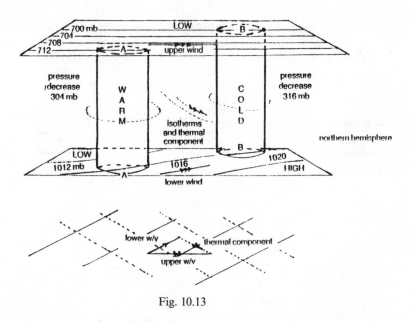

Fig. 10.13

10 000 ft, in fact the appropriate chart would be the upper contour chart for the 700 mb level. Similarly the isotherms of mean temperature would be available in the meteorological office but in the guise of 'thickness charts' where for standard layers (such as 1000 to 700 mb) the value h of the pressure-height formula (in this case 'thickness') is ascribed to each isotherm of mean temperature T, i.e.:

$$h \text{ (thickness)} = 221.1 \times T \left(\frac{\text{mean temperature}}{\text{isotherm}} \right) \times (\log 1000 - \log 700)$$

The thermal wind component is thus parallel to the thickness isopleths and proportional to their gradient.

Variation of upper wind with height

Above the friction layer of the lower atmosphere, the following rules may be deduced.

1. If the lowest upper air mean temperatures are in the area of low pressure at low level, then the wind speed will increase with height with no change of direction (fig. 10.14).

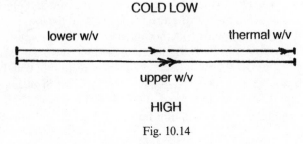

Fig. 10.14

2. If the lowest upper air mean temperatures are coincident with the area of high pressure at low levels, then the wind speed will decrease with height from the same direction. Ultimately it will become zero and then start to increase from the reciprocal direction (fig. 10.15).

Vectorially, in sequence

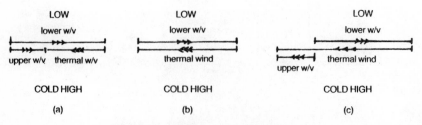

Fig. 10.15   Wind reversal with height

3. If the lower wind is blowing towards the area of coldest upper air temperatures then the wind will veer with increase of height in the northern hemisphere and back with height in the southern hemisphere (fig. 10.16). The opposite applies when the lower wind is blowing towards the warmest air.

4. Away from low latitudes where geostrophic force is nil or negligible and the upper winds are light easterly, in the troposphere winds become increasingly westerly with height. This applies in both hemispheres and up to the tropopause where upper winds are often 100 knots or more. On entering the lower stratosphere, the wind speeds start to decrease again. In summer over NW Europe, it is almost invariably the case that the lower stratosphere in higher latitudes is warmer than it is in lower latitudes so reversing the temperature gradient and eroding the thermal component. This is often true too in spring and

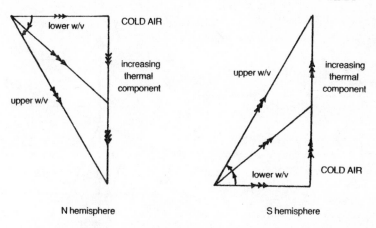

Fig. 10.16   Wind change with height

autumn. In mid-winter however, with the very disturbed conditions of the troposphere the gradient of mean temperature of the lower stratosphere is not constant, but even so the thermal component (and upper wind) decreases on entering the stratosphere.

5. In areas where upper air mean temperatures change appreciably in a short distance there will be a relatively localised large gradient of mean temperature producing a big thermal component and hence a strong upper wind. These strong winds of 100 knots or more are called jet streams and are referred to again in Chapter 12.

Jet streams occur in sub-tropical latitudes and near the fronts of depressions associated with the polar front. Although they may be well over 1000 miles in length, they are comparatively narrow (often 100–250 miles wide) and shallow (10 000 feet thickness is typical). Because of their very high speeds, near fronts where the wind gradient horizontally between the jet core and the frontal surface may be appreciable (see fig. 12.7, p. 146) there is often clear air turbulence.

Winds below 2000 feet
Leaving aside for the moment local winds which are associated with the topography of the area, e.g. sea breezes at a coastal aerodrome on a summer afternoon, certain general rules apply to the winds encountered in the lower atmosphere.

Effect of surface friction
It has been seen that, from the balance of forces acting horizontally on the air, at 2000 feet the wind would be geostrophic or gradient depending upon whether the isobars are straight or curved. At the surface, the friction between the air and the underlying surface has also to be considered and may be represented vectorially as a force acting in a reciprocal direction to that of the air's motion. The force will decrease the wind speed and, because it is proportional to the wind speed, the geostrophic force (fig. 10.17).

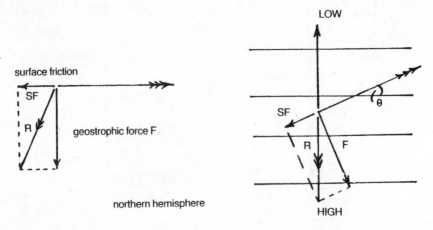

Fig. 10.17   Effect of surface friction

The resultant of geostrophic and surface friction forces then balances the pressure gradient force with the wind blowing slightly across the isobars (θ) towards the lower pressure. On an average:

Over the land   *Over the sea*
   θ = 30°   θ = 15°
speed = $\frac{1}{3}$ of 2000 ft wind   speed = $\frac{2}{3}$ of 2000 ft wind

However, to be realistic, friction is irregular even over the sea and the precise value of the surface wind at a particular point and time will depend not only on the friction but also on the degree of turbulence mixing the air in the lower

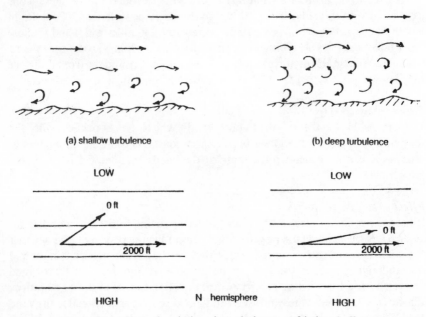

(a) shallow turbulence   (b) deep turbulence

Fig. 10.18   Effect of variations in turbulence on frictional effect

atmosphere. If conditions are very stable and turbulence is weak (fig. 10.18(a)) the concentrated frictional effects on the surface wind are greater than when there is a deep and vigorous turbulence layer (fig. 10.18(b)) distributing the frictional effect through the deeper layer.

Apart from variations in lapse rate, there is over land a diurnal variation in the vertical extent of the turbulence layer, being a deep layer by day, a shallow layer by night (fig. 10.19).

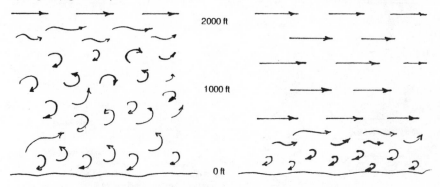

over land in the northern hemisphere

(a) by day   (b) by night

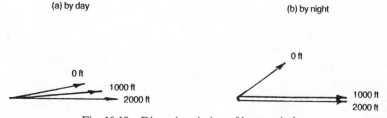

Fig. 10.19   Diurnal variation of lower winds

From day to night, for a given isobar pattern:
  Surface wind backs and lulls
  1000 ft wind veers and increases to become geostrophic
  2000 ft wind has no variation
From night to day:
  Surface wind veers and increases
1000 ft wind backs and decreases when it becomes absorbed within the turbulence layer
2000 ft wind has no variation.
In the southern hemisphere, the direction of wind variation is opposite to that of the northern hemisphere.

Wind gradient
Not to be confused with the primary cause of wind, pressure gradient, nor with the gradient wind around curved isobars, wind gradient is the term used to

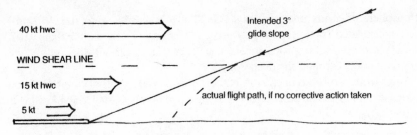

(a) aircraft landing in wind shear conditions

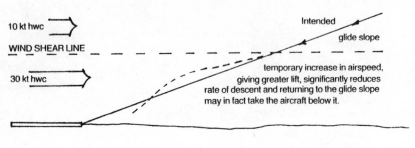

(b) aircraft landing in wind shear conditions

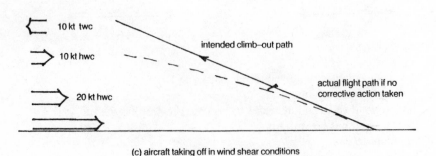

(c) aircraft taking off in wind shear conditions

Fig. 10.20 Effects of varying wind shear conditions

describe the decrease of wind speed as an aircraft descends on the approach to the runway. The term is more likely to be used by flying instructors than by meteorologists.

Wind shear
Although there has always been the wind gradient with height from the surface

to, say, 2000 feet, in recent years our greater knowledge of cause and effect has highlighted problems which can be met during the critical phases of a flight immediately after take-off and on the approach to land due to wind shear. The problems are worse too for jet aircraft compared to propeller-driven aircraft. This is because when the pilot of a propeller-driven aeroplane encounters a marked wind gradient, i.e. a wind shear, and experiences loss of airspeed and lift, increasing the power immediately results in greater propeller slipstream over the mainplanes and increased lift. Increasing the power of a jet engine, however, produces a relatively slower 'spool-up' time, there is no propeller slipstream and the airspeed and lift recovery is correspondingly slower.

Generally a wind shear will be associated with a marked meteorological feature so its presence can be anticipated. Also, as investigations have identified accidents which have primarily been caused by wind shear, major airports give wind shear warnings to pilots about to make an approach if there is any reason to suspect one's presence. Conversely, if a pilot encounters a wind shear he should report it to air traffic control giving particulars of the relevant height(s), what effects were experienced (vertical speed, airspeed, etc.), any visible weather phenomena and if possible an assessment of the vertical wind temperature structure. Airborne and ground equipment is constantly being developed and researched to provide a timely warning of wind shear near aerodromes. Some aerodromes have taken advantage of nearby television or radio masts or hills to install anemometers to measure the wind directly at various levels and so obtain a vertical profile of the airflow in their area. Apart from micro-bursts and downdraughts associated with thunderstorms, mountain wave systems and deflected low level winds around buildings and large structures near runways already discussed, low level wind shear arises at warm and cold fronts and at sea breeze fronts with usually a marked temperature inversion near the ground. Some researches suggest that a temperature difference of 5°C or more between the air masses across a front, or an active front moving at 30 knots or more, is most likely to produce a significant wind shear.

Ignoring crosswind effects which can require large corrections for drift, consider the effects on aeroplanes taking off and landing when there is a sharp wind shear as shown in fig. 10.20. In each case, when the aeroplane flies into the wind shear, the inertia of the aeroplane will maintain its ground speed but the airspeed will change by the amount of change of headwind component. A reduction of airspeed also means reduced lift which in turn causes the aeroplane to descend below the intended flight path.

As more research is carried out the various wind shear possibilities are being incorporated into modern simulators. However, the problem remains that low level wind shear is basically inconstant and pilots must be vigilant whenever potential conditions exist. If the aircraft has an Inertial Navigation System (INS) with a ground speed read-out which can be compared with the indicated airspeed, then a ready appreciation of changing headwind/tailwind component can be made. A DME (distance measuring equipment) derived ground speed can similarly be used. Otherwise, guidance must be sought from any of the following: vertical speed, pitch attitude, deviation from the glide slope, need to change power settings or aircraft attitude; even sudden or large drift changes can be indicative of the presence of wind shear.

Company operating drills vary but essentially are designed to keep the aircraft from colliding with the ground, maintaining safe airspeeds and full handling control. Take-off should be delayed until the weather conditions producing the micro-burst or wind shear have cleared the aerodrome. In the event of encountering either of them on the approach to landing, an early decision to overshoot must be made if at decision height the aircraft is still departing below the desired glide path by using maximum power as soon as possible.

Local surface winds

Ravine, valley and headland winds
Not only are winds deflected in direction but their speeds may also be increased when substantial high ground is encountered. If the obstruction occurs at a steep headland on the coast or at a similar topographical feature inland (fig. 10.21) then the streamlines near to it become closer and the wind speed increases.

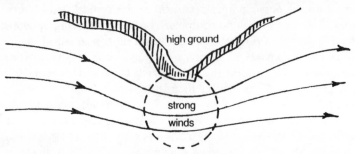

Fig. 10.21   Headland effects

Should the airflow be across high ground, then the wind will flow most readily through any valleys, mountain passes, etc., that traverse the mountain range. The speed of the wind through the valley due to this channelling or 'funnel' effect may reach well over gale force. Generally, of course, in narrow valleys, the wind

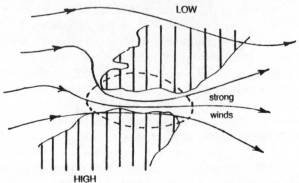

Fig. 10.22   Ravine winds

tends only to blow up or down the valley anyway, with only a tenuous adherence to Buys-Ballot's Law (fig. 10.22).

Mountain and lee wave systems

The hazards arising from this topographical effect upon the airflow at low and middle levels has prompted the Civil Aviation Authority to issue pink Aeronautical Information Circulars drawing pilots' attention to them from time to time.

The conditions suitable for the development of standing waves may be summarised as:

1. Wind at right angles (or within ±30°) to a continuous mountain range.
2. Little change of wind direction with height.
3. Wind speed 20 knots or more at the mountain summit and increasing with height.
4. Very stable layer several thousand feet thick just above the mountains, with less stable air above and below the stable layer.

The airflow then takes the form illustrated in fig. 10.23.

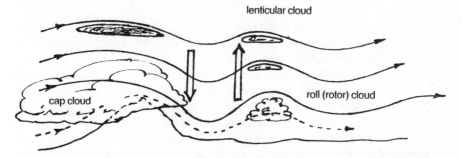

Fig. 10.23   Mountain and lee-wave system

The orographic cloud formed on the mountains is called cap cloud (but may have a particular local name) and above it and downwind there is lenticular cloud. Clouds also form in the rotor zone and these clouds while perhaps appearing innocuous do in fact conceal extremely turbulent flying conditions. The surface turbulence layer in these circumstances is in no way limited to the 2000 feet assumed for general purposes earlier in this chapter. Immediately downwind of the mountains (and through a substantial depth of atmosphere) there is a strong down-draught followed very quickly by a strong up-draught. The motion remains turbulent downwind resulting in either roll (rotor) cloud which, like the lenticular cloud, appears to remain stationary in its position in relation to the mountains, or rotor streaming where there is a continual streaming away down-wind of low-level rotors of severely turbulent air.

Together with the attendant problems of icing in IMC, if the region cannot be avoided an appreciable increase in safety height margins must be allowed for. It is not safe to assume in any mountainous region that the conditions generated by one mountain range will be cancelled out when they meet the next range. This next range may in fact produce mountain waves in phase, so worsening the situation even further.

Anabatic and katabatic winds

These winds also occur in hilly or mountainous countryside and may be called valley or mountain winds. Generally, however, to avoid confusion the term valley wind should be reserved for the funnel effect already described.

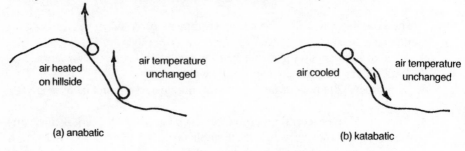

(a) anabatic   (b) katabatic

Fig. 10.24

If the pressure gradient is slack and the day is relatively cloudfree, the sun-facing slopes become warmer and in turn warm the air in contact with them. This air then becomes warmer than the free air at the same level of which the temperature is relatively unchanged. The warmer lighter air on the hillside then tends to rise as a light anabatic wind. Sometimes the irregularities of convection give an irregular flow, while near to coastlines the anabatic winds may be stronger because the flow is supplemented by a sea-breeze.

The reverse katabatic flow may be much stronger (well over gale force), more widespread and persistent. In the case of katabatic winds, although the free air temperature remains unchanged the air on the hillside is cooled by conduction and flows downwards. Any heating adiabatically in the descending air is also quickly conducted away. On gently sloping ground the katabatic flow at night may not amount to much more than a breeze. On the other hand, if mountains are snow-covered and long winter nights are interspersed with cold days, then katabatic winds may be very strong and persistent. The Bora, described in Chapter 15, is an example. Flight conditions if not prohibited by the actual wind speed itself can be extremely rough, especially for light aircraft, in the take-off and landing phases.

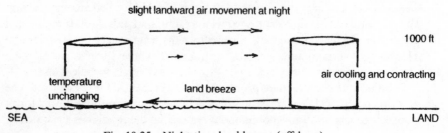

Fig. 10.25   Night-time land breeze (offshore)

Land and sea breezes

These breezes arise from the diurnal variation of temperature of the lower atmosphere over land and sea. Consider first the lighter land breeze which blows off-shore (fig. 10.25). At night, the sea temperature and that of the air above it hardly changes. However in relatively cloudless conditions with a slack pressure gradient the land cools by radiation and the lowest layers of air are cooled in turn by conduction. In this colder denser air, by about 1000 feet there will be slightly lower pressure than over the nearby sea and there is a gradual drift of upper air from over sea to over the land. This in turn causes sufficient rise in surface pressure over land for a surface flow of air off-shore to result, called the land breeze. It dies out around dawn, is limited to the 300 to 500 feet up to 10 miles either side of the coast, and rarely exceeds 10 knots.

In contrast, the sea breeze (fig. 10.26) is a daytime phenomenon. In the UK it does not usually extend to more than 500 to 1000 feet and speeds of 10 knots but in tropical countries speeds may reach 20 knots and the breeze penetrate to 20 to 30 miles inland as opposed to the 10 to 15 miles more usual in NW Europe. Generally, because they are less vulnerable to the cloudiness and strong pressure gradients of temperate latitudes, sea breezes are a regular feature of the climate of tropical coastal aerodromes.

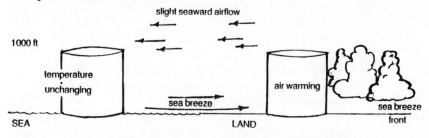

Fig. 10.26   Day-time sea breeze (onshore)

In on-shore sea breezes, the land air warms and expands producing a relatively higher pressure than over the sea at, say, 1000 feet and higher. A drift of upper air from over the land to over the sea then causes a slight surface pressure rise over the sea and a slight fall over land. As a result of this local cross-coastline pressure gradient, an on-shore sea breeze sets in. Sometimes if the general pressure gradient had previously been producing a slight off-shore wind, the onset of the sea breeze can be quite sudden with a noticeable drop in temperature, especially if it brings in any mist that may have been lying just out to sea. In fact, the boundary between the previous warmer land air and a deep sea breeze – say 3000 feet thick – may well be defined as a sea breeze front defined by small cumulus clouds.

The sea breeze on a hot summer's day may well develop by late morning and during the afternoon Coriolis effect starts to apply turning the sea breeze increasingly along the coastline with the land on the left (in the northern hemisphere, on the right in the southern hemisphere). Generally, as sunset approaches, the sea breeze weakens and disperses soon after dark.

The actual pattern of surface winds at an aerodrome near to the coast with high ground not too far inland can in fact be quite complex. Even where there is a basic airflow due to the overall pressure distribution over the area, local topographical features do influence landing conditions appreciably – probably most where there are fjords and marked indentations in the coastline.

Test questions

Q1.   A changing wind direction from 315° through to 015° is:
    (a) veering
    (b) backing
    (c) veering if N hemisphere, backing if S hemisphere.

Q2.   The windspeed suddenly increases for a few seconds from 10 knots to 30 knots and then falls to 15 knots. This is a:
    (a) gust
    (b) squall
    (c) gale.

Q3.   Due to the increasing effect of surface friction on the wind, on a straight-in approach to a UK aerodrome which starts directly into wind at 1500 feet, the drift during the descent will:
    (a) increase to port on an easterly heading
    (b) increase to port on a westerly heading
    (c) increase to starboard on all headings.

Q4.   A significant wind shear can be associated with:
    (a) a surface inversion with calm conditions
    (b) south-westerly gales away from low pressure systems
    (c) thunderstorms or line squalls.

Q5.   A reported wind shear identifies for an aircraft on the approach to runway 09 a wind of 090/40 knots at 1000 feet decreasing to 20 knots at 800 feet; if the pilot takes no corrective action, the aircraft will:
    (a) deviate appreciably above the intended glide slope and land beyond the runway
    (b) deviate appreciably below the intended glide slope
    (c) encounter severe clear air turbulence and an appreciable deviation to one side of the glide path due to a large change in drift.

Q6.   The small rotor clouds down-stream of a mountain range:
    (a) are not a hazard to aviation as they never obscure high ground
    (b) are less hazardous than the cap cloud as the vertical motion is diminished away from the mountains
    (c) should not be flown through because of their severe turbulence.

Q7.   If on a certain chart, straight isobars 1 centimetre apart give a geostrophic wind of 40 knots, the same isobars when 0.8 centimetres apart will give a geostrophic wind of:
    (a) 32 knots
    (b) 50 knots
    (c) 40 knots.

Q8.   The cyclostrophic wind equation gives a practical approximation to:

    (a) the 2000 ft wind speed in an intense tropical storm

    (b) the correction to apply to the geostrophic wind speed around an anticyclone to obtain the 2000 ft gradient wind

    (c) the effect of the earth's rotation (Coriolis) force.

Q9.   Over the North Sea, the 3000 ft w/v is 330/30 kt and the gradient of mean temperature from 3000 ft to 30000 ft is 13°C in 300 nm with the coldest air in the direction of 030°T. The 30000 ft w/v will be:

    (a) 270/130 kt

    (b) 300/117 kt

    (c) 306/144 kt.

Q10.   The diurnal variation of the surface wind at an inland aerodrome in level countryside will be:

    (a) veer and increase during morning, back and lull in the evening in the northern hemisphere, vice versa in the southern hemisphere

    (b) back and increase during the morning, veer and lull in the evening in the northern hemisphere, vice versa in the southern hemisphere

    (c) veer in the northern hemisphere (back in the southern hemisphere) and increase in morning; back in the northern (veer in the southern) hemisphere and lull in the evening.

11:   Air Masses

Having considered the various individual meteorological elements that are significant to a pilot when operating his aircraft, attention can now be given to taking an overall view of the weather conditions prevailing in a local flying area or along a particular route. This is synoptic meteorology. There are two broad lines of approach: air mass analysis and pressure type-frontal analysis. This chapter is devoted to the former.

From time to time in earlier chapters reference has been made to a mass of air, for example in considering stability and instability together with the subsequent motion of air displaced vertically in relation to its environment. An 'air mass' means something completely different to such small masses or parcels of rising air.

An air mass is a large body of air hundreds of miles across, usually occupying the whole troposphere in a region, in which there is horizontal uniformity (or approximately so) of temperature and humidity. These two properties are fundamental to the type of resultant weather conditions. The uniformity of temperature, i.e. lack of a horizontal gradient of mean temperature and hence a thermal wind component, means that the wind varies little with height and the air mass can move along with little distortion.

Source regions

Within an air mass, the mean sea level pressure may be low or high and the QFF at an aerodrome has little significance in this connection. However, the regions in which air masses originate, their source regions, are always areas of high pressure. This is because in order to establish the uniformity of its temperature and humidity the air has to remain stationary or slow-moving for a week or two over a fairly uniform area of the earth's surface, e.g. sub-tropical ocean or polar ice-cap, etc. As will be seen in Chapter 15: Climatology, there are large anticyclones permanently or seasonally situated over certain areas of the earth's surface which provide just such stagnant conditions. Depending upon the source locations, air masses are classified by temperature as Arctic (A) (or Antarctic), Polar (P), Tropical (T), Equatorial (E) and by humidity as maritime (m) or continental (c).

Modification of air masses

Although it is not intended in this book to consider the many sub-classifications of air masses that specialist meteorologists may require in particular geographical locations, pilots should be aware that the weather to be expected in a particular air mass depends not only on its source region but also upon its track to the forecast area. Consider first the modifications of temperature, starting with an air mass moving into a warmer surface area (fig. 11.1).

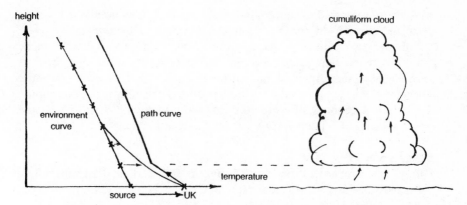

Fig. 11.1   Air mass moving to warmer area becoming unstable

In this case, the surface temperature rise increases the lapse rate in the lower levels, producing increasing instability. If the air is and also remains moist, this instability and the convection currents generated will produce towering cumuliform cloud.

Conversely (fig. 11.2), if the air mass is moving to a progressively colder surface area, it will be cooled from below, decreasing the lapse rate to a stable value. This stability opposes vertical motion so helping to confine the cooling to the surface layers and perhaps creating a low level inversion. If the air is and remains moist, any cloud formed will be stratus and stratocumulus and any prolonged cooling will probably produce advection fog.

Similarly the trajectory of the air after leaving the source region can also help to determine its humidity by the time it reaches another area. If a continental air mass moves continuously over open ocean it will gradually become maritime. The required distance does depend to some extent upon the prevailing temperature. Typical of this modification would be a flight departing from Copenhagen or Helsinki in clear cloudless conditions on a January day, remaining in the same air mass while crossing the North Sea to arrive at Aberdeen or Newcastle in snow showers. The opposite situation occurs when a

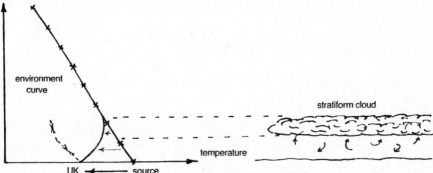

Fig. 11.2   Air mass moving to colder area becoming stable

maritime air mass crosses high ground and its humidity is reduced by orographic cloud and rain. The higher the mountains, the greater is the drying out.

Although, as mentioned earlier, the prevailing mean sea level pressure value is not of any real significance in an air mass once it has moved away from its source region, one aspect of pressure may have a part to play – pressure tendency. If within an air mass surface pressure is generally rising this implies that there is probably subsidence occurring and a stabilising effect on the lapse rate, while generally falling pressures imply lessening stability.

Air mass properties

The air mass properties experienced in Britain (fig. 11.3) are dealt with below. Other parts of the world are considered in Chapter 15: Climatology.

Tropical maritime air (Tm)

With the prevailing wind in NW Europe being south-westerly, this is a common air mass in the UK. Originating near the Azores, it becomes progressively more stable and humid on its track north-eastwards. When the winds are light there

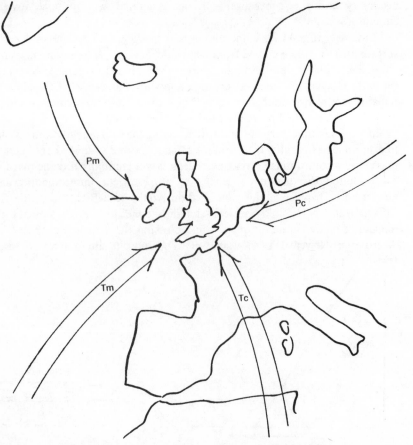

Fig. 11.3   Main air masses affecting the British Isles

may be an isothermal layer or inversion near the surface; when they are fresh to strong the inversion is found above the surface turbulence layer when the air mass arrives in the south-west approaches. In winter the dull, drizzly weather with low stratus or advection fog moves inland, especially at night, and all high ground is obscured. However by the time that the tropical maritime air reaches north-east England and east Scotland it is descending on the leeside of high ground of northern Britain and breaks in the cloud may appear. In the summer, although at night there may be advection or hill fog and widespread stratus or stratocumulus cloud, inland there is usually enough solar heating to disperse the stratus and perhaps be followed by isolated small cumulus in the still stable conditions. The visibility is usually no more than moderate at best and in light winds there may be local radiation fog patches around dawn if the stratus has not reformed.

Polar maritime air (Pm)

Originating often in the Greenland region, polar maritime air frequently spreads across Britain from a north-west direction. On its track it will have become more unstable and maintained its humidity. The relative humidity, however, is not as high as that of tropical maritime air (which may be 90% to 100% in the UK) as although there is continual evaporation into the air from the sea below, at the same time the air is being warmed up from its slowly increasing dew point temperature. Relative humidities of 70% are typical. The increasing instability permits active convection and helps to distribute the added moisture upwards.

In winter, polar maritime air brings cool weather with wintry showers with good visibility away from the showers. Surface winds are gusty and flying is bumpy. Clouds are large cumulus and cumulonimbus over the sea and all coasts, with turbulent flying and a risk of severe icing. Inland the clouds tend to clear at night and if the winds are light, there may be frost or radiation fog. In summer, as the air mass moves over land by day, the instability is increased and there is widespread convection. Cumuliform is general with heavy showers of rain and hail often accompanied by thunderstorms. Again turbulence and icing are problems in cloud. Often the thunderstorms become more severe the further south-east the air moves over Britain. Visibility outside the showers is good to excellent.

There is one particular case of polar maritime air which is worthy of special mention, occurring when there is a slow-moving low pressure system situated to the north-west of the British Isles. In this case the trajectory of the polar air takes it into latitudes much further south than the UK so that it arrives here as a south-west wind and is known specifically as 'returning polar maritime air' (rPm). Its lapse rate reflects the effect of this trajectory (fig. 11.4).

Having become unstable by the time it has travelled from its source (1) to the most southerly point (2) on its track, the lowest layers of the rPm air are then cooled from below as it moves north-eastwards to the seas (3) off south-west England. This cooling is confined to the lowest layers and stabilises that part of the previously unstable lapse rate making the air mass similar to tropical maritime air with that air mass's characteristics. At night and in winter, if the rPm air moves inland it spreads the low stratus, drizzle and poor visibility in with it. The upper air is, however, still unstable (and cool) so if the air is forced upwards by substantial high ground then large cumulus, cumulonimbus and showers develop. In summer by day, the low cloud that moves inland (4) with rPm air disperses and in the warm, moist airstream, unstable conditions and widespread convection develop. The stratus and stratocumulus are replaced by large cumulus and cumulonimbus with squally showers, thunderstorms and turbulent flying conditions.

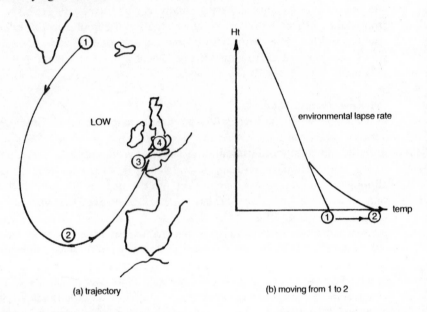

(a) trajectory   (b) moving from 1 to 2

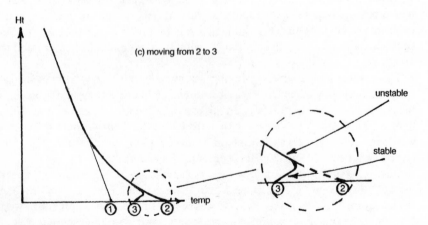

Fig. 11.4   Trajectory and lapse rates of 'returning' polar maritime air arriving in the UK

Polar continental air (Pc)

This air mass has its source region in continental eastern Europe and Siberia and brings very cold weather to Britain in winter. At that time, low surface temperatures and subsidence give a stable lapse rate and relatively low humidities in the source region. Easterly winds with a short sea track continue into Britain the cloud-free cold conditions particularly at night. Further north along the east coast of Britain, the air mass will travel further across a relatively warmer North Sea (even if the sea temperatures are only single-figure °C) absorbing heat and moisture. The lapse rate gradually becomes unstable and snow and sleet showers fall over the coastal regions of eastern Britain with little diurnal variation. Inland the showers become more scattered dispersing to the lee of high ground and at night.

Air from the same source region in summer tracks across a warm continent and may therefore not be considered 'the genuine article' by the time that it arrives in the UK. In south-east England, with a short sea track, it arrives as a cloudless warm dry airstream with a large diurnal range of temperature inland. Further north along the east coast, the moistening and cooling effect of a longer path over the North Sea (now relatively cold) will produce advection fog or low stratus in the modified polar continental air.

Tropical continental air (Tc)

Because a suitable trajectory is rare and even if it did occur the multiple modifications caused by its passage across the Mediterranean Sea, the high ground of southern Europe, e.g. the Alps, and the cold continent itself, preclude tropical continental air from the Sahara Desert arriving in Britain in winter.

At its source the air is stable, hot and arid. Tracking northwards to Britain in summer, tropical continental air brings 'heat-wave' conditions. The air is cooled as it travels, so stabilising the lapse rate especially at night. The daytime temperatures even fail to produce extensive clouds due to the dryness of the air. Visibilities are hazy due to the dust and smoke collected from the source and continental industrial regions respectively.

Equatorial air never reaches the British Isles but in mid-winter sometimes Arctic air is experienced, which then gives more extreme cold than Polar air.

Test questions

Q1.   A south-westerly wind with low stratus cloud, drizzle and poor visibility spreading into SW Britain indicates that the incoming air mass is:
(a) tropical maritime
(b) polar maritime
(c) tropical maritime or returning polar maritime.

Q2.   Polar maritime air masses are characteristically:
(a) cold, dry, unstable with poor visibility
(b) cold, humid, increasingly unstable with good visibility except in showers
(c) infrequent over Britain in summer but when they occur they produce radiation fog at night.

Q3.   In summer, steady easterly winds from north Germany produce on the
       NE English coast:
       (a) a deterioration in visibility
       (b) an improvement in visibility
       (c) a marked drop in the freezing level.

Q4.   In winter over southern Britain, returning polar maritime air will
       probably produce:
       (a) overcast skies of stratus and stratocumulus
       (b) clear skies and radiation fog
       (c) towering cumuliform cloud and thunderstorms.

Q5.   Tropical continental air over central Britain in summer will probably
       produce:
       (a) hot hazy weather
       (b) widespread thunderstorms
       (c) layers of altocumulus and cirrocumulus (mackerel sky).

Q6.   Clear night skies, with convection cloud and showers over the whole UK
       during the day, is typical of:
       (a) tropical maritime air
       (b) polar maritime air
       (c) returning polar maritime air.

Q7.   If in January the weather conditions on a short cross-Channel flight from
       Dover are: wind 110/20 kt, visibility 3 km; the prevailing air mass is:
       (a) tropical maritime air
       (b) tropical continental air
       (c) polar continental air.

Q8.   In an ideal air mass, with an increase of altitude:
       (a) the wind becomes progressively more westerly
       (b) the wind becomes progressively stronger
       (c) there is little variation of wind velocity.

Q9.   Within an air mass:
       (a) pressure is uniformly high to preserve its homogeneity of temper-
           ature and humidity along its track
       (b) one particular mean sea level isobar bounds the limits of that air
           mass's specific temperature and humidity
       (c) pressure is lower on one side of its trajectory than on the other.

Q10.   An air mass in summer over southern England which is experiencing the
       following conditions at the surface in the evening: wind 220/15 kt; QFE
       1010 mb; no cloud; visibility 5 km; temperature 15°C; dew point
       temperature 13°C; will probably by dawn in the same locality be
       experiencing:
       (a) cumuliform cloud and thunderstorms
       (b) low stratus and poor visibility
       (c) unchanged conditions.

12: Low Pressure Systems and Fronts

Although the concept of air masses and their associated weather was introduced by Norwegian meteorologists in 1928, the association of particular weather conditions and identifiable pressure systems pre-dated the air mass concept by many years. In 1883, in his *Principles of Forecasting by Means of Weather Charts*, the Hon Ralph Abercromby first delineated a depression by mean sea level isobars and annotated it with its direction of motion and its related cloud, weather and surface winds. In 1918, at the end of World War I, the Norwegian meteorologists who had been working on both mathematical and empirical studies of meteorology introduced the term 'front' and the concept of a frontal surface.

A frontal surface may be defined as a sloping surface separating two air masses of different temperatures (and hence of different air densities). In practice, the transition between adjacent air masses will probably occupy a small mixing zone and the term 'frontal zone' may be preferable. The angle of slope is variable and probably averages around 1 in 100 so it is greatly exaggerated in fig. 12.1 *et seq*. The line on the earth's surface where it is intersected by a frontal zone is called a front.

Where at a front, warm air is overtaking colder air, the front is called a warm front (shown on a chart as a red line or the symbols ⬤⬤⬤) while if cold air is overtaking warmer air the front is called a cold front (shown by a blue line or by ▲▲▲). Sometimes a front may become stationary or quasi-stationary and at other times the motion reverses (called retrograde) and the cold front becomes a warm front or vice versa.

Because the major characteristics of an air mass are its temperature and its humidity, in practice it may be easier to determine the change from one air mass to another by comparison of the dew point temperatures (which combine both attributes) rather than the reported air temperatures alone.

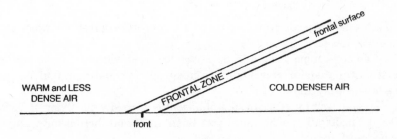

Fig. 12.1

The global atmospheric circulation produces a number of areas around the world which regularly experience this discontinuity between air masses:

Arctic front – boundary between arctic and polar air masses located mainly near to the Arctic Circle.

Polar front – boundary between polar and tropical air masses, found in temperate latitudes in all of the great oceans of northern and southern hemispheres, its position varying with the season and from day to day. In the North Pacific it lies to the south of the Aleutian Islands while in the North Atlantic is lies from Florida to SW Britain in winter and from Newfoundland to Scotland and Scandinavia in summer.

Inter-tropical front (ITF) – boundary between the trade winds of the two hemispheres. It is, however, modified by the seasonal monsoons and because often the two trade winds have similar air and dew point temperatures, the term 'inter-tropical convergence zone' (ITCZ) is preferred in Chapter 15: Climatology.

Active fronts, whether cold or warm, lie in troughs of low pressure. A weak front produces only a shallow trough and the isobars may well be U-shaped, while a front with a large difference between the air masses will have V-shaped isobars with a well-marked change in isobar direction (fig. 12.2).

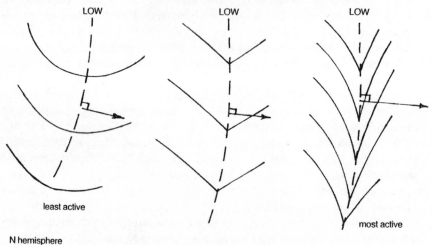

Fig. 12.2   Isobars at a front

The trough shape determines certain basic properties of fronts of which pilots should be aware.

1. At an aerodrome when a front passes, the wind will veer (in the northern hemisphere) so a pilot returning after a cross-country could easily find that there is a new runway in use.

2. The same wind veer means that if a front is crossed while flying at 2000 to 3000 ft, an alteration of heading to starboard (in the northern hemisphere) will be necessary to maintain the same track.

3. Although a satellite picture will clearly show the belt of frontal cloud, on a

synoptic chart in a meteorological office the plotted observations usually enable the front's position to be located fairly accurately by a study of the station reports of:

(a) wind direction, which will veer
(b) pressure tendency, which will usually change from a fall to become steady or rise
(c) dew point temperature, which will change from one air mass to the other
(d) air temperature, which will also change.

Perhaps even more important to pilots than the horizontal characteristics of fronts and frontal surfaces are the associated vertical conditions, of which cloud types and their distribution have already been mentioned in Chapter 6. The clouds are primarily associated with the ascent of the warm air which is an element in the general circulation of the troposphere as depicted in fig. 12.3.

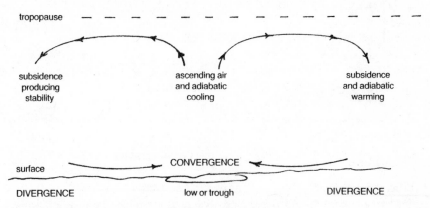

Fig. 12.3   Vertical circulation of the troposphere

The clouds are associated with the frontal zones (see fig. 12.7), so the worst flying weather, e.g. airframe icing, wind shear, etc., may be experienced some distance away from the surface position of the front. The height of the frontal zone will be readily identifiable from upper air temperature and dew point temperature readings (fig. 12.4).

The movement of the trough is at right angles to the trough line (front) with the lower pressure on the left in the northern hemisphere (right in the southern hemisphere). Its speed is dependent upon the isobar spacing along the front (fig. 12.5). If the winds are exactly geostrophic, the speed will be that obtained by measuring the distance apart of isobars at the front and taking the corresponding speed from the geostrophic scale.

If the speed of movement obtained from the geostrophic scale is small, say less than 10 knots, then the rule is less reliable and such slow-moving situations may in fact result in the front moving away from an area of rising pressure towards an area of falling pressure (isallobaric movement).

The speed of cold fronts generally corresponds to the geostrophic scale value but in the case of warm fronts the actual speed of translation is usually only two-thirds of the geostrophic component measured as shown in fig. 12.5.

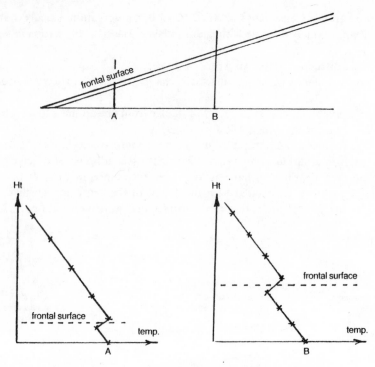

Fig. 12.4   Slope of frontal surface from upper air observations

Frontal depressions

The great majority of depressions which determine flying conditions in temperate latitudes are 'lows' formed on the polar front. The sequence of development is shown in fig. 12.6. The process was first described by J. Bjerknes of the Norwegian group of meteorologists, so is sometimes called the Bjerknes or Norwegian Theory of polar front depressions.

Initially a small wave of warm air intrudes into the cold air (fig. 12.6 (a), (b)

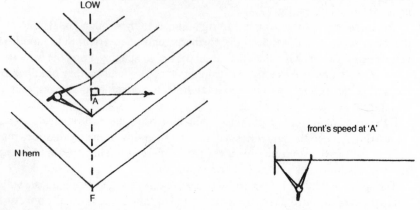

Fig. 12.5   Speed of movement of frontal trough

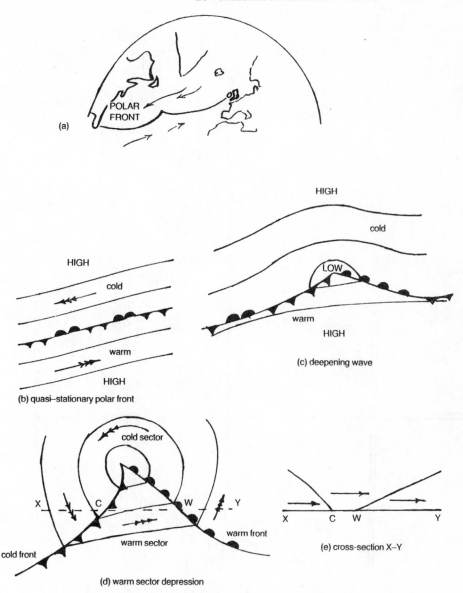

Fig. 12.6   Development of a warm sector depression

and (c)) which is called a frontal wave and is associated with a fall of pressure at the tip of the wave. This wave tends to ripple its way along the polar front at the velocity of the warm air stream. The wave may be stable and only have a temporary effect, but if it is unstable the pressure fall at the tip of the wave continues and the deepening frontal depression then develops a life cycle of its own. The advancing portion of the polar front becomes the warm front and the rear portion becomes the cold front. The warm air in the wave between the warm

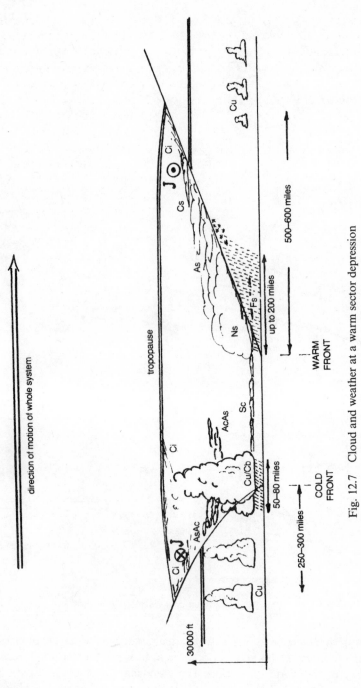

Fig. 12.7 Cloud and weather at a warm sector depression

and cold fronts is known as the warm sector of the depression and the polar air constitutes the cold sector. The clouds, weather, winds, etc., vary in degree from one warm sector depression to another but follow a general pattern which may be considered by reference to a vertical cross-section through the system, such as XY in fig. 12.6(d). Cold sector air XC is overtaking and lifting warm sector air CW at the cold front and in turn, the warm sector air CW is over-running the cold sector air WY. The whole system is moving along the polar front at the speed of the wave which is the 2000 ft w/v in the warm sector (or possibly slightly slower). Typical associated conditions are shown in fig. 12.7.

For ease of illustration, the vertical scale is exaggerated from that for the horizontal dimension. The warm front slope really is of the order of 1 in 100 to 150 while the cold front slope is usually steeper at around 1 in 50. The accompanying jet stream will be located at J [$\odot$] (where it is travelling out of the page) at the warm front while behind the cold front it will be located at J [$\otimes$] (where it is travelling into the page).

The sequence of events for an observer ahead (to the East) of a frontal depression starts with the appearance of cirrus clouds usually at 30 000 feet or higher. Within the cold air there will still be conditions characteristic of polar air – usually cumuliform cloud and showers. The cirrus clouds gradually become cirrostratus which spreads until the sky is overcast and although the sun may be visible upwards, the ice crystals of the cirrostratus will produce a 22° halo around it. Similarly when flying at heights of, say, 40 000 feet, coastlines of land masses will be visible initially when looking down through the cirriform cloud.

Gradually the clouds thicken and lower so that at some 400 to 500 miles ahead of an active warm front the cloud layer(s) have become altostratus with small supercooled water droplets. To a ground observer, the sun takes on a 'watery' outline before being obscured completely. At altitude, a pilot will find that once the cloud base is down to 20 000 feet or lower, slight snow or perhaps rain will start to fall but soon evaporates, so never reaching the ground. The tropopause has now risen in the warm sector air and the core of the jet stream will be between the frontal surface and the warm sector tropopause, with the maximum probability of clear air turbulence between the jet core and the warm frontal surface. Even if the upper winds do not reach the speed of a jet stream, they are still strongest in this area and a ground observer may see low clouds moving steadily north-eastwards while the medium and high clouds are moving rapidly south-eastwards (fig. 12.8).

The 8/8 altostratus continues to thicken and lower with the precipitation from it steadily intensifying. Eventually some 150–200 miles ahead of the surface warm front when the cloud base is down to 6000 to 7000 feet, the precipitation reaches the surface. The altostratus now becomes nimbostratus and the precipitation continues for several hours until the warm front passes. In summer, the precipitation is as slight then moderate rain but in colder conditions it will be of snow, sleet or, worst of all, freezing rain. The degree of activity of fronts is very variable so while on some occasions the altostratus/nimbostratus cloud system may extend from near to the surface (and obscuring high ground) to heights well in excess of 20 000 feet, at other times the altostratus may be layered with some

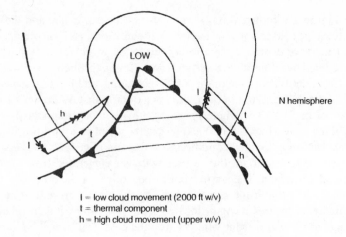

N hemisphere

l = low cloud movement (2000 ft w/v)
t = thermal component
h = high cloud movement (upper w/v)

Fig. 12.8   Cloud movement at different levels in a frontal low

clear lanes. Beneath the lowering warm front cloud, the cumuliform cloud activity of the cold sector gradually diminishes. However, further cloud may be found in the cold air in rain beneath the nimbostratus caused by evaporation from the falling raindrops. In extreme cases, the evaporation can give a belt of frontal fog. The transition at the surface into the warm sector will also be marked by the wind veering (northern hemisphere), the barometric tendency's large falls of pressure ceasing and the dew point and air temperatures rising. There may in fact already have been some gradual rise in temperature ahead of the front. At upper levels, say, 30 000 feet above the surface position of the front, the wind will have gradually backed (northern hemisphere) and decreased in speed. In practice, while most warm fronts will show the foregoing features of primarily stratiform cloud structures, there are a few exceptional cases where the warm air rising up the frontal surface becomes unstable and as a result produces warm front thunderstorms.

The warm sector will be warm and humid. The typical tropical maritime air mass characteristics of stratus, stratocumulus, drizzle or slight rain with hill fog and possibly advection fog will prevail at night and in winter. The flying conditions above the lowest levels will be stable and smooth and mostly cloudfree. On summer days, there may be little cloud (except on south-west coasts) with poor visibility generally.

Depending upon how near the centre of the depression is to the observer, so the interval before the cold front is experienced will vary. As already mentioned, the slope of the cold frontal surface is steeper than that of the warm front and the cloud and weather are not just a simple reversal of that of a warm front. The conditions vary considerably from one cold front to another. Because surface friction retards the lowest part of the frontal surface, there is often a 'nose' of warm air at 1500–2000 feet over-running the surface air. This 'nose' is continuously being destroyed and re-developing with attendant squalls or severe gusts.

The ascent of the warm air due to the under-cutting effect of the wedge of cold air will produce cumuliform cloud along the line of the front. As shown in fig. 12.7, the towering cumulus and cumulonimbus may be found over a band some 30 to 50 miles wide with some altocumulus carried forward ahead of the main frontal cloud mass. The presence of the line of cumulus/cumulonimbus may not be readily visible to a ground observer because of the warm sector low cloud, but will be easily identified on weather radar (ground or airborne) and visible to aircraft in flight which are clear of the altocumulus. Penetration of cold fronts, particularly if they are very active, should be made as near as possible at right angles to the front.

At the surface, in addition to the gusty or squally winds, rain or hail falls from thickening cloud from just ahead of the front and continues for a belt some 30 to 50 miles wide. After the front passes, pressure rises rapidly, the temperature falls and the wind direction veers (northern hemisphere). As the cumulus and cumulonimbus clear, some altocumulus and altostratus may linger for a while with some cirrostratus on the frontal surface. The final cloud clearance can be quite clear-cut and, out of precipitation, the visibility greatly improved. Overall, the frontal surface probably extends some 250–300 miles back from the surface front. At high cruising levels the wind (in the northern hemisphere) will be found to have backed further and again between the warm sector tropopause and the sloping frontal surface there is every prospect of a jet-stream from a south-westerly direction with its associated clear air turbulence. Such active cold fronts with unstable warm air are called ana-fronts while cold kata-fronts are far less active. Sometimes then the cloud structure is layered and resembles a warm front in reverse and may amount to nothing more than a very thick layer of stratocumulus. At such times, there is correspondingly little change in surface wind direction, only slight and perhaps sporadic rain at the front itself together with a small drop in temperature.

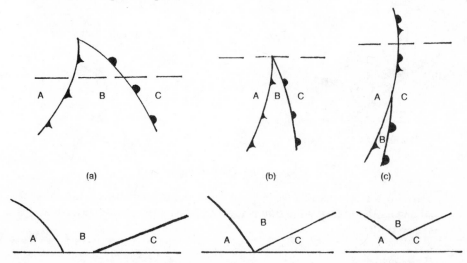

Fig. 12.9   Occluding of a frontal depression

The occluding process

A depression occludes due to the gradual decrease of the warm sector as the warm air is lifted upwards along the frontal surfaces to diverge at altitude. Successive surface charts show the cold front gradually overtaking the warm front until, when no warm sector air is left at the surface, an occlusion is formed (fig. 12.9). Occlusions are also named cold or warm depending upon the characteristics of the two cold air masses. They are unlikely to have the same temperatures, lapse rates and humidities because of the two air masses' differing recent histories and trajectories. Whichever they may be, the occlusions still lie in troughs of low pressure but as shown in fig. 12.12 (a) to (e) and fig. 12.13, various isobar patterns are possible overall.

Cold occlusion

This occurs when the overtaking cold air mass (A) (fig. 12.10) is colder than the retreating cold air mass (C) so that not only is the warm sector (B) lifted off the surface but the warm front and air mass (C) is too. The associated cloud and weather are found on both sides of the occlusion and in the later stages of its life the cold occlusion tends more and more to resemble a cold front. Because it marks the forward surface limit of the overtaking cold air, the trough line for a cold occlusion runs smoothly on from the cold frontal trough.

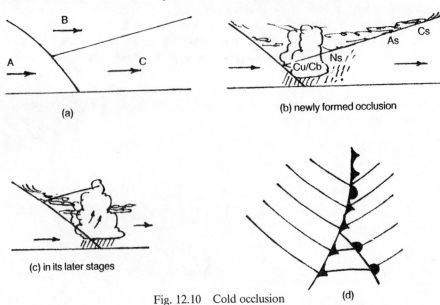

(a)

(b) newly formed occlusion

(c) in its later stages

Fig. 12.10   Cold occlusion   (d)

In NW Europe, because the North Atlantic ocean is relatively colder than the land mass to the east in the summer, cold occlusions are most frequent at this season of the year.

Warm occlusion

This occurs when the overtaking cold air (A) (fig. 12.11) is relatively warmer than

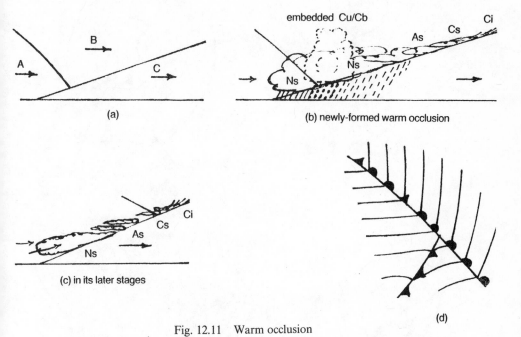

(a)

(b) newly-formed warm occlusion

(c) in its later stages

(d)

Fig. 12.11   Warm occlusion

the retreating cold air (C), which is most likely in winter in NW Europe. At this season, the cold air in the east is mainly cold continental polar air while the overtaking air is the less cold maritime polar air. The warm sector air (B) slides up the warm frontal surface followed by the cold front itself.

Superficially, with the rain and main cloud structure ahead of the surface position of the warm occlusion, its weather resembles that of a warm front. In fact in its later stages this approximation is valid. However, during the first 24 to 36 hours of the occluding process, there may be active large cumulus and cumulonimbus left still on the residual cold frontal surface which are 'embedded' in the layer cloud. Although readily detectable on an aircraft's weather radar, for an unsuspecting pilot believing that his IMC is due to layer clouds only, sudden entry into severe turbulence, heavy icing, thunderstorms and hail may come as an unpleasant and unwelcome surprise.

Back-bent occlusions
Several common alternative isobar patterns occur when a warm sector depression occludes. The occluded low can remain at what was the original tip of the warm sector with all of the occlusion lying on its warmer side (fig. 12.12 (a)). When this happens the low usually slows down, becomes a mass of rotating polar air and the occlusion weakens and finally loses its identity as a significant feature.

Alternatively the occluded low can remain at what at any time is currently the tip of the warm sector (fig. 12.12 (b), (c), (d)). In this case the subsequent

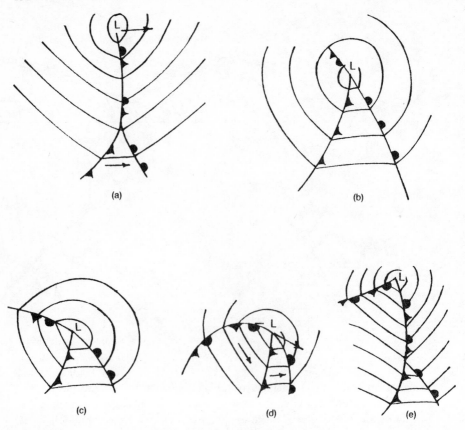

Fig. 12.12   Isobars at occluded depressions

movement of the occlusion is determined by the winds in the cold air on the polar side of the low. Together with the continued movement of the occluded low, the occlusion becomes 'back-bent' following the cold front from the north-west or west. Often the area between the cold front and the occlusion is similar to a second warm sector and a good approximation of the direction of motion of the low at this time is gained from an average of its two warm sectors.

At other times, the isobars may assume a pattern intermediate between the two just described, as shown in fig. 12.12 (e). This still produces a back-bent occlusion.

Families of depressions
Often as one depression occludes so another will form, perhaps as a variation of the system illustrated in fig. 12.12 (a). In such a case (fig. 12.13), the new low will be secondary to the original (primary) low and starts to circulate about it. If as often happens the new secondary deepens quickly and the occluded primary fills, then the secondary assumes the greater importance with the 'old' centre moving about it. If the two lows have the same intensity they pirouette about each other. The isobars around a secondary are often closest together on the side away from

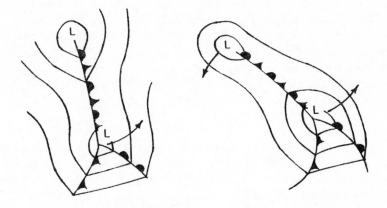

Fig. 12.13   Movement of occluded low and secondary

the primary low. Frequently the extensive drifting of snow in winter over SW England occurs when there is an occluded low over northern Britain with a frontal secondary over the SW approaches to the English Channel or in the Bristol Channel.

The trailing cold front of an occluded low extends west-south-west as the polar front but the cold air has moved it further south than its original latitude. Conditions then become suitable for a new frontal wave to form. Typically, some

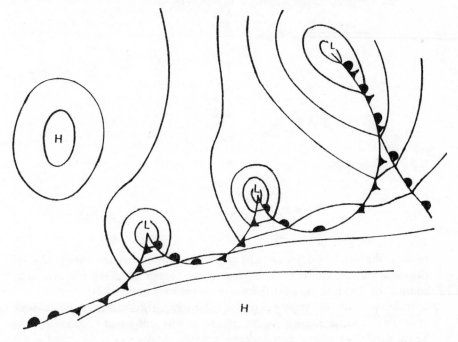

Fig. 12.14   Family of depressions

four or five depressions form one after another along the polar front, each at a successively lower latitude. The sequence ends with an anticyclone building up in the polar air. Cold air moving behind the last of the series of depressions spreads so far southwards that it flows on into the trade wind system. At the same time, a new family of depressions starts to form on the new polar front becoming established to the north-west of the anticyclone and the whole process repeats (fig. 12.14).

Frontal activity

The process of development of fronts is known as frontogenesis, and their process of decay as frontolysis. The actual degree of activity of a front at a particular time will, from a pilot's point of view, depend upon where he meets the front in the course of his flight. For example, if it is met in a mountainous region, orographic uplift will supplement the frontal uplift so worsening icing, turbulence, etc., as already described. The activity does also depend upon whether the depression is deepening rapidly and, in the case of a cold front, upon the degree of (in)stability of the warm sector air.

The convergence of low level air in a depression is most concentrated at the V-troughed isobars at a front. If a depression has not been deepening for some time, the winds will tend to approximate to geostrophic and convergence will be negligible. In fig. 12.15 the front F_1F_2 will be weak with little or no rainfall

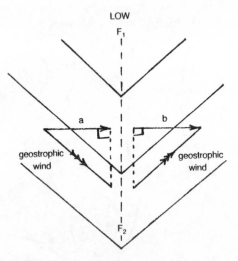

Fig. 12.15   Non-convergence of geostrophic winds at a front

because the winds are geostrophic and when this occurs the component 'a' perpendicular to the front in its rear is no greater than the perpendicular component 'b' ahead of it, so there is no overtaking motion.

However, with a deepening depression the winds are not geostrophic because of the constantly increasing pressure gradient. The amount of unbalance in the actual wind is known as the isallobaric component (fig. 12.16). Applied to the frontal situation, the isallobaric component of actual ageostrophic wind will be

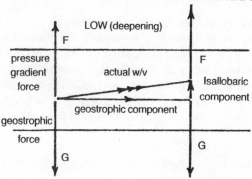

Fig. 12.16   Ageostrophic wind due to isallobaric effect

directed to the front F_1F_2 at the trough line (fig. 12.17). Although the geostrophic component will produce no convergence the isallobaric component will do so, with which there will be the attendant ascent of air, adiabatic cooling, cloud and precipitation associated with active fronts.

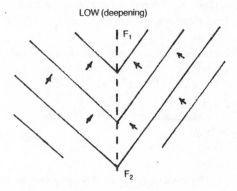

Fig. 12.17   Isallobaric components at a front

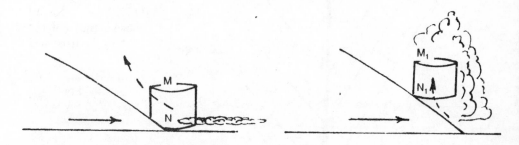

Fig. 12.18   Potential instability at a cold front

At a warm front, conditions are usually stable with successive layers of warm sector air sliding gently upwards to produce layers of cloud with progressively lowering bases. At a cold front, the undercutting wedge of cold air effectively lifts a whole mass of warm sector air (MN) bodily upwards (M_1N_1) (fig. 12.18). If, as is often the case, the stable warm sector air has a high humidity at low level but is much drier aloft, then it is potentially unstable and the bodily lifting produces large cumulus and cumulonimbus along the cold front.

Test questions

Q1.   If for a westbound flight at a position 500 miles east of a warm front the following winds are forecast:

30000 ft 315/135 kt
2000 ft 235/ 35 kt

it is probable that the warm front will be:
   (a) quite weak
   (b) quite active
   (c) quite probably occluded by the cold front.

Q2.   At an aerodrome in the UK, when an active warm front passes:
   (a) the surface wind veers
   (b) the surface wind backs
   (c) the surface wind direction may veer or back.

Q3.   The three best elements to use to locate a cold front on an unanalysed synoptic chart are:
   (a) MSL pressure, air temperature, surface wind velocity
   (b) air temperature, dew point temperature, visibility
   (c) barometric tendency, surface wind direction, dew point temperature.

Q4.   The symbol ⌃⌃ on a chart denotes:
   (a) warm front
   (b) cold front
   (c) an occlusion.

Q5.   At midnight, the geostrophic winds measured at A, B and C in the diagram are respectively 40, 20, and 30 knots. For position D, 120 nautical miles ahead of the front, the ETA of the front will be:
   (a) 0300 hrs
   (b) 0400 hrs
   (c) 0600 hrs.

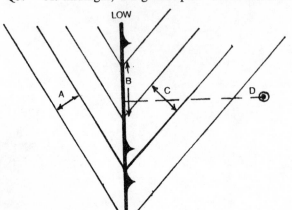

Q6.　If an observer notes that while low clouds are dispersing upper clouds are changing from cirrus to cirrostratus then altostratus, he can assume that:

    (a) a warm front is approaching

    (b) a cold front is approaching

    (c) a warm front or an occlusion is approaching.

Q7.　If a pilot notes that his flight forecast shows he will meet a front in a mountainous area of his intended route, he should assume that:

    (a) the front will be weakened by orographic drying out of any moist air

    (b) the föhn effect will make the front lose its activity

    (c) the orographic uplift will supplement the frontal uplift and worsen flying conditions.

Q8.　It is true to say of occlusions that:

    (a) if back-bent, they always tend to move more northerly

    (b) cold occlusions are most common in the UK in winter

    (c) when newly-formed, the layer clouds of a warm occlusion may conceal embedded cumulonimbus.

Q9.　With a family of depressions in the northern hemisphere, the track of each successive depression tends to pass:

    (a) further to the east

    (b) further to the north-east

    (c) further to the south.

Q10.　Overflying an active warm sector depression from New York to London at 33 000 ft, the associated jet stream will:

    (a) be from 270°T throughout

    (b) initially be from 240°T, later becoming 300°T

    (c) initially be from 300°T, later becoming 240°T.

13: Non-frontal Depressions

Although the majority of depressions affecting NW Europe are frontal in origin, some depressions are 'non-frontal' and in fact in some parts of the world, all of the low pressure systems experienced are of this type. Generally, the non-frontal lows are categorised as:

(a) orographic lows, or
(b) thermal lows

and may appear as either secondaries to other systems or as distinct entities on their own.

Orographic depressions

Sometimes called 'lee depressions', these lows form to the lee, i.e. downwind, of a substantial barrier of high ground in a steady airflow (fig. 13.1). Where the high ground comes near to the coast, e.g. Scandinavia or parts of the Alps, the resultant low may be situated over the sea. Sometimes the effect may not be sufficient to produce an individual depression with its own isobar system, in which case there will be a leeside trough.

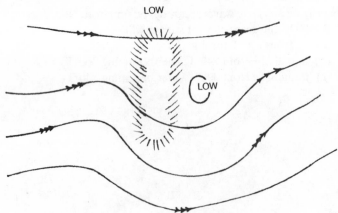

Fig. 13.1   Orographic depression

The weather in the low (which remains relatively stationary) is influenced by the föhn effect and is fine and dry. If a cold front is borne along in the airstream and part of the front is able to skirt around the end of the mountain range while the rest of the front is held up by the high ground, then the low will probably intensify with accompanying bad weather. The depression then of course is no longer non-frontal. The hazards to aviation of mountain lee-wave systems have already been described in Chapter 10. The presence of active orographic depressions with frontal weather adds to the difficulties of aircraft operations in mountainous regions, where deteriorations can be very rapid.

Thermal depressions

Thermal depressions vary considerably in size and their accompanying weather. Because such depressions can occur with either heating at the surface producing a reduction in surface pressure or by the generation of an unstable lapse, some authorities categorise 'instability depressions' as a separate group. For the purposes of this chapter, they will be treated as a variant of the thermal low type.

(a) Equatorial low pressure

This will be dealt with in Chapter 15: Climatology. It is convenient to note here that in the lowest latitudes where the sun is overhead, or nearly so at mid-day, it is regularly hot, the lapse rate is unstable and mean sea level pressures are relatively low.

(b) Monsoon low

In large continents (e.g. Indian sub-continent), summer heating gives rise to a seasonal thermal low which establishes a circulation over the whole region and is known as a monsoon low. Again this will be covered in detail in Chapter 15.

(c) Summer lows over land

Whereas monsoon lows become a regular feature of meteorological charts for weeks at a time, in other land areas (e.g. Europe) in slack pressure gradients, summer heating over successive days can produce shallow depressions. If the air is humid enough, the instability generated together with the surface heating produces towering cumuliform clouds, thunderstorms and squalls. Often such lows forming over France and the Iberian peninsula drift slowly northwards to cross the Channel and bring severe thunderstorms to southern and central England to put an end to a few days of 'heat-wave' conditions.

(d) Tropical revolving storms

These storms, which are discussed in detail in Chapter 15, are large stormy depressions known variously as hurricanes, typhoons, cyclones, etc., in different parts of the world. Although most likely to be encountered in low latitudes, they can occasionally migrate to temperate latitudes.

(e) Tornadoes

In contrast to tropical revolving storms, tornadoes are very intense localised depressions characteristic of the climate of certain localities and seasons.

(f) Winter lows over the sea

The counterpart to (c) above, albeit at much lower temperatures. They form over large inland waters such as the Mediterranean when the arrival of a polar airstream behind a cold front from a cold land area can lead to the cold air being so heated by the relatively warm sea that it becomes very unstable and depressions are formed in the polar air. On flying through the cold front into the polar air there is then not a rapid improvement in flying conditions, but in the depression there are further thunderstorms, turbulence, icing and squalls.

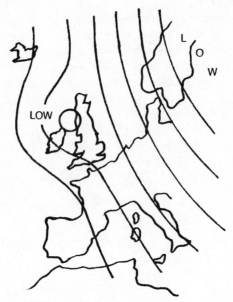

Fig. 13.2   Polar air depression

(g) Polar air depressions

It was noted in Chapter 11 that polar maritime air moving into NW Europe is unstable. Sometimes the instability is enough to produce a small circular depression in the airstream (fig. 13.2). Because such depressions are associated with areas of particular instability they will also be areas of large cumulus and cumulonimbus clouds, heavy showers or thunderstorms, turbulence, icing and squally winds which move along with the low. As with the orographic depression, instead of an individual, separate depression with its own system of isobars, sometimes a polar trough will be formed within the airstream.

Test questions

Q1. A thermal depression:
  (a) only occurs over land
  (b) only occurs over land during daylight hours
  (c) may occur over land or sea.

Q2. Orographic depressions occur:
  (a) only in valleys
  (b) to the windward of high ground
  (c) downwind of high ground.

Q3. The weather in non-frontal lee depressions is:
  (a) fine due to föhn effect
  (b) overcast due to orographic uplift
  (c) squally due to anabatic/katabatic effects.

Q4. A polar air depression:
  (a) remains stationary or nearly so
  (b) moves with the polar airstream
  (c) moves towards the pole.
Q5. Over inland seas, thermal depressions form most frequently:
  (a) during winter months
  (b) during summer months
  (c) in spring and summer.

14:   Anticyclones and Cols

In an earlier reference to the general circulation of the troposphere it was stated that areas of low pressure experienced convergence at low levels and ascending air while regions of high pressure experienced convergence of air at upper levels, subsiding air and divergence at low levels (see fig. 12.3). The effects of subsidence in anticyclones and ridges of high pressure upon flying conditions are now considered in more detail.

In an anticyclone the area over which subsidence is occurring may be very substantial, for example in mid-summer a high may extend for the whole width of the North Atlantic ocean at 40°N. The rate of subsidence in an anticyclone is relatively slow when compared with the rate of ascent of convection in towering cumuliform clouds, and may amount to no more than 2000 feet in a day. Nevertheless, despite this slow downward rate of movement spanning a large region the subsiding air warms adiabatically, establishing two major characteristics of high pressure systems, namely humidity and temperature distribution vertically.

As the subsiding air warms, any cloud that it contains or encounters in its descent will be evaporated, so producing cloudless skies. In these cloudless skies all subsequent subsidence brings about warming at the dry adiabatic lapse rate and reducing the relative humidity. This process continues down to the lowest few thousand feet of the troposphere, where the upward transport of water vapour from the surface may be sufficient to offset the drying effect of the subsidence in the lower atmosphere.

The warming effect of the subsiding air gradually but steadily establishes a stable environmental lapse rate and an anticyclone is usually characterised by a substantial inversion. In fig. 14.1, ABC represents an initial environmental lapse rate approximating to ISA temperature conditions.

If the air originally at 20000 feet (C) subsides to 6000 feet (C_1) and the air in the middle of the layer subsides to 3000 feet (B_1) before diverging, the respective temperatures produced by warming at the DALR will be +17°C and +16°C.

The flying conditions experienced in any particular anticyclone are therefore determined by:

(a) the relatively low humidities of medium and high levels. The humidity near the surface depends upon the site of the high. It should be remembered that they are the sources of air masses.

(b) the stable lapse rate.

(c) the light winds or calm near the centre of the high with light to moderate divergent winds nearer its edges.

Although the terms tropical or polar high are used in a climatological sense or when referring to the source region of an air mass, an anticyclone moving to cover the British Isles is more likely to be described as a warm or cold

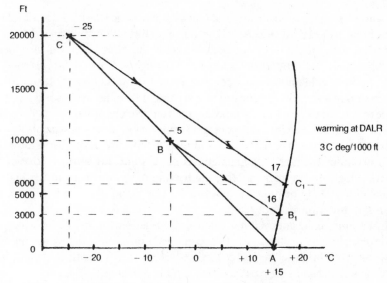

Fig. 14.1   Subsidence producing stability

anticyclone. The other descriptive terms applied to anticyclones are 'permanent' or 'temporary' which are self-explanatory, and sometimes a high may be referred to as a 'blocking high'. This latter term is applied to an anticyclone situated over or off the coasts of NW Europe in such a way that it effectively 'blocks' the usual west-to-east passage of warm sector depressions along the polar front, diverting them either much further north or much further south than their usual track and giving quiet anticyclonic weather over Britain.

Cold anticyclones

The polar regions, especially Antarctica, are regions of permanent cold anticyclones although the north polar high does collapse at times when invaded by fronts from temperate latitudes. In the winter months there is a 'seasonally-permanent' anticyclone over Siberia and a less intense tendency to high pressure over North America.

Because of the density of the very cold air at low levels, the rate of decrease of pressure with increase of height is much greater than standard and by 10000 ft (700 mb) often the pressure at that level is no longer higher than that of surrounding areas, i.e. there is no high on the 700 mb chart.

Such cold anticyclonic regions have very low surface temperatures and the subsidence inversion is very pronounced. On its outer edges, especially if nearby depressions are bringing moist air into its circulation, the anticyclone will still have no medium or upper cloud but there are often widespread sheets of stratus or stratocumulus cloud. If the winds are lighter, dull foggy weather prevails. Above the fog or low cloud, fine smooth flying conditions occur. In central areas of continental cold anticyclones brilliant frosty weather is the rule.

Sometimes in mid-winter, the Siberian high becomes so intense and extensive that the British Isles are encompassed in its circulation and UK aerodromes in the south-east such as Heathrow and Gatwick experience these cold anticyclonic conditions in easterly winds. At UK aerodromes further north such as Aberdeen and Newcastle, the passage of the air across the North Sea will produce a modification of its properties, as already described in Chapter 11: Air Masses.

Temporary cold anticyclones occur over the British Isles at any season. Each depression in a family of depressions is separated from its successor by either a ridge of cold air or by a small temporary cold anticyclone and the last depression of a family is followed by a rather bigger temporary cold anticyclone until a new polar front becomes established. In summer, 'temporary' is of shorter duration than in winter when the high sometimes merges into the western edge of the Siberian high. In summer months, the heating of the polar air in the high by subsidence and by heating from below by both land and sea will gradually change it into a warm anticyclone.

In autumn, cold anticyclones often give radiation fog or, if the winds are stronger, widespread stratus or stratocumulus. For most of the winter months, however, cold bright cloudless conditions are most likely with overnight frost needing to be cleared off parked aircraft in the morning.

In summer, although cold anticyclones are not long-lived, the surface heating generates convection currents as the day warms up. These will be inhibited by the general stability of the environment and dryness of the upper air so only small fair weather cumulus result from the convection.

Warm anticyclones

Permanent warm anticyclones are found over the oceans at latitudes around 25° to 40°. In such regions they are subject to little diurnal variation in temperature, experience virtually no surface cooling and are very stable and persistent. Flying conditions could not be better as they are usually warm and cloudless with excellent visibility and surface winds at island aerodromes determined by land and sea breezes.

In temperate latitudes such as the British Isles, a temporary warm anticyclone may either have evolved from a cold anticyclone as already described or be an extension of a sub-tropical anticyclone. The evolution from a cold anticyclone is the frequent occurrence and in the summer leads to a period of fine weather. Sometimes there is fair weather cumulus and at coastal aerodromes, especially at night, there may be stratocumulus in the tropical maritime air. In autumn there is radiation fog inland in suitable conditions of wind speed. Where a warm anticyclone develops from an extension of the sub-tropical high (and this will not occur in the UK in winter because that high will then have moved towards the Equator), the air mass within it will be tropical maritime air. Above the inversion flying conditions are fine and smooth. Below it there will be a high probability of sea fog, especially on its western flanks and in spring and summer, while over land in late summer and in autumn radiation fog is very likely.

Ridge of high pressure

A ridge is an extension outwards from an anticyclone. It may be quasi-stationary but in the British Isles is more likely to be a transitory feature between two

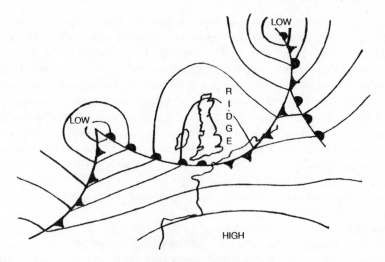

Fig. 14.2   Ridge of high pressure

frontal depressions. In the former case, the ridge will tend to reflect the weather characteristics of its parent anticyclone and the air mass of which it is the source. In the latter case (fig. 14.2) the subsidence in the polar air gives fine clear weather. Unfortunately the ridge's movement is determined by the motion of the two depressions each side of it, so it is unlikely to persist for more than 24 to 36 hours.

Col

A col is not bounded by any one isobar but is in fact the region of almost uniform pressure between two highs (or areas of higher pressure) and two lows (or areas of lower pressure) (fig. 14.3). As such, winds are light and variable, tending to flow in on two sides (AB, CD) and flow outwards on the other two sides (BC, DA) (northern hemisphere).

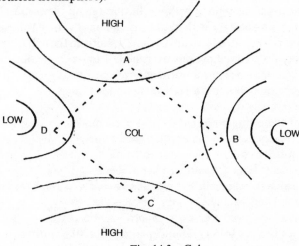

Fig. 14.3   Col

With the exception of a strong wind or gale forecast, a pilot should be prepared for any type of flying weather in a col. In general, a col in autumn or winter will probably experience fog or low cloud while in summer after possibly a misty start, large cumuliform clouds are likely to build up over land with a risk of thunderstorms. Sometimes a front or occlusion may cross a col (as in fig. 12.13), particularly if the col lies between a primary and a secondary depression. In this case, the light winds mean that the associated belt of cloud and precipitation will also be very slow-moving. Any aerodromes near the front will have persistent low cloud and the rain (or snow in winter) will be prolonged.

If it is noted that over the region of the col, the surface pressures are rising, then any fronts or occlusions will gradually die out. Conversely if the col is a region of steadily falling pressure, the converging (and differing air masses) will intensify the frontal activity.

In summary, because of its very shape (or lack of it), its extent and existence depend upon other adjoining pressure systems, a col can produce a wide variety of weather conditions and the forecaster keeps an alert eye open to the adjoining pressure systems as well as barometric tendencies and upper air conditions in the col itself.

Test questions

Q1.   In an anticyclone that is intensifying, there is:
    (a) divergence at low levels, convergence at upper levels
    (b) divergence at all levels
    (c) convergence at low levels, divergence at upper levels.

Q2.   From the centre of an anticyclone outwards, the surface winds:
    (a) gradually decrease in speed
    (b) gradually increase in speed
    (c) show no significant change in wind speed.

Q3.   At an aerodrome in the British Isles experiencing a cold anticyclone, an easterly wind at 2000 ft will:
    (a) increase in strength with height throughout the troposphere
    (b) remain constant with height throughout the troposphere
    (c) decrease with height and become westerly in the upper troposphere.

Q4.   A temporary cold anticyclone over the UK in summer will:
    (a) gradually become a warm anticyclone
    (b) gradually become a permanent anticyclone
    (c) gradually develop into a col.

Q5.   Around an anticyclone winds at low level circulate:
    (a) anticlockwise in the northern hemisphere
    (b) anticlockwise in the southern hemisphere
    (c) clockwise in the southern hemisphere.

Q6.   In a warm anticyclone in summer at UK coastal aerodromes:
    (a) land and sea breezes are a frequent occurrence
    (b) land and sea breezes are an infrequent occurrence
    (c) sea breezes bring in thunderstorms from the warm sea.

Q7.   Typical of anticyclonic weather are:

(a) gales and low cloud in winter

(b) thunderstorms in late afternoon and evening in summer

(c) radiation fog in autumn.

Q8.   A small cold anticyclone moving south-eastwards across the British Isles in January will bring:

(a) increasingly colder weather across the country over a period of a few days

(b) increasingly milder weather across the country over a period of a few days

(c) widespread snow across the country for a period of a few days.

Q9.   Around a col the isobar pattern is such that:

(a) one isobar joins all places with the same mean sea level pressure

(b) the isobars on the high pressure sides have one interval greater value (e.g. 2 mb, 4 mb, etc.) than the isobars on the low pressure sides

(c) the isobars enclose an approximately square area defining the col.

Q10.   If, for a winter flight, the forecast chart shows a col at your destination which is in the Midlands, for a landing around midnight, you should expect:

(a) gales and low cloud

(b) radiation fog

(c) cumulonimbus, thunderstorms and squalls.

15: Climatology

The first ten chapters were devoted to individual meteorological elements which are significant to aircraft operations and the four subsequent chapters to synoptic meteorology when the interaction of these elements to give the overall weather conditions on a flight were considered. However, aviation is an international profession operating on a year-round basis and a pilot should be aware of conditions usually to be found on any route at any season if he is to extract maximum value from the forecast provided for a particular overseas flight. It also ought to go without saying that a pilot should have more than a passing acquaintance with general geographical and topographical features; for example, does the alignment of mountain ranges near his proposed route allow air masses to move more readily in latitude than in longitude?

It is convenient first to consider the climatic zones which it is believed would occur on an 'ideal earth' composed of uniform surface material, the sun with zero declination (overhead the Equator at mid-day) and geostrophic force negligible below about latitude 15°, but fully effective at higher latitudes. In such circumstances, the greatest solar heating would always occur at the Equator and least at the poles. In turn, because of the uniformity of the surface material, i.e. a world covered entirely by ocean or sand or grasslands, the surface polar air would be coldest and densest and the warmest air at the Equator would be the least dense. It would be unrealistic to ignore the earth's rotation (because the lowest temperatures on a non-rotating earth would also occur on the Equator,

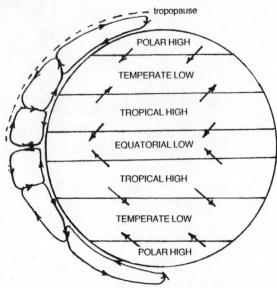

Fig. 15.1   Climatic zones of an 'ideal world'

180° removed from the hottest point where the sun was overhead) so geostrophic force cannot be ignored. The resulting circulation of the troposphere would be as shown in fig. 15.1, together with the surface pressure zones of an 'ideal' earth.

In addition to the dense cold air producing a polar high and the hottest air producing a thermal low or trough at the Equator, the idealised circulation includes two other major zones – low pressure at temperate latitudes and sub-tropical high pressures. This is because the earth's rotation prevents a simple circulation of air rising over the Equator and in a single cell, travelling at altitude to polar regions to subside and pass back to the Equator at low levels to redress the balance of a net gain of heat energy at low latitudes and a net loss of heat at high latitudes.

Air in the upper troposphere over the Equator will have the highest upper level pressure at that level of anywhere on an ideal earth. It will move polewards and gradually, by subtropical latitudes, geostrophic force will have become sufficiently great for the upper winds to have become predominantly westerly while the surface pressure in these latitudes then rises and subsidence occurs. At the surface, divergence at the sub-tropical anticyclones supplies the trade winds on their Equatorial side and tropical air on the poleward side moving towards the polar front. At the polar high, the subsiding air diverges to supply the polar air to the poleward side of the polar front. The ascent of warm air at frontal depressions of temperate latitudes (and of cold air when they are occluded) then supplies upper air to above the sub-tropical and polar highs in this 'idealised' situation.

In reality, these basic zones can be recognised on maps of average mean sea level pressure and surface winds, and the names already stated – Equatorial trough, sub-tropical high, etc. – are actually used in practice. To approximate more closely to reality, refinements of two of the basic assumptions of an 'ideal world' can be made by making allowances for (a) seasonal changes, and (b) land and sea distribution.

Seasonal changes: climatic zones

Throughout the year, the sun's midday overhead position varies from the tropic of Cancer in the northern summer to the tropic of Capricorn in the summer of the southern hemisphere. The effect of heating by the sun is, however, cumulative so in the northern hemisphere it is hottest not in June but some 6 to 8 weeks later in late July and early August. Similarly the southern hemisphere is hottest and the northern hemisphere coldest at the end of January and in early February.

With the change of seasons, so the Equatorial trough moves too, to reach its most northerly position by late July. At this time, the Arctic regions are enjoying permanent daylight and the north polar high is at its weakest, while in the southern hemisphere, Antarctica is permanently dark and its high intensifies. The relative positions for January and July of the four main pressure belts are shown in fig. 15.2. Some parts of the ideal earth will remain within the same pressure zone throughout the year in spite of the seasonal changes. At other places, the change of season shows a change of pressure type.

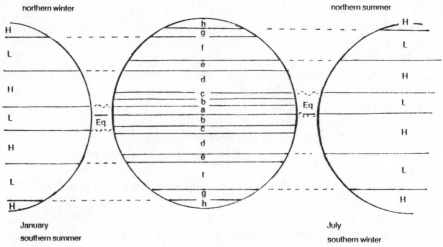

Fig. 15.2   Seasonal changes on an 'ideal world'

The resulting seasonal climatic zones can therefore be recognised and their climate summarised as follows.

(a) Equatorial low or trough
In fig. 15.2 this zone has been offset slightly northwards to correspond more closely with actual conditions arising from the greater preponderance of land in the northern hemisphere. In this zone the thermal Equator is overhead twice a year when the conditions are hottest, most unstable and precipitation greatest. Although there are perhaps two 'rainy seasons', conditions are hot and humid in all months with much convective cloud and thunderstorms. Further consideration is given to special features of Equatorial weather later in this chapter.

(b) Savannah climate
This is a seasonal zone in which there are regular summer rains from the Equatorial low and then a dry season (it would be inappropriate to call it winter as the dry season temperatures often exceed the wet season's). The length of the dry season increases with increase of latitude and in this season, flying conditions over land are hot, dusty and bumpy.

(c) Steppe climate
The edge of the Equatorial low pressure area is far from clear-cut, the low pressure arising as it does from local heating and convection. In the summer therefore, on the poleward side of the savannah climate zone there is an irregular semi-arid zone which only receives sporadic rainfall and in some years may produce only cloudiness and no summer rain at all. Throughout the rest of the year, conditions are controlled by the sub-tropical anticyclone and resemble those of the deserts which steppe regions border.

(d) Sub-tropical high: desert climate

This region is permanently influenced by anticyclonic conditions which have already been considered in Chapter 14 as far as the effects of permanent warm anticyclones occurring over the oceans are concerned. Overland, the continuously fine, virtually cloudless and rainless weather conditions lead to deserts forming and a quick reference to an atlas will show that most of the world's deserts do in fact lie in this zone.

(e) Mediterranean climate

This zone is also distinctly seasonal. In the summer the conditions are anticyclonic, hot, fine and sunny with land and sea breezes on coasts. In winter the area is affected by frontal depressions and consequently has cloud and precipitation in association with their air masses and fronts, with a possibility of gale force winds near the lows.

(f) Disturbed temperate climate

This is in the temperate low zone throughout the year. In the winter months, the travelling lows produce freezing levels on or near the surface so snow or freezing rain is a distinct hazard. In the summer, precipitation is in the form of rain, or hail when in association with thunderstorms. Winds of gale force can occur with the frontal lows at any season but are most frequent in winter.

(g) Tundra climate

This is the area of high latitudes which 'enjoys' the frontal weather and gales of travelling depressions in the summer when the mean temperatures rise above 0°C. The sub-soil remains frozen but the aerodrome surfaces are clear of snow and ice. In the winter, the polar high predominates with very cold, clear weather.

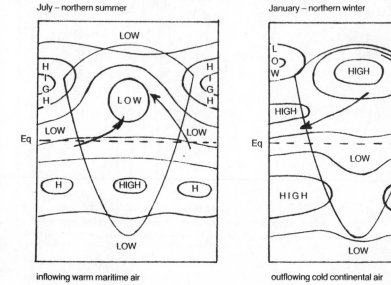

Fig. 15.3   Land-sea distribution effect on climate

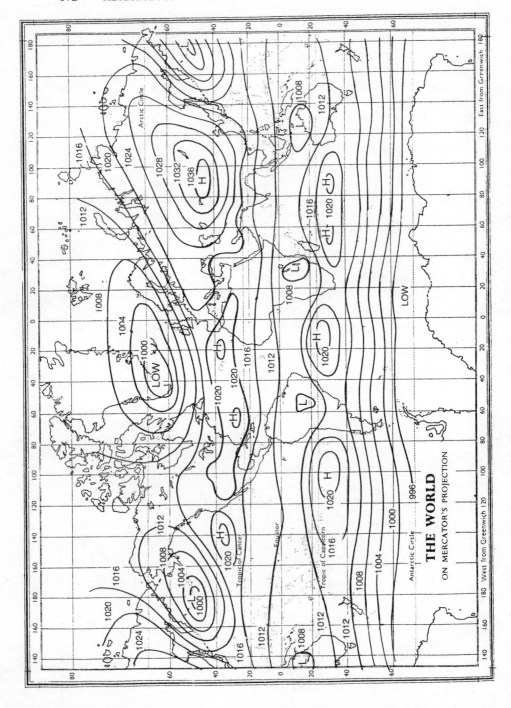

Fig. 15.4   Mean sea level pressure distribution – January

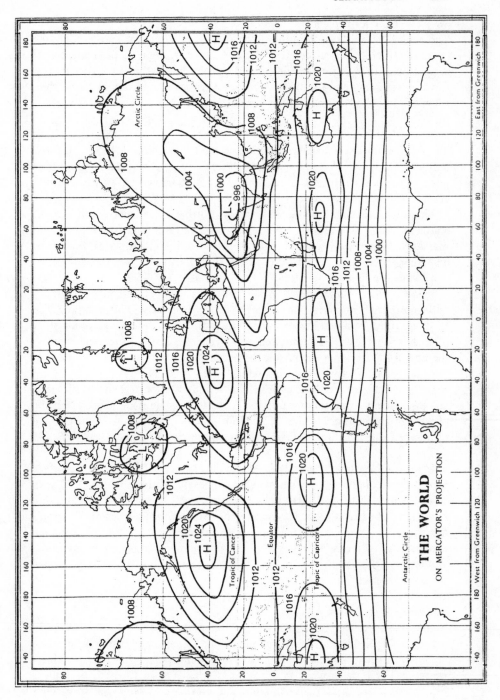

Fig. 15.5   Mean sea level pressure distribution – July

(h) Polar high: ice-cap climate

The area is within the cold anticyclone throughout the year experiencing the conditions considered in detail in Chapter 14 in relation to permanent cold anticyclones. In practice, the high is eroded from time to time so that then there is widespread cloud and snow from frontal weather being brought nearer than usual to the poles by travelling depressions.

Land-sea distribution

The distribution of continents and oceans is not conveniently aligned with either latitude or longitude and so imposes a further modification of the climatic zones just enumerated. In fact it is often convenient to categorise an aerodrome's climate as maritime or continental.

There is appreciably more land in the northern hemisphere than in the southern hemisphere and fig. 15.3 represents an idealised distribution of land masses – schematically it could apply to North and South America, to Europe and Africa or to Asia and Australia – while figs 15.4 and 15.5 represent observed conditions for January and July.

In the northern summer, the isotherms of mean temperature in low latitudes of the northern hemisphere will not lie parallel to the Equator and the tropic. The land will produce much higher temperatures than the tropical ocean (at 30°N often averaging over 30°C compared with an oceanic 25°C average) so distorting the Equatorial trough to lie outside the tropic, and at the same time, weakening the sub-tropical high over the continent.

In the northern winter, the continent near and even south of the Arctic circle will lose far more heat than it gains in the reduced daylight and this distorts the polar high and confines frontal depressions mainly to the ocean. In the average northern winter, the Siberian High is often actually centred between 40°N and 50°N.

In the southern hemisphere, the great predominance of uniform ocean surface means that conditions approximate more closely to those of fig. 15.2 with relatively little distortion of the basic pressure zones. At places in low latitudes, in the northern hemisphere particularly, the result of the land-sea distribution's distortion of the pressure zones and hence of the airstreams is that seasonal climatic changes can be related to the prevailing continental or maritime airstreams. These are the lands of the monsoon (a name derived from the Arabic word for season).

Monsoons of south-east Asia

Figure 15.6 depicts a typical airflow on a January day and on a July day in south-east Asia. In July, the SE trade winds cross the Equator and with the change of direction of geostrophic force with change of hemisphere, they become south-westerly. These then sweep in across the Indian Ocean to bring the humid Equatorial air to the Indian sub-continent, Burma and Malaysia. In practice there are troughs in the airstreams circulating around the Baluchistan Low so that occasional breaks occur in the south-west monsoon which are followed by the renewed onset of further convectively unstable air, with towering cumuliform clouds, torrential rain and thunderstorms. Flying conditions are turbulent,

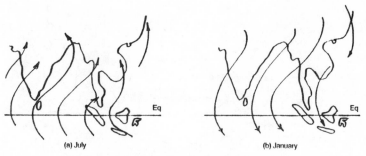

Fig. 15.6   Monsoon flow in south-east Asia

cloud bases are low and visibility poor. At any particular aerodrome, e.g. Bombay or Calcutta, the initial onset of the SW monsoon is quite sudden and varies little in date from one year to another. Equally, the retreat at the end of the SW monsoon also takes place on a regular basis.

In the northern winter, the development of the Siberian High and of a thermal low over northern Australia reverses the pressure gradient and the airflow. By December the NE monsoon is established over India, although the Himalayas prevent the direct flow of air from Siberia to airports such as Delhi and Calcutta. Further east, air from central China has a similar path, ultimately reaching Malaysia and Indonesia, as depicted in fig. 15.6 (b). Although in northern India the NE monsoon is fine and dry, the continental air becomes maritime by the time it reaches SE India and Sri Lanka, producing cloud and rain.

Although south-east Asia and northern Australia are the major examples of a monsoon climate, the land-sea effect also applies on a smaller scale to parts of the east and west coasts of Africa.

Equatorial weather

Of the four pressure belts depicted in fig. 15.1 of the ideal world's circulation, three have been considered in earlier chapters under frontal depressions and permanent cold and warm anticyclones. The fourth zone, the Equatorial trough or low, had no part in the synoptic meteorology of temperate latitudes and is now considered in greater detail as there are considerable variations in its activity. In each case subsided air from the sub-tropical anticyclones is fed by the trade-winds into the inter-tropical convergence zone (ITCZ). Along some relatively short parts of its length, the two trade-winds feeding in to the ITCZ have dissimilar characteristics (fig. 15.10 below) when the name inter-tropical front (ITF) may be a relevant description, but for most of its length the term ITCZ is preferred.

Except where continental airstreams are involved, the trade winds are remarkably steady, producing similar flying conditions over thousands of miles of ocean in low latitudes. It was their constancy which was such a boon to the ancient mariners who relied on sail. They should not be visualised as a very light, gentle breeze but as a steady wind of some 20 knots or so. Unless continental influences prevail, they blow from the north-east in the northern hemisphere and from the south-east in the southern hemisphere to the Equator.

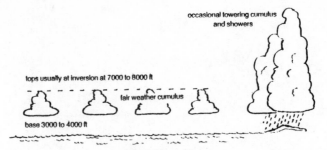

Fig. 15.7   Trade wind weather

As the trade winds move away from the sub-tropical high they retain the stability (probably an inversion around 7000 to 8000 feet) that they gained from subsidence in the high. As they track across the ocean they usually produce ⅛ to ⅜ small cumulus but over islands and in any troughs, the cumulus may build up into towering cloud and produce showers. Typical of this latter condition is Hawaii situated in the north-east trade winds, where Waikiki Beach may be enjoying fine weather while the north-east sides of the Hawaiian Islands are experiencing orographic and afternoon convectional rain showers. On the last part of their track the trade winds converge into the Equatorial trough or low, bringing their warm moist air.

Doldrums: weak ITCZ
If the pressure gradient on the Equatorial side of the sub-tropical anticyclones is slack (fig. 15.8) and the trade winds become progressively lighter along their

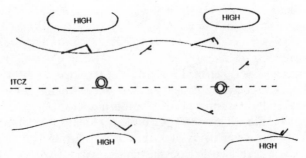

Fig. 15.8   Slack airflow and convergence in Doldrums

track, the rate of convergence is slight. As a result, a north-south flight through the ITCZ will then only encounter individual cumulus clouds, only some of which will be giving showers, with light winds both at the surface and at altitude. This is not an unlikely occurrence and actually representing the position of the ITCZ on a forecast chart in these circumstances is not easy.

Equatorial trough: active ITCZ
In this case, the ITCZ shown on the chart will denote an active zone of cloud and weather to be flown through. Figure 15.9 depicts such a situation where there is sufficient gradient to produce steady converging trade winds from the sub-tropical anticyclones of both hemispheres. In this case, over the ocean flying

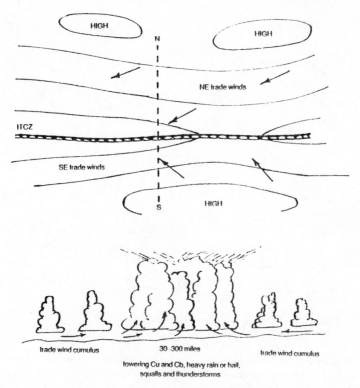

Fig. 15.9   Active inter-tropical convergence zone

conditions are similar whether the ITCZ is approached from the north or from the south. The trade winds are potentially unstable as they converge upon each other and cumuliform clouds quickly develop by night as well as by day. Sometimes this belt of large cumulus and cumulonimbus is 30 nm wide, sometimes it is 300 nm wide. The tops of the cloud can reach the tropopause which is 50 000 – 55 000 feet, but at other times it is possible to fly over or between the upper parts of the clouds at 30 000 feet. It should be remembered that sometimes some of the areas of severe turbulence of the upper parts of towering cumulonimbus will be hidden from direct view by the cloud's anvil cirrus, but will still be painted on the aircraft's weather radar. The height of the 0°C isotherm is generally around 17 000 feet. Surface winds may produce sudden squalls.

The inter-tropical convergence zone moves north and south with the changing seasons but it moves irregularly from day to day, as well as showing varying degrees of activity. Often troughs aligned north-south move slowly westwards within the ITCZ. Most tropical revolving storms seem to originate on the edge of the ITCZ at the time that it is furthest from the Equator and is about to return to the lowest latitudes.

Inter-tropical convergence zone: the ITF case
As most of the world in Equatorial latitudes is open ocean, the general weather

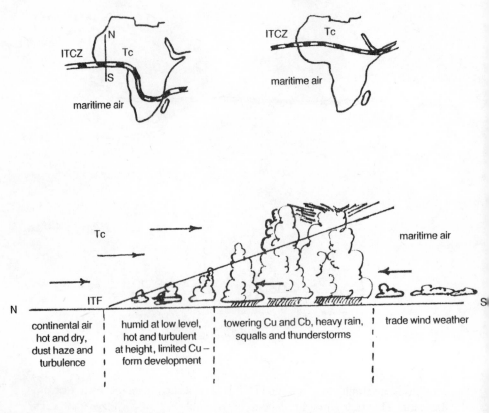

Fig. 15.10   Inter-tropical front over West Africa

conditions of two moist, potentially unstable airstreams converging into the ITCZ as described above will usually apply. However, where one of the airstreams has had a continental track there will be different temperatures and humidities between the air masses converging on the Equatorial trough. The term inter-tropical front (ITF) could then well be used to describe the situation. Such conditions apply in West Africa (fig. 15.10) throughout the year.

In West Africa, considering a north-south flight, the north-east airstream to the north of the ITF consists of continental tropical air so a southbound aircraft will initially be flying in hot and dusty conditions. Locally the north-east trade wind is known as the Harmattan and, as shown in fig. 15.10, because of its higher temperatures it overlies the moist oceanic trade winds. Because after leaving the sub-tropical anticyclone of the southern hemisphere the south-east trade winds have crossed the Equator their direction will have changed to become south-west 'deflected' trade winds on arrival in West Africa. On a southbound flight in July the inter-tropical front's surface position will probably be around 15°N but in January it will be crossed around 5° to 8°N. On crossing the ITF position shown

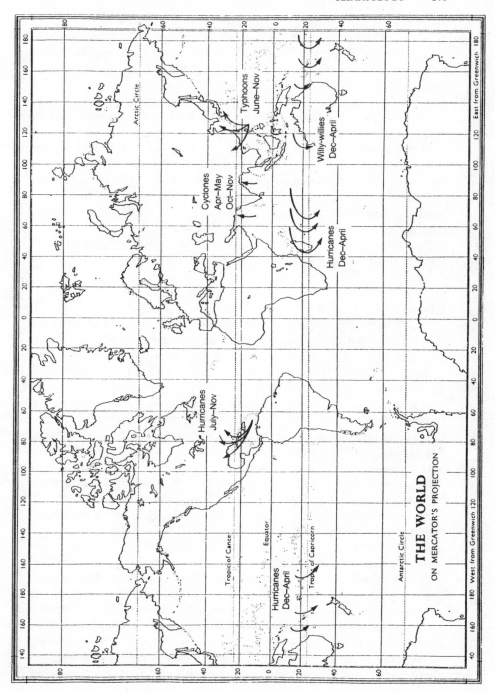

Fig. 15.11   Locations, seasons and tracks of tropical revolving storms

on the flight forecast documents, although the surface wind will change, flight conditions at medium and high cruising levels will remain cloudless and hazy.

However, as flight progresses south of the ITF and as the vertical extent of the deflected trade winds increases so convection builds up cumuliform cloud. After some 100 to 200 nm and depending upon the distance of the route inland from the coast, the cloud becomes towering cumulus in the afternoon and evening and flying is bumpy. Further flight southwards gives a sufficient vertical extent of moist air for widespread building-up of large cumulus and cumulonimbus which break through the frontal surface and there is a belt of heavy rain, thunderstorms and hail. Further south still of the inter-tropical front, conditions then revert to the usual trade wind conditions of fair weather cumulus or stratocumulus. In summary, the effect of the continental air at the ITF is to offset the weather conditions normally found roughly symmetrically about the Equatorial trough, to some distance to the maritime side of the ITF. Although West Africa has the ITF throughout the year some other regions of the world, both northern and southern hemisphere, only have an inter-tropical front situation for one part of the year.

Tropical revolving storms

These are particularly hazardous conditions which can occur on routes in low latitudes (although the occasional rogue storm breaks through into higher latitudes). They are known locally by a variety of names: Cyclone, Hurricane, Typhoon, Baguio, Willy-willy. Typical regions affected and tracks are shown in fig. 15.11.

In forecasts for the media, individual storms are identified by forenames. Originally they were all girl's names but modern equality has decreed an equal use of male and female forenames. As mentioned earlier, tropical revolving storms mostly start in the edge of the ITCZ when it is late summer and autumn of that hemisphere. The exceptions are the cyclones of the Arabian Sea and the Bay of Bengal which occur as the Equatorial trough is moving through, before and after the south-west monsoon. That the storms do not originate in the South Atlantic Ocean is consistent with the fact that the ITCZ (because of the effect of the enormous land mass of West Africa) never lies to the south of the Equator in the Atlantic Ocean.

In trade winds on the east sides of oceans, the air has only recently subsided in the sub-tropical anticyclones and is stable and dry aloft. After the trade winds have progressed across hundreds of miles of ocean, their humidity will have increased and they will have lost some of their initial stability and it is on the west sides of oceans at sea temperatures of 28°C (82°F) or more that tropical revolving storms start. They require some geostrophic force to impart the circulatory motion to the air, so the storms are not found within 5° of the Equator. Whatever their location, the storms have similar life histories and characteristics (fig. 15.12).

Initially the tropical revolving storm will become apparent in the Equatorial trough in a particular area when freshening winds start to become circulatory, the normal semi-diurnal variation of pressure gives way to a continuous fall of

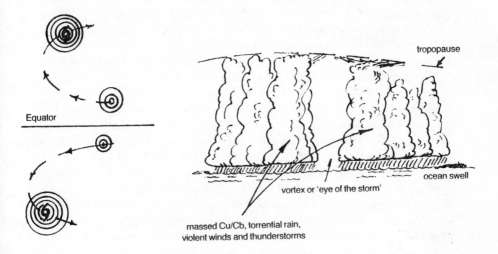

massed Cu/Cb, torrential rain,
violent winds and thunderstorms

Fig. 15.12   Tropical revolving storms

pressure and there is an increase in thundery activity with masses of cumulonimbus cloud. There are no fronts associated with the storm and when first identified on a chart it will have quite circular isobars and probably a diameter of 50 to 100 nm. In the Equatorial trough the upper winds are light easterlies and the storm initially moves westwards and perhaps polewards (see fig. 15.12), gradually deepening and increasing in diameter so that ultimately it may be 500 nm across. The isobars remain concentric circles, close together, so the winds soon reach hurricane force. Despite the high wind speeds in its circulation the storm itself moves only slowly, often around 12 knots and probably no faster than 15 knots. The storm has a life of several days and its track gradually turns polewards and it eventually re-curves towards the east. If it encounters land it will cause a lot of structural damage, especially on the coasts. If the land comprises only islands, the storm goes on its destructive way with its vigour relatively undiminished. However, if it moves into a substantial land mass, e.g. the north shores of the Gulf of Mexico, the hurricane winds are slowed by friction and the supply of water vapour appreciably reduced, so the tropical revolving storm soon degenerates. Also if in its re-curvature the storm's path brings it towards a cell of the sub-tropical high pressure, the storm slows down and fills. On occasions, the storm's track takes it around the sub-tropical anticyclone so it moves into temperate latitudes when it joins on to the sequence of polar front depressions.

Apart from the high wind speed which prohibits operations out of affected aerodromes, tropical revolving storms produce other hazards so that en-route aircraft should give them a wide berth. If anything, the flying conditions are worst on the leading inside sector of the storm where particularly fresh supplies of very humid unstable air are drawn into the storm's circulation. Mariners who do not have the advantage of the speed and manoeuvrability enjoyed by the aviator call this sector the 'dangerous quadrant'. Apart from the substantial damage caused by the violent winds, much of the damage at coasts is caused by the ocean swell. The strength of the wind moves the surface water so that a large swell builds up. Even large vessels in port have received substantial damage so owners or operators of flying boats, seaplanes and amphibians must arrange for their aircraft's removal to sheltered situations.

Flying conditions

Except for a very small area, a few miles in diameter, at its centre called the 'eye of the storm', where winds fall calm and cloud clears temporarily, tropical revolving storms are areas of dense cloud extending from below 1000 feet to at least 30 000 feet usually and with a possibility of reaching the tropopause at 50 000 to 55 000 feet. In torrential rain, the cloud base is almost on the surface. The cloud comprises masses of towering cumulus and cumulonimbus which have dense cirrus on the outer edges of the storm. Visually, a pilot at altitude can recognise the edge of a tropical storm by the bands of dense cirrus and if operating at low level, by the marked ocean swell. In both cases his navigation will have identified an increase in drift and the thunderstorms will be shown on the weather radar. Satellite pictures and weather radar in fact show the convective clouds to be massed in bands spiralling inwards to become a solid mass of cloud (except for the 'eye') in the main central storm area. All of the hazards of thunderstorm flying apply and they go on for hundreds of miles. Turbulence is severe, lightning frequent, precipitation in the form of rain and hail is torrential, visibility is very poor, the freezing level is usually around 16 000 to 18 000 feet and instrument flying is very difficult especially as the performance of navigational aids and the flight instruments themselves may be impaired.

Tornado

This is not one of the names given to a tropical revolving storm for a particular area but an entirely different meteorological phenomenon. At one time in West Africa the name was used for the squalls associated with the passage of line squalls moving from east to west at the beginning and end of the wet season (p. 207), but on flight forecasts these are identified as troughs or line squalls. Where the term 'tornado' is used in a meteorological warning, usually in the United States of America and only rarely in north-west Europe, it is referring to a violent whirlwind associated with a cumulonimbus cloud (fig. 15.13).

If the basic conditions for thunderstorms are present – high humidity, instability, and trigger action – in the extreme, convection inland on summer afternoons is so great that an intense local depression forms under an individual cumulonimbus. Sometimes more than one may occur if there are several strong convective cells. The intense depression is far too small to be shown on a synoptic chart, typical diameters being only 50 to 250 metres. The air ascending in the cumulonimbus cannot be replaced from below as fast as the great instability and the winds at altitude are removing it so surface pressure falls, often to below 1000 millibars. The resulting pressure gradient is of tens of millibars in only a very short distance. Air converging under the cumulonimbus spirals inwards and

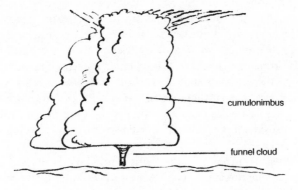

Fig. 15.13   Tornado

speeds of 100 to 200 knots are experienced (c.f. cyclostrophic wind, Chapter 10).

The decrease of pressure beneath the main cloud base also causes adiabatic cooling and condensation which produces the 'funnel' cloud hanging from the cloud base and which often has a writhing motion in the violent winds. The thunderstorm and associated tornadoes move along with the general airstream, causing great havoc along their narrow path. Sometimes the track finishes in less than one mile; at other times it may exceed 100 nm. Unfortunately too, there may be several tornadoes crossing a particular area at the same time.

In open country, tornadoes uproot trees, devastate crops and haystacks and demolish buildings. When they strike developed areas such as aerodromes, apart from the high wind damage the enormous pressure gradients literally cause buildings to explode, removing roofs, demolishing walls, etc. There have been cases of picketed-down aircraft being lifted on to airport buildings! In addition, the thunderstorms themselves are particularly active and often accompanied by large and heavy hail.

When tornadoes occur in Britain, which is only rarely, the conditions are not so severe as in the United States but nevertheless considerable damage is done to property and aircraft must avoid the tornado area.

Waterspouts are similar in origin to tornadoes but because of the lower surface temperature of the sea over which they form they are not so intense nor normally so large. The funnel cloud comprises most of the waterspout but its lowest section is composed of sea spray whipped up in the vortex of the storm. More than one waterspout can occur under a particular cumulonimbus but they do not last more than 30 minutes at the most. Again flight conditions are very turbulent and structural damage can occur if they are inadvertently mistaken for a heavy shower when on the approach under cumulonimbus to an island or coastal aerodrome. The higher the latitude, the less likely are waterspouts to be encountered.

Effect of ocean currents
Oceanography is a major subject for study on its own and it is only intended here

to touch lightly on general points of which a pilot should be aware in so far as the climatology of the route(s) he may fly are affected by nearby major ocean currents. Generally, an ocean current can be caused by differences in the specific gravities of sea water in an area or by friction from a surface wind blowing consistently from one direction. These latter currents are called 'drifts'. An inspection of a world map in an atlas showing ocean currents will reveal that usually there are cold currents on the west sides of land masses and warm currents on the east sides. The exception is the Gulf Stream which not only warms the east side of north America but also carries on to bring its warmth to the eastern Atlantic.

The main ocean currents are the 'drifts' caused by the surface wind blowing regularly from one direction, moving the surface water along by friction. The areas of steadiest winds are around the sub-tropical centres of high pressure and,

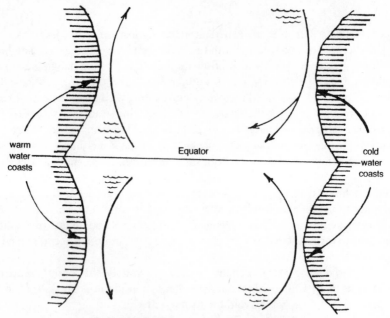

Fig. 15.14   Idealised ocean current circulation

as shown in fig. 15.14, these produce the 'warm water coasts' on the west sides of oceans and the 'cold water coasts' on the east sides of oceans.

In areas of persistent off-shore winds, 'upwelling' of colder water from the ocean depths occurs (fig. 15.15). This upwelling accentuates the effect of cold water currents but reduces the effectiveness of a warm water current.

The general features of the modification of climate may be summarised as follows.

(a) Cold water coasts

Over land, due to the low rate of evaporation from the nearby relatively cold ocean, the air in these areas has a low water vapour content. As a result, there is

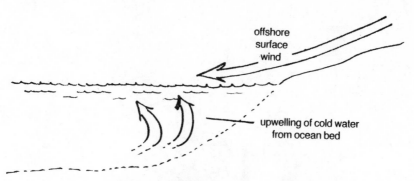

offshore
surface
wind

upwelling of cold water
from ocean bed

Fig. 15.15   Upwelling from ocean depths

little or no cloud or precipitation and deserts can extend right up to the coasts. Night-time cooling may be sufficient to produce low stratus by dawn but it soon disperses after sunrise. Over the sea, the air that has moved to over the cold current will have experienced appreciable surface cooling and widespread advection fog (or low stratus and drizzle) often occurs both by day and night. This fog may drift over the adjoining land when the land cools at night.

(b) Warm water coasts

Over both land and sea, humidities are high due to the rapid evaporation from the relatively warm ocean. Over land by day and over the sea, surface temperatures are relatively high and cumuliform cloud with thunderstorms, squally winds, heavy precipitation, etc., result. Over land at night, the diurnal variation of surface temperature can cause clouds to collapse into stratiform cloud which will then re-develop to cumuliform cloud again the following day. Over sea at night the cumuliform cloud persists. As already mentioned, these areas are particularly suitable for the formation of tropical revolving storms.

Local winds

In Chapter 10 reference was made to the ways in which local topography could modify or even generate winds in certain terrain and to the fact that the term 'föhn effect' is used to describe a particular meteorological phenomenon anywhere in the world rather than just in one alpine valley. There are other 'local winds' of which pilots should be aware as they spread their effects over a fairly wide area and their name used in a report or forecast context tends to imply not only the wind itself but also its associated weather. The selection covered below is based on the author's experience of such practice and is by no means exhaustive.

Mistral

This is a strong cold N or NW wind which blows down the Rhône valley into the Gulf of the Lion in the NW Mediterranean in the winter and early spring. Gale force is common and at times the Mistral reaches 70 to 80 knots. Frequently

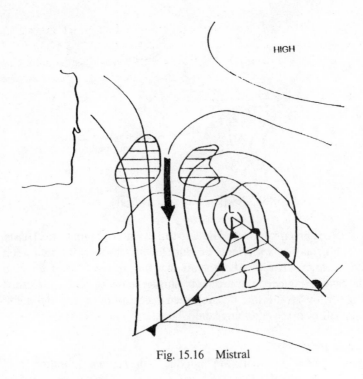

Fig. 15.16   Mistral

associated with a depression over the Gulf of Genoa, the strength arises mostly from a combination of:

1. the pressure gradient. A cold front held up by the Alps can produce a very active orographic low near N Italy,

2. the canalisation of the airstream down the Rhône valley, i.e. 'funnel effect', and

3. the katabatic effect of air flowing off the Massif Central and the other high ground to the side of the river valley.

Over the land the wind is strong, turbulent and usually dry and cloudless.

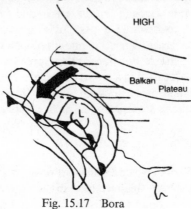

Fig. 15.17   Bora

However, as it flows out over the sea it rapidly picks up moisture. An aircraft northbound from Africa meeting Mistral conditions in the NW Mediterranean will first meet the cold front with active cumuliform cloud and then in the following Mistral, further turbulent conditions with more large cumulus and cumulonimbus, icing and thunderstorms often themselves in troughs, before nearing the European coastline when the airstream reverts to clearer continental air but still turbulent conditions.

Bora

This is a similar wind to the Mistral, which occurs over the Adriatic and its eastern shores particularly. Again it is a very strong wind and with gusts which have exceeded 100 knots, strong enough to prohibit operations at Balkan and nearby airfields. Over the Balkans it is often very dry and cloudless but nevertheless very squally and turbulent. It mainly occurs in the winter months and is basically due to the katabatic flow off the cold, high Balkan Plateau which extends almost to the Adriatic shores. The katabatic effect is accentuated when the continental high is well established giving a pressure gradient as shown in fig. 15.17 and locally the deeply indented coastline also produces ravine effects.

Where the airstream out over the Adriatic and Eastern Italy is humid (usually in association with a depression over the Adriatic Sea) the Bora has dense cloud, thunderstorms, icing and heavy snow or rain, in addition to its basic turbulence and strong squally surface winds (fig. 15.18).

Fig. 15.18   Bora blowing from the eastern shores of the Adriatic

Sirocco

The spelling of the English name of this wind tends to vary with the translator but it applies to a hot wind blowing northwards from Africa in the winter months, usually in advance of a frontal depression moving from west to east through the Mediterranean. Over the land and near to the coast, the Sirocco is dry and dustladen. In fact, the airstreams on both sides of the warm front trough over N Africa may be drawn from a dry and dusty source. When it progresses northwards over the Mediterranean to, say, Malta, Sicily or Italy, the airstream picks up moisture and the cooling of the surface layers also produces a stable lapse rate. The moistening, cooling and stabilising continues with the passage northwards and eventually leads to widespread low stratus and drizzle or advection fog.

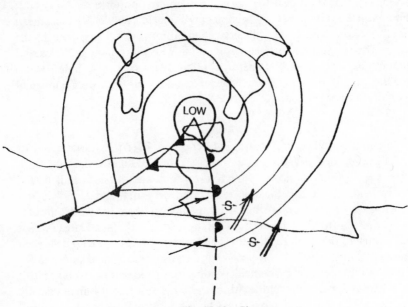

Fig. 15.19   Sirocco

Khamsin

Similar to the Sirocco in its nature, the Khamsin (which is Arabic for 50) according to folklore blows for 50 days and nights. In fact it is a mainly southerly wind of late winter and spring in Egypt and the eastern Mediterranean, generally occurring ahead of eastward moving depressions. It is hot and dry bringing much dust from the desert and in April and May it may well blow for many days

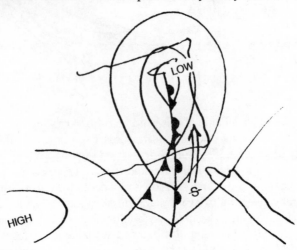

Fig. 15.20   Khamsin

in succession. Again, once it passes over the sea it picks up moisture so that by the time it reaches, say, Cyprus or Turkey the same airstream will be producing a sheet of stratocumulus or stratus. In Israel, the hot desert southerly wind is known as the Sharav.

Harmattan

This NE wind has already been referred to in connection with the inter-tropical front over West Africa (fig. 15.10) and is the name given to the flow of continental tropical air flowing from the Equatorial side of the Sahara Desert. It is dry and dusty and very hot by day. Its aridity however often makes it more acceptable to visitors to West Africa than the humid conditions which prevail in the rainy

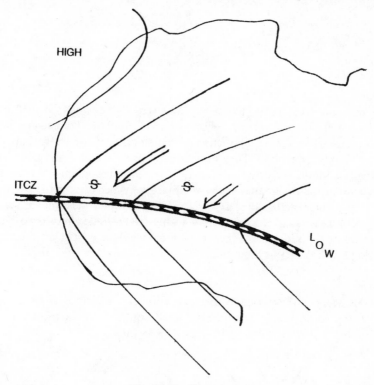

Fig. 15.21   Harmattan

seasons. Because of the annual movement north and south of the ITF the months when the Harmattan is experienced varies from one aerodrome to another. Those to the north of about 18°N which remain always to the north of the inter-tropical front have Harmattan conditions throughout the year. Aerodromes further south such as Dakar and Kano experience months when the ITF lies to the south of the field and the visibility is poor due to dust haze. Further south still, at the coastlines of Nigeria, Ghana, and the Ivory Coast, the ITF only moves to just off the coast for a few weeks so the Harmattan period is very short, with its attendant dry and hazy conditions.

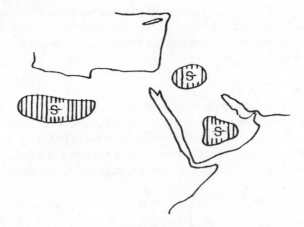

Fig. 15.22   Simoom

Simoom

Simoom is the name given to the hot and very dusty winds (in fact, often described as choking or suffocatingly so) which occur in the Arabian and North African deserts, or to the convectional dust/sandstorms or whirlwinds with which they are associated. They occur in spring or summer and completely prohibit operations in their immediate locality. The Simoom may last no more than 20 minutes although the shallow thermal lows which form in the afternoon may be 30–40 miles across and last for 2 to 3 hours. Visibility near the surface due to the wind-blown sand is down to a few metres but en-route aircraft can overfly the storms at altitude. Being a local circulatory wind, no particular direction is associated with the name Simoom.

Haboob

Haboobs occur in the hot dusty areas of the Sudan around Khartoum in the afternoons and evenings of the summer months of May to September when the

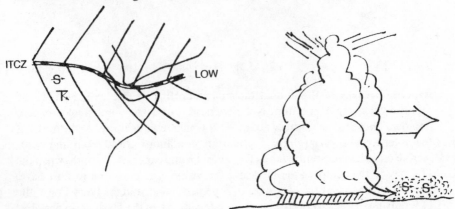

Fig. 15.23   Haboob

ITCZ is to the north. Moist air flows in from the Indian Ocean at both low and upper levels. Convection produces large cumulonimbus clouds and the strong squall winds blowing from the clouds raise dust and sand ahead of the clouds to considerable heights. As it approaches an aerodrome, the Haboob is associated with an increase in surface wind speed and a reduction in visibility. The duststorm is followed by a torrential downpour and thunderstorm before conditions improve again.

Southerly Buster

This is a strong and squally wind of south and south-east Australia, associated with the passage of a line squall at a cold front following which the wind backs to a southerly direction. There is a sudden and appreciable drop in temperature, together with thunderstorms and often a line of roll cloud along the front edge of the cumuliform cloud. Apart from the violent winds at the surface, flight conditions at all levels are very turbulent. The Southerly Buster is most frequent from October to March. Similar conditions occur in Uruguay and Argentina where the line squall and strong southerly winds are known as the Pampero, and in the southernmost parts of Africa where they are called 'South-Easters'.

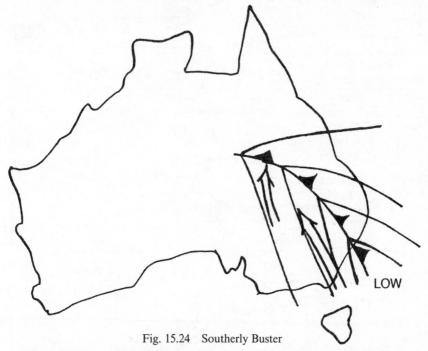

Fig. 15.24 Southerly Buster

As stated at the outset, it is a matter of opinion which local winds to include and which to exclude and pilots will add to their store of knowledge as their careers progress. There is really no substitute for experience but the following sections on the aviation climatology of various parts of the world are provided in a modest endeavour to try, at least in part, to remedy this deficiency for the student pilot.

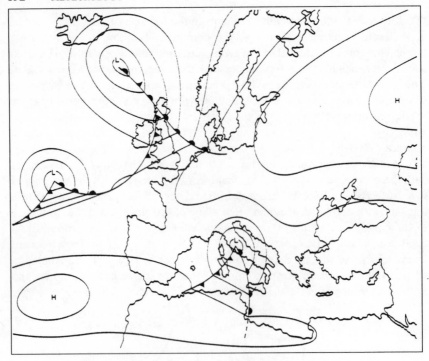

Fig. 15.26   Europe and the Mediterranean – typical July day

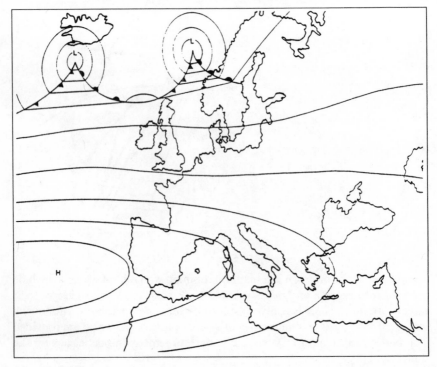

Fig. 15.25   Europe and the Mediterranean – typical January day

REGIONAL AVIATION CLIMATOLOGY

When interpreting the flight and landing forecasts for a long flight it is a great advantage to have in the back of one's mind the usual conditions that can be expected at various stages of the route and what extremes could be encountered.

Consider in turn what pressure systems and air masses dominate the area to be overflown; what lower and upper winds are likely, together with the probable cloud, precipitation, icing and height of the 0°C isotherm, visibility and fog. Is there any risk of thunderstorms or other phenomena at any stage, including the destination and any intermediate landings? For convenience, five areas of operations are identified:

Europe and the Mediterranean
N Atlantic and N America
Asia and Australasia
Africa and South America
Pacific Ocean

In each case, a typical synoptic situation is sketched for a day in January and for a day in July which will depict the seasonal changes over the area. It is assumed that the positions of the major topographical features (mountains, rivers, etc.), and also, of course, of the international aerodromes, are known.

Europe and the Mediterranean

Pressure systems

On a typical January day, NW Europe including the British Isles and Iceland is usually affected by frontal depressions which have travelled along the polar front which at this time is in its most southerly position. Eastern Europe is under the influence of the Siberian high which extends a strong ridge westwards, which also at times covers the British Isles as well as the European mainland. Depressions track from west to east through the Mediterranean Sea but are not as numerous as those coming into NW Europe from the N Atlantic.

During the spring, the Siberian high gradually declines while the sub-tropical anticyclone over the Azores and north Africa intensifies and moves slowly northwards. By midsummer, a typical July day's synoptic chart will usually show frontal depressions only affecting the NW part of the area with a longer interval between the fronts passing over Britain and N European countries. The bulk of Europe and the whole of the Mediterranean is dominated by a ridge of high pressure extending eastwards from the Azores high. From time to time this ridge collapses to allow thundery lows or cols to develop. In the autumn, frontal lows start to move through the Mediterranean again while the North Atlantic polar front lows track progressively further south and are able to move their frontal systems well into Europe before the Siberian high reasserts itself. Although not shown on the typical January day depicted, sometimes eastern Europe has frontal depressions in winter and spring that have originated in the Black Sea – Danube area and then track NW to Poland, Germany and even the North Sea.

Winds

Surface winds in January often reach gale force at the terminals of NW Europe although the direction for take-off and landing for a particular flight will depend upon the position of the frontal lows at that particular time, but the prevailing wind direction is from the south-west. Whenever the Siberian high becomes dominant, surface winds are easterly or north-easterly and may be persistent. In the Mediterranean and the countries bordering it, again the winds are very variable due to the passage of the frontal depressions and gales can occur at and behind their cold fronts. In July, average wind strengths are lighter but gales and very variable winds still occur in the north-west. Away from the frontal areas, surface winds are light and land sea breezes are a feature of anticyclonic weather. Where thermal lows or thunderstorms break out, surface winds can become blustery and squally.

Upper winds throughout the year are mainly from a generally westerly direction, increasing with height up to the tropopause. In January, due to the effect of the Siberian coldness which dominates the thermal component, over western Europe the upper winds tend to be frequently from north of west, while in July the relative warmth of south-east Europe compared to the north Atlantic tends to produce upper wind directions from rather south of west. Throughout the year, but most frequently in winter, upper winds exceed 100 knots in jet streams associated with depressions moving along the polar front. The sub-tropical jet-stream occurs in the eastern Mediterranean in January but although it moves slightly north to the Cyprus–Turkey area in July it is then weaker and unlikely to exceed 80 knots.

Weather (including cloud, visibility and icing)

The cloud and weather of this area may be summarised as due to fronts in the winter, giving way to cold anticyclonic conditions in eastern Europe and warm anticyclonic conditions along the southern shores of the Mediterranean, while in summer NW Europe still has frontal weather while the Mediterranean enjoys anticyclonic weather and high temperatures. In southern Europe, particularly mountainous areas, and sometimes further north, cloud then is mainly convective and at times builds up sufficiently to produce thunderstorms. In the autumn, before the Siberian high is fully established, frontal depressions that have passed over Britain or France can carry their low cloud and precipitation right across to eastern Europe and as autumn gives way to winter so the frequency of snow increases. By January, the probability of cold cloudless weather over eastern Europe is high and the frontal cloud is confined to the maritime countries further to the west and south. From spring onwards, airstreams flowing in from the Atlantic and North Sea pass over the warmer land and cumuliform cloud rather than frontal cloud is more common. Over and around the Mediterranean in the anticyclonic conditions, fair weather cumulus is most likely but in temporary collapses of the high pressure large cumulus and cumulonimbus develop over high ground of southern Europe.

For a pilot who has not learnt to fly in this area, visibility poses a problem over Europe, especially in winter. When fronts are moving across, visibility is poor in precipitation and the hill fog where the low cloud obscures high ground. Warm sectors give widespread advection fog while in anticyclonic conditions between depressions, widespread radiation fog affects most airports in autumn and winter. In some industrial areas, smoke may thicken the fog and make it more persistent. In the summer only hill fog really poses any problem.

The height of the 0°C isotherm (freezing level) is important for aircraft operations especially in January, when it is usually on or very near the surface over Europe, particularly by night. Even over southern Britain it averages around 3000 to 4000 feet. With the large amounts of dense cloud, airframe icing is therefore a permanent winter hazard, especially over high ground such as the Alps, the Pyrenees and in Scandinavia. In the Mediterranean the freezing level in winter is usually around 10 000 feet. By July, the freezing level over the Mediterranean and southern Europe is usually around 15 000 feet and icing only a problem in thunderstorms when they break out. In northern Europe, the freezing level has risen to average around 10 000 feet but unfortunately the risk of severe icing still remains in thunderstorms and in frontal cloud, especially where the front is passing over hilly terrain.

Local phenomena
The local phenomena likely to be met when operating in this area are the local winds of the Mediterranean mentioned earlier in this chapter – the Mistral, Bora, Sirocco and Khamsin. Tropical revolving storms do not enter the area and tornadoes are extremely rare.

North Atlantic and North America
As ranges of aircraft have increased so the routes across this area have increased and now vary from direct flights from terminals well in Europe to destinations well into north America via high latitudes to routes to holiday and business destinations in low latitudes such as the Caribbean. The trans-Atlantic crossings from West Africa to Brazil are considered in the later section, 'Africa and South America'.

Pressure systems
In considering flights into North America, it should be remembered that while in Europe the arrangement of high ground allows the ready movement west to east of pressure systems and air masses, in North America the alignment of high ground is mainly north-south. Although exhibiting the characteristics therefore of a continental climate, it is often the case that here either very warm air moves northwards or very cold air moves rapidly southwards through quite a wide band of latitude. In January, the polar front lies at its most southerly limit in the North Atlantic with its depressions tracking from Florida towards south-west Britain and the Bay of Biscay, occluding as they move generally east-north-eastwards. Many of the deepest centres track between Iceland and Scotland, giving the average low pressure of the 'Icelandic low'. However, later depressions of the same family will have their fronts swinging well to the south so that they affect the Azores and Bermuda. In addition to the frontal lows there are also

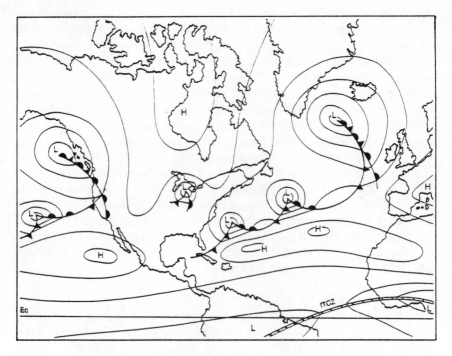

Fig. 15.27   N Atlantic and N America – typical January day

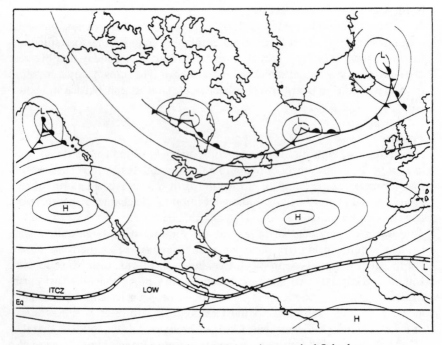

Fig. 15.28   N Atlantic and N America – typical July day

polar air depressions which develop over the ocean. Eastern America experiences both the lows passing along the polar front and lows which have formed and moved west to east across the continent. Further west, frontal depressions bring bad weather to terminals near the Great Lakes before polar air behind their cold fronts swings well to the south. In the extreme west, the Pacific polar front will bring depressions to these terminals, with ridges or cols between. Many of these depressions are occluded but some very bad weather occurs when a new series of depressions forms near to the coast on a trailing cold front and they move inland towards the mountains. During the spring, the sub-tropical high intensifies and moves northwards so that by July the Atlantic polar front lies from Newfoundland to NW Scotland and similarly the Pacific coast of North America is dominated by the oceanic high. In summer, frontal depressions not only track further north but also are usually less intense and less frequent. In the extreme south of the Atlantic-North America area, the Caribbean generally has NE trade wind conditions throughout the year, with the ITCZ affecting the southern part of the Gulf of Mexico in July.

Winds
Surface winds in January over the Atlantic and the aerodromes around it are very variable in direction as the intense frontal depressions bring gale force winds as they move along the polar front. At the European terminals, as a low moves in from the west so the winds freshen from the south, veer to south-west or west in the warm sector and become squally north-west or north behind the cold front. If the low is to the south, as for example it may well be at Reykjavik, the surface wind is easterly, which is also the direction which prevails in NW Europe when the Siberian high extends that far to the west. On the North American stage the wind direction is again dependent upon the position of frontal depression, whether forming on the Atlantic or Pacific polar fronts or over the continent. Between depressions, winds are light and variable in ridges and cols over the whole area. In North America surface winds are mainly northerly in cold continental conditions of high pressure. In the winter, at the Azores and Bermuda the surface winds vary with the passage of fronts mainly to the north of the aerodromes but are mainly light south-westerlies. Further south to the Equator, north-east trade winds prevail. Upper winds are very strong and from a mainly westerly direction with usually a jet stream in association with the polar front. In the western Atlantic and the eastern parts of North America, the upper air temperature gradients are particularly great, so giving high jet stream speeds and clear air turbulence in this area.

By July, the gales associated with the depressions are normally only experienced at the more northerly terminals and although the surface wind directions are still variable at fronts, on the average they tend to be north-westerly over Europe, south-westerly in the eastern parts of North America and north-west again on the Pacific coast. At the Azores and Bermuda and in any extension of the oceanic anticyclones to cover the European and American aerodromes, winds are light and variable with land-sea breezes occurring on coasts. Where summer thunderstorms occur, sudden squalls should be expected.

The north-east trade winds continue to dominate the southern part of the area. Upper winds are still westerly and although usually not quite so strong as in the winter there are still jet streams regularly in association with the polar front. In the extreme south of the area where the trade winds are feeding into the inter-tropical convergence zone, the upper winds are light easterlies.

Weather

The cloud and weather over and near the oceans is poor in January, being controlled by the depressions and their fronts. Usually there is extensive cloud up to the tropopause, with very low base heights and belts of precipitation at each of the fronts. At the more northerly aerodromes there is extensive snow and when deep lows form off Canada and north-east USA, deep snow from slow-moving warm fronts may close aerodromes in this area. Freezing rain can also produce serious hazards in the same area. Frontal depressions passing eastwards across North America bring periods of bad weather and low cloud, but of shorter duration, to the region of the Great Lakes but more often the flying conditions are fine and clear although temperatures are well below freezing. Away from frontal depressions, polar maritime air in any part of the more northerly section of the North Atlantic–North America–North Pacific area will give cold showery weather with turbulence, snow and icing. Overland when cols or ridges of high pressure prevail, radiation fog is likely to occur and be slow to clear during the day. Where the winds are just too strong for fog, sheets of stratus or stratocumulus may be expected. Generally the freezing level is likely to be between the surface and 4000 feet. On Atlantic crossings further south via the Azores and Bermuda, frontal weather is usually less severe and more widely spaced although some very intense lows with severe icing can be encountered over the Bay of Biscay and on the stage from Bermuda to the eastern seaboard of America. In the Caribbean and further south, there are scattered fair weather cumulus in the trade winds with only a slight chance of a light shower over high ground in the afternoon.

In the summer, polar front depressions track further north, are weaker and less frequent. The Azores–Bermuda area enjoys settled anticyclonic conditions which often extend to the adjoining continents in the same way that the Pacific oceanic high extends to over the western parts of the area. As a result, with a freezing level of 8000–10000 feet near Iceland and some 15000 feet in the south, frontal cloud and rain are unlikely to produce prohibitive operating conditions. When pressure gradients are slack over NW Europe or over North America convection of moist air causes thunderstorms and these are particularly severe in eastern USA. Off the American coast, both the Californian and the New England, there is often extensive advection fog so that the onset of a sea breeze at, say, Los Angeles or Boston may bring surface visibility down to below minima at exposed aerodromes on or near the coast.

Local phenomena

Clear air turbulence was mentioned in connection with the polar front jet streams. In the south-west states of the USA in winter when jet streams blow eastwards over the high mountains, lee-waves and their attendant hazards are common. The other local phenomena to be mentioned are violent thunderstorms and tornadoes of the summer months in the USA in the Mississippi-Missouri basin especially, with structural damage at the surface, violent hailstorms, etc., and hurricanes in the summer and autumn. The hurricanes (of which typical tracks were shown in fig. 15.11) form in or to the east of the Caribbean Sea and move west-north-west, then north-west and then north. If they enter the Gulf of Mexico near the Mississippi delta they then soon start to decline. If however they re-curve to cross Florida or the Bahamas, then in addition to inhibiting operations at aerodromes here they continue to take up moisture from the warm Gulf Stream and have much longer lives and may affect other routes further north.

Asia and Australasia

This area is dominated by the large monsoonal changes of climate. It extends both sides of the Equator so to avoid confusion, the terms summer and winter will not be used but instead are substituted January (as typical of mid-winter of the northern hemisphere) and July (mid-summer of the northern hemisphere, mid-winter in the southern hemisphere).

Pressure systems

In January in the north-east of the region, polar front depressions form over the Pacific and may be encountered on routes into Japan where they move mainly east or north-east. Depressions also pass into the west of the area from the Mediterranean, travel down The Gulf, gradually becoming less active and generally dying out near or over northern India where they are known as western disturbances. Mainly, however, over this region, pressure in January is high to the north and decreases southwards to Sri Lanka and Singapore which are on the edge of the Equatorial low. This is centred over Indonesia and north-west Australia with the inter-tropical convergence zone just to the south of Djakarta and near to Port Darwin. At the same time, over Australia there is a belt of high pressure with anticyclonic centres moving slowly from west to east, separated by cols or troughs extending from the south. By April-May, the 'western disturbances' no longer reach the area, the Asian continental anticyclone is collapsing and the inter-tropical convergence zone is moving northwards with the Equatorial low pressure and is overhead Sri Lanka and Singapore.

By July, the northerly movement is complete and the ITCZ extends along the Arabian coast to the monsoon thermal low centred over Baluchistan. Pressure is high both to the west over the Mediterranean and to the east over the Pacific Ocean but here the ITCZ extends south-eastwards from the Korea area to north of the Philippines. Over the southern hemisphere, the belt of sub-tropical anticyclones now affects central and northern Australia while frontal depressions passing over or to the south of Tasmania extend their fronts northwards over south-east Australia. By September-October the Equatorial low has moved sufficiently far south again to be located over Sri Lanka and Indonesia once more.

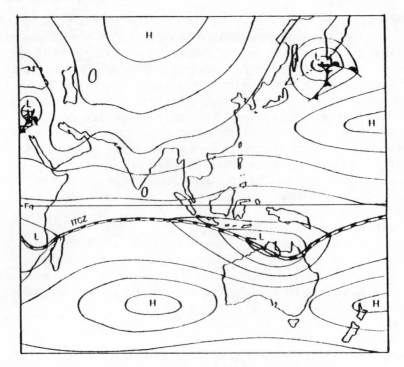

Fig. 15.29 Asia and Australasia – typical January day

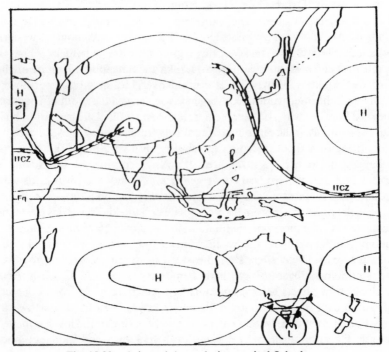

Fig. 15.30 Asia and Australasia – typical July day

Winds

Surface winds conform to the monsoonal flow so that in January there is a general northerly or north-easterly flow from the northern hemisphere to the southern hemisphere. As depressions pass from the west through The Gulf so winds ahead of them become southerly but revert to northerly again after the passage of the cold front. Over the Indian sub-continent, Thailand, etc., the winds are north-easterly but near to Japan they may be northerly or north-westerly. Here they are likely to become gale force and cyclonically variable with the passage nearby of polar front depressions. At, and just south of, the Equator the surface winds back north or north-west as they feed into the ITCZ. Over Australia south of the ITCZ the south-east trade winds prevail, gradually becoming light and variable near south-east Australia unless any frontal systems intrude from the south (Southerly Buster).

In July under the influence of the south-west monsoon, the surface wind directions are reversed almost everywhere. From the Mediterranean eastwards to the ITCZ surface winds are steadily northerly becoming south-westerly over India. Near Japan and near to the Equator, the wind backs to southerly or south-easterly. By central Australia, the south-east trade winds fall to light and variable and by New South Wales, conditions depend on the prevailing synoptic situation. Ahead of the warm fronts winds are mainly north-westerly, westerly in warm sectors and southerly, often strong, behind cold fronts. Throughout the year in conditions of slack pressure gradients, coastal regions experience fresh land and sea breezes. In the Equatorial low pressure, particularly in spring and autumn, the usual light winds may suddenly be replaced by squally winds of which the direction is largely determined by local topography.

At normal cruising altitudes over the whole area north of the Equator in January, upper winds are westerly and may be very strong between Bangkok and Tokyo due to the large temperature contrast between continent and ocean in this region at this season. From the Equator to the ITCZ upper winds are easterly then reverting to westerly with flight southwards over Australia. In July, upper winds are westerly everywhere south of the Equator and also in the northern hemisphere to the north of the ITCZ. Otherwise over Asia from the ITCZ to the Equator upper winds are easterly, usually less than 30 knots.

Weather

As regards cloud and weather in January, the Himalayan mountains prevent the direct outflow of very cold air from the interior of Siberia across India so that winters there are only relatively cool but fine. From Karachi to Bangkok there may be fog or mist patches or very low stratus around dawn on coasts and in river valleys, but this soon clears to be followed by a fine, sometimes hazy day. In the west of the region, similar conditions prevail in high pressures but as a depression approaches so the increasing southerly winds bring dust and sand storms to the stage from Cairo to Bahrain. Warm fronts are weak but cold fronts bring cumuliform cloud and heavy showers and these conditions prevail for a further day or two in the polar airstream behind the front. In these conditions, rain or hail showers occur at low level but over high ground in the extreme north-west of the region there is snow with severe icing and turbulence above the freezing level of approximately 5000 feet. Similarly in the north-east of this region over the China Seas and Japan, there is much cumuliform cloud in a north-westerly polar airstream while, if a frontal low affects the Tokyo area, warm fronts give widespread layer cloud with bases down to 1000 feet or less, much low stratus in the warm sector and showers, icing, etc., at the cold front.

Flying southwards to aerodromes such as Colombo and Singapore, increasing cumuliform cloud is encountered and in their vicinity large cumulus and cumulonimbus give showers and thunderstorms, particularly overland in afternoons and evenings. Over Indonesia and Australia north of the ITCZ it is also hot and humid with thunderstorms, torrential rain or hail and squalls over both land and sea, with the storms intensified on the windward sides of mountains in Indonesia.

In central Australia south of the ITCZ it is hot, cloudless and bumpy, with dust often up to 15000 feet. Further south towards Sydney, turbulence over high ground can be severe. Otherwise the worst flying conditions occur with the arrival of a cold front from low pressure to the south. This then can bring in severe duststorms to be followed by a southerly buster. During the transitional months of April and May, the northward movement of the ITCZ brings a season of heavy rains to Sri Lanka and Singapore. At the same time, temperatures are rising over Arabia and India and in this part of the region flying becomes very bumpy with much dust haze. In the large river valleys of northern India very violent but fortunately mainly isolated pre-monsoon thunderstorms develop during the day and must be avoided.

As the summer of the northern hemisphere advances, so the south-west monsoon steadily extends north and west so that by the end of July the whole of south-east Asia is covered. The weather in this south-west airstream is bad with massed thunderstorm clouds and heavy rain and particularly so in troughs circulating around the main monsoon centre of low pressure. At the same time, flying from the Mediterranean to Pakistan and north of the ITCZ, conditions are dry, very hot, dusty and bumpy. Dust storms are likely to develop in the afternoons while at Bahrain on The Gulf, surface air moistened locally by The Gulf makes conditions hot and humid.

During July on the other side of Asia when flying from the Philippines northwards to Japan, the monsoon airstream is cooled from below as it moves over the Pacific Ocean and has small cumulus clouds. However, over land, surface heating by day soon produces enough convection to give large cumulus and cumulonimbus with heavy rain showers. Near Japan there may be advection fog over the sea. In the Tokyo area, the main thundery rains occur in June and early July (the 'plum' rains) as the south-west monsoon first sweeps into the area. Later the large Pacific oceanic anticyclone can give fine sunny days.

South of Indonesia, the monsoon low of Asia is relatively ineffective and there are trade wind conditions of scattered small cumulus on the routes to Australia. Over Australia itself, the mainly anticyclonic weather gives small amounts of cloud but there is often extensive haze due to dust or smoke up to 10000 feet. Between the anticyclonic cells, fronts from depressions passing to the south of the continent give periods of cloud and rain mostly from the cold fronts. There is also the risk of mountain waves downwind of high ground.

In October and November, as the south-west monsoon retreats from India, so a period of renewed heavy rains occurs at Sri Lanka and Singapore as the Equatorial low pressure and ITCZ move south across this region.

Local phenomena

There are a number of important phenomena that affect this area. Tropical revolving storms seriously disrupt flights in many areas and, as may be seen from fig. 15.11, they may be experienced somewhere in this large region in any month of the year. Important local winds have already been mentioned in this chapter. Finally there are some very violent thundersqualls, two of which have local names which it is as well to know. Near Calcutta, in April and May, i.e. pre-SW monsoon, these thunderstorms and violent squalls set in during the late afternoon. They are called 'Nor-westers', indicating the direction from which they appear. Similarly, 'Sumatras' are squalls which occur in the Malacca Strait. They occur between April and November in the south-west monsoon. At night, air flows katabatically out over the warm waters of the strait, towering cumulonimbus develop with lightning, thunder and torrential rain together with a sudden squall and drop of temperature from the south-west, usually between 2300 and 0300 hours.

Africa, South Atlantic, South America

As with the preceding region, to avoid confusion the months January and July will be used instead of mid-winter in the northern hemisphere (mid-summer, southern hemisphere) and mid-summer in the northern hemisphere (mid-winter, southern hemisphere) respectively.

Pressure systems

The synoptic charts for typical days at the extremes of seasons have been drawn for sea level isobars. In some areas the height of the terrain makes this unrealistic, for example in north-east South America and south-eastern parts of Africa, and the practice then is to use the appropriate contour chart and streamlines. In January, frontal depressions move from west to east through the Mediterranean Sea but their fronts do not extend very far inland into Africa, having their greatest activity in the west of north Africa over the Atlas mountains. Significant cloud is normally only associated with the cold fronts and warm fronts may be ill-defined. Usually a weak ridge of high pressure extends from the west across Africa north of the Equator and then pressure decreases southwards south of the ridge to the Equatorial low and inter-tropical convergence zone (ITCZ) at and south of the Equator. For a very short period in West Africa the ITCZ moves just across the coast to lie a few miles off-shore in the Gulf of Guinea but for almost all of this season the ITCZ is north of aerodromes such as Accra and Lagos. From central Africa to Zimbabwe, and also over most of Brazil, Equatorial low pressures occur.

Further south over the two continents the sub-tropical high pressure is

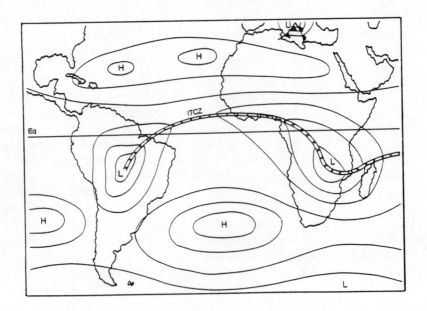

Fig. 15.31   Africa and South America – typical January day

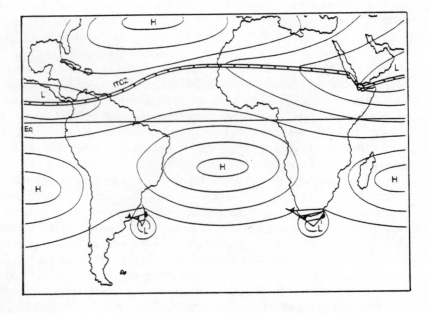

Fig. 15.32   Africa and South America – typical July day

dominant from a large anticyclone centred over the adjoining ocean. Frontal depressions affect the southern and south-western parts of South America. As the year advances, so the ITCZ moves northwards most rapidly in the continents and most slowly over the open oceans so that for example, from March to May it is virtually overhead at aerodromes such as Nairobi. In September-October it is overhead again, moving southwards. By July, frontal depressions do not affect the Mediterranean shores of Africa and a ridge of high pressure from the Azores anticyclone extends its influence both here and southwards across the desert until the ITCZ's surface position is reached just to the north of aerodromes at Dakar, Kano and Khartoum. From the ITCZ to the Equator, Equatorial low pressure conditions are experienced, gradually becoming less active as the Equator is reached. Both Africa and South America from the Equator southwards to about 25° to 30°S are normally under anticyclonic conditions. The remaining, most southerly parts of the region, at this time of the year are likely to be affected by fronts of depressions passing offshore to the south.

Winds

In January on the north African coast, surface winds are mainly south-westerly or land and sea breezes. When a depression moves through this area from the west, surface winds freshen from the south or south-east and after the depression has cleared to the east the winds become north-westerly. Inland over the rest of Africa north of the Equator and in South America in northern latitudes, the winds are north-east trade winds backing to north on crossing the Equator to feed into the ITCZ. In Africa south of the ITCZ there are south-east trade winds (sometimes as south-west 'deflected' trade winds at Lagos) although these become lighter and more variable in the extreme south where land and sea breezes occur on coasts. In South America, the Andes mountains and the large oceanic anticyclones over the South Pacific and South Atlantic have quite a large influence. On the west coast, surface winds are usually southerly from the Equator to the tropic and then become south-west or west except when fronts are present. On the east side of the continent there is a steady backing of wind direction with flight southwards from south-east trades to east or north-east in northern Brazil to mainly north-westerly by the time the River Plate estuary is reached. Further south, although generally from a westerly point, the surface winds over South America back from north-west to west then south-west as fronts pass by.

In July, the surface winds over Africa north of the ITCZ are north-easterly, while in the same area of South America they are more easterly. Further south over South America they are predominantly southerly or south-westerly on the west coast but on the east coast the regime is much as before with a steady backing from east to north and then north-west as one flies from the equator to the River Plate estuary, and thereafter mainly westerly winds varying as fronts pass by. Over Africa from the ITCZ to the Equator there are south-west 'deflected' trade winds which back to south-east in southern latitudes. South of the tropic, wind directions are more variable. As depressions pass eastwards to the south of the continent winds are initially north-west backing to west and then to south or even south-east with squalls at the cold front passage.

Upper winds are strong westerlies in the sub-tropical jet-streams which occur over the most northerly and most southerly parts of this region. In January, the line of the jet-stream is around 30°N and it is strongest in north-east Africa while to the south, it lies across South America at approximately 40°S and just to the south of South Africa. Because of the presence of the Equatorial low and the ITCZ, much of the region has easterly winds at altitude, often less than 30 knots. These winds prevail over South America from the north coast to about 20°S while in Africa, they are found from around 10°N to about 20°S before giving way to the upper westerlies. In July, the northern hemisphere sub-tropical jet stream is to the north of Africa and the upper winds are only modest westerlies from the north coast to the ITCZ. Then light easterlies prevail over both Africa and South America to 10°S before reverting to westerlies with a possible jet stream between 30°S and 40°S.

Weather
In January, north-west Africa has periods of cloudy weather with rain as depressions pass by. Warm fronts are not active as regards precipitation but the freshening southerly winds may cause duststorms between Tripoli and Cairo. Cold fronts give more precipitation and over the Atlas mountains this may be heavy with snow and severe icing. Inland over north Africa the desert gives hot, dry, bumpy conditions by day with duststorms or dust haze which may extend up to 15 000 feet. Near the Equator, increasing cumuliform clouds are encountered with showers and thunderstorms. Along the Nile and the Mediterranean coast, radiation fog sometimes forms around dawn but is very quickly dispersed by solar heating. From the Equator to almost 20°S in both continents it is the rainy season, under the influence of the Equatorial low and ITCZ. There may be low stratiform cloud in the early morning but it soon builds up into large cumulus and cumulonimbus and there is heavy rain during afternoons and evenings with squalls, thunderstorms and turbulence. Further southwards towards Cape Town and Buenos Aires there are usually only small fair weather cumulus and settled fine weather but occasionally very scattered heat thunderstorms may develop in the evenings.

Later in the year, as the ITCZ passes northwards so the main rainy season occurs in central Africa (e.g. Nairobi) in April-May and eventually by July this Equatorial weather extends to 15° to 18°N so affecting terminals such as Dakar, Kano and Khartoum. Over all of Africa north of the ITCZ it is now very hot and dusty, with the bumpiness diminishing at night, and skies are mainly cloudless. To the south of the ITCZ as far as the Equator, at the surface it is hot and humid and although there may be low cloud overnight, by day there are towering cumuliform clouds and thunderstorms which may go on into the early hours of the morning. Flying conditions become particularly bad when line squalls, orientated north-south, move westwards across the continent between 15°N and the Equator.

Considering Africa south of the Equator, it is the dry season and days become increasingly dusty and bumpy. Near the tropic, periods of moist air coming in from the Indian Ocean lasting several days can produce low cloud at night ('guti'). However, in the area near to Cape Town frontal cloud and rain occur with the worst conditions at cold fronts.

In South America in July in the most northern parts it is the rainy season with well-developed cumulus and cumulonimbus and heavy showers and thunderstorms, again worst in line squalls or easterly waves as referred to above for central Africa. The visibility is generally very good, deteriorating only for short periods in heavy rain. From the Equator to about 30°S it is the dry season even though very occasionally there is an isolated thunderstorm, especially in coastal areas near the tropic. At night too the same aerodromes are liable to low stratus around dawn. The remainder of the continent is subject to frontal weather. Warm fronts give overcast skies, low cloud bases and continuous rain, especially to the west of the Andes, while warm sectors have very low stratus and drizzle. Cold fronts may well develop line squalls with cumulonimbus, turbulence, icing and heavy showery rain. With no fronts in the immediate area there is a risk of radiation fog forming overnight, or low stratus in slightly stronger winds.

The passage of the ITCZ southwards in October and November brings a second rainy season as it passes overhead, to aerodromes in countries on or very near to the Equator such as in Ecuador and Kenya, with thunderstorms and generally unpleasant flying weather.

Local phenomena

There are a number of local phenomena, apart from the following local winds already mentioned earlier in this chapter: Sirocco, Khamsin, Simoom, Haboob, Harmattan, South-Easter and Pampero. Tropical revolving storms only have an indirect effect. When they occur in the Indian Ocean they normally re-curve by the Mozambique Channel. However, even though they do not normally pass over land they supply very humid warm air at both low and high levels from the east to the routes such as Nairobi to Harare, intensifying the bad weather from the ITCZ whenever they occur between January and April. The other intensification of bad weather in the ITCZ occurs in easterly waves or line squalls which pass from east to west near the Equator. Often particularly active over a belt some 30 miles wide they move in sympathy with the upper wind at speeds of some 20 to 30 knots although the squalls at their sudden onset have higher speeds. In contrast, in the dry seasons of the continents, visibilities are poor in the very dry air aloft due to dust and smoke carried upwards by convection. Finally, pilots should remember that the Atlas mountains in Africa and the Andes in South America, to mention but two ranges of significance, are massive and extensive and extend to above the freezing level especially in winter. Flying conditions, particularly if fronts are crossing the mountains, can be very poor in IMC with severe icing and turbulence and mountain lee-wave systems.

Pacific Ocean

Although physically this region is the largest being described, in fact all the surrounding continents have featured in the descriptions of the preceding regions and as far as possible repetition will be avoided although some will be inevitable.

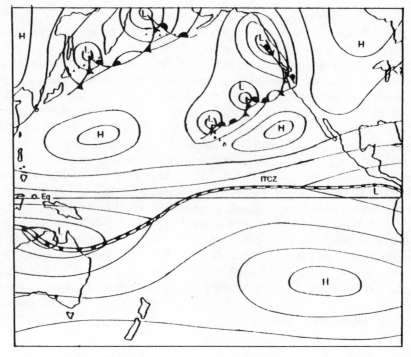

Fig. 15.33   Pacific Ocean – typical January day

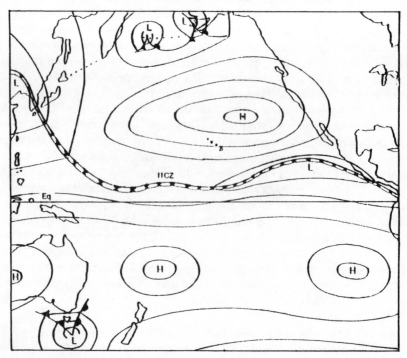

Fig. 15.34   Pacific Ocean – typical July day

Pressure systems

From October to March in the northern hemisphere, while winter anticyclones dominate the continents, depressions form off the Chinese coast and along polar fronts to the east. Their fronts can also affect the Hawaiian Islands when the north Pacific anticyclone declines from time to time. The inter-tropical convergence zone (ITCZ) lies across northern Australia, extends eastwards into the ocean to swing north-east to the north-east of Fiji and then lie west-east at about 5°N to South America, with the belt of sub-tropical high pressure on its southern side. From April to September the ITCZ is exclusively in the northern hemisphere. It emerges from the mountainous interior of Asia in the vicinity of Korea, swings south-east to lie east of the Philippines and then eastwards across the North Pacific only slightly north of its January position until nearing land again, when it swings north-east to central America. To the north, the sub-tropical anticyclone has intensified and extended east-west to dominate the ocean and often overlap the coasts on both sides too. Pressure is still low near the Aleutians so fronts can still affect the Canadian west coast. Similarly, because the Equatorial low is north of the Equator, all of the southern hemisphere's major oceanic routes are normally within the southern sub-tropical high except for the occasional intrusion northwards of fronts from depressions even further south.

Winds

In January, surface winds near the Asian and Australian coasts are controlled by the monsoon as already described. Over the open ocean from the ITCZ to about 20° north or south latitude there are steady trade winds. Over the latitude band 20° to 40° the winds gradually fall lighter and eventually reverse direction to variable westerlies and in higher latitudes depend upon passing fronts for their specific direction on a particular flight. By July, the western part of the region will be dominated by the south-east trade winds feeding in to become the south-west monsoon of Asia. Over the open ocean there is again on both sides of the ITCZ the steady transition from steady trade winds to light winds in the sub-tropical highs. Off the west coast of the USA there is a northerly flow while off the coast of Peru and Ecuador there is a southerly flow becoming south-east near the ITCZ. At upper levels, in January the winds are westerly except near the Equator where they are easterly and light. Between Hong Kong and Tokyo where the sub-tropical jet stream augments the polar jet stream, speeds of 200 knots occur at times. Over the southern hemisphere in central and southern Australia and eastwards at the same latitude over the ocean, upper winds are westerlies at speeds mainly of 50 to 60 knots. In July, almost everywhere south of the Equator has westerlies which are strongest in the sub-tropical jet stream across central Australia. From the Equator to the ITCZ there are light easterlies and then from the ITCZ northwards, westerlies gradually increase in strength although not quite as strong as in January.

Weather

The weather in January in Asia and southwards to northern parts of Australia is controlled by the north or north-east monsoon as already described. Very cold and dry in northern China, the airstream becomes polar maritime by the time it reaches Japan to give showery, unstable weather which alternates with frontal conditions from depressions passing nearby. The same airstream parallelling the China coast or turning slightly back onshore gives under the edge of the 'Siberian high' low stratiform cloud, drizzle and poor visibility (Crachin) in the Hong Kong area. By the time it reaches Indonesia, towering cumuliform cloud, thunderstorms and their associated turbulent flying conditions occur.

Flying eastwards on the trans-Pacific crossings, those parts of routes in the southern hemisphere experience cumuliform cloud and thunderstorms in the Equatorial low pressure in January, with particularly bad conditions, in fact curtailing or prohibiting operations, in tropical revolving storms in the Fiji-Queensland area. Away from such areas, trade wind conditions of scattered fair weather cumulus prevail. North of the Equator again large expanses of the ocean also have trade wind conditions until beyond 20°N and then those of warm oceanic anticyclones, until the Hawaii–North America stage. Although Hawaii usually has scattered cumulus and any rainfall is usually over exposed north-east slopes of the islands, occasionally the Pacific high declines sufficiently for cold fronts of depressions to bring gale force southerly winds (Kona storms) and heavy rain. Further east the situation is determined by the passage of polar front depressions from the west or north-west and conditions from British Columbia to California are broadly similar to the January conditions of north-west Europe. Between the fronts and particularly in California, there are periods of quiet but foggy weather. Visibility is also poor in other parts of the region in January at times. In Japan, fog, rain and snow may give limiting conditions and along the China coasts and in valleys there is stratus or fog. Elsewhere there are poor visibilities in torrential rain.

In July, the very large northern oceanic anticyclone gives much of the region settled fine weather. The Asian coastline has its summer monsoon weather but the western coastline of north America is much drier than in winter. In the north there are still fronts from depressions travelling further to the north but California is practically rainless although it suffers from the advection fog offshore which drifts inland, later to lift into low stratus. The ITCZ gives an area of thundery rain north of the Equator and to its south there is a broad band of fair weather cumulus in the south-east trade winds. In the most southerly parts of the region the weather is very changeable. There is a continuous flow of frontal depressions to the south of Australia and New Zealand, of which the cold fronts are most active, separated by cols or temporary cold anticyclones.

Apart from the squally winds associated with thunderstorms and those with cold fronts in higher latitudes the most important local phenomena associated with this region are tropical revolving storms. They occur mostly in the western section as shown in fig. 15.11.

Test questions

Q1. Cold water coasts are found mainly on:
    (a) the east sides of continents
    (b) the north sides of continents
    (c) the west sides of continents.

Q2. The Doldrums are:
    (a) another name for the sub-tropical anticyclones
    (b) cols between weak fronts encountered in low latitudes
    (c) weak inter-tropical convergence zones.

Q3. At the tropopause over the Atlantic and Pacific oceans, the strongest westerly winds are experienced at 40°N in January:
    (a) on the west sides of both oceans
    (b) on the east sides of both oceans
    (c) on the east side of the Pacific and the west side of the Atlantic.

Q4. At 5°N 140°W in the Equatorial low pressure zone, the probable wind at 40 000 feet will be:
    (a) 090°/20 kt
    (b) 180°/40 kt
    (c) 270°/30 kt.

Q5. On a flight from Heathrow to Fiji in February, with a night's stop-over in Hong Kong, there is a risk of tropical revolving storms:
    (a) in the Fiji area
    (b) at both Fiji and Hong Kong
    (c) in the Hong Kong area.

Q6. Which of the following storms is not a tropical revolving storm:
    (a) cyclone
    (b) tornado
    (c) typhoon.

Q7. Harmattan is the name given to:
    (a) duststorm and thunderstorm in the Sudan
    (b) wind-blown duststorm blowing onto the Mediterranean Sea
    (c) dusty north-east trade winds of West Africa.

Q8. Flying the route Darwin to Sydney in January could mean a possibility of there being:
    (a) tropical storms at Darwin and/or a Southerly Buster at Sydney
    (b) tropical storms at Darwin but no risk of a Southerly Buster at Sydney
    (c) no risk of tropical storms at Darwin but a risk of a Southerly Buster at Sydney.

Q9. The surface wind at Recife (NE Brazil) is usually from:
    (a) the south in winter, north in summer
    (b) the north in the winter, south in the summer
    (c) an easterly direction.

Q10. In Nigeria in May, thunderstorms associated with the inter-tropical front
are located:
- (a) entirely to the north of the ITF
- (b) approximately symmetrically about the ITF
- (c) entirely to the south of the ITF.

16: Organisation, Observations, Reports and Forecasts

The efficiency of the service provided by any organisation is dependent upon the quality of the data it receives and how well it is processed. This is certainly true of the meteorological service offered to aviation in the form of forecasts and warnings, which depends upon a global system of observations and reports.

In order to avoid any possible confusion from the outset between the use of the terms 'report' and 'forecast', they may be defined as:

A meteorological report is a statement of the weather conditions which are prevailing, or have prevailed, at a particular place and time. In aviation, it is often given in a standardised code form for brevity, sometimes called an 'actual'.

A meteorological forecast is a statement of the weather conditions which are expected to prevail at a particular place and time. It also may be given in code form for brevity.

It is an unfortunate fact that a slip of the tongue or a temporary lapse of concentration does from time to time lead to the misuse of the words 'report' and 'forecast' when a moment's thought would clarify that, literally, one can only report something which has occurred or is occurring while to forecast means to anticipate future conditions. It is an even more unfortunate fact that fatal

Table 4

Element	How measured
Pressure	Barometer or barograph
Temperature	Dry-bulb, maximum, minimum, grass minimum thermometers and thermograph
Humidity	Wet and dry-bulb thermometers and hygrograph
Cloud type	Visual
amount	Visual
base height	Visual or cloud-base recorder (ceilometer), pilot balloon, cloud searchlight (by night only) and alidade
Wind direction	Wind vane
Wind speed	Cup-generator or pressure-tube anemometers
Visibility	Visual of known objects at fixed distances, transmissometer or (at night only) Gold visibility meter
Precipitation	Rain-gauge, rate of rainfall recorder, weather radar (for storm movement)
Weather	Visual or weather radar
State of ground	Visual
Sunshine	Sunshine recorder

accidents have occurred where pilots have assumed that a report has been a forecast.

Considering firstly the observations made at a meteorological station (and remembering that there are many more reporting stations than forecasting offices), the main elements observed and the methods commonly used are given in Table 4.

Pressure

Barometer

The pressure of a column of mercury is balanced against the pressure being exerted by the atmosphere on the mercury in the barometer cistern (fig. 16.1). The greater the atmospheric pressure, the greater the column of mercury. The instrument is calibrated assuming standard conditions, so to obtain QFF it is necessary to apply corrections for index error, temperature error, latitude (gravity) error and to 'reduce' the reading to mean sea level.

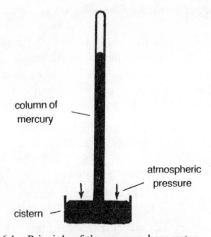

column of
mercury

atmospheric
pressure

cistern

Fig. 16.1   Principle of the mercury barometer

Barograph

A block of capsules almost completely evacuated of air will be compressed when atmospheric pressure increases and will expand when it decreases. The motion is magnified by a lever system and the variation of pressure recorded by a pen on a rotating drum.

It is quite satisfactory for the barometer and barograph to be located in the meteorological office out of a draught. However, the elements of the instruments measuring temperature and humidity must be out of doors and they are housed in a 'thermometer screen'. The screen has slatted sides, a split base and a double top to allow free circulation of air around the instruments and is painted white to keep absorption of solar radiation to a minimum. In the northern hemisphere the screen door is on the north side (vice versa for southern hemisphere) and the instruments at 4 feet above ground level.

Temperature

Dry-bulb thermometer
The air temperature is measured by a mercury-in-glass thermometer in which the mercury expands up the capillary tube as the air temperature rises.

Maximum thermometer
This is similar to the dry-bulb but it has a constriction in the capillary tube so that although the mercury when expanding can force its way through as the temperature rises, it is unable to contract into the reservoir as the temperature falls. Like the doctor's clinical thermometer it is reset by a brisk shake.

Minimum thermometer
This is an alcohol-in-glass thermometer with a small index in the capillary of alcohol. Although the spirit flows round the index as the temperature rises, when the temperature falls the index is dragged by the spirit's meniscus towards the thermometer bulb. Provided the thermometer is not disturbed from its horizontal position before the reading is taken, the high temperature end of the index indicates the minimum temperature.

Thermograph
Usually the recording on the rotating drum via a system of levers is of the movement of the 'free' end of a bimetallic strip of which the other end is fixed to the instrument frame.

Humidity

Wet-bulb thermometer
The wet-bulb is the same as a dry-bulb except that it is wrapped with a muslin bag kept damp by distilled water from a wick leading from a small jar. If the relative humidity is 100% there is no evaporation from the muslin bag and the dry-bulb and wet-bulb read the same. If the air is unsaturated, the depression of the wet-bulb reading below the dry-bulb increases as the relative humidity decreases.

Hygrograph
The sensitive element is commonly a bunch of human hairs of which the length varies with the relative humidity. Over normal temperatures, the changes in humidity are reasonably reflected but the exact relative humidity cannot be relied upon.

Apart from the above temperature and humidity instruments kept in the thermometer screen, a grass minimum thermometer is put out at night on grass on two pegs to record the minimum temperature there, and hence 'ground frosts' as opposed to 'air frosts' noted from the screen minimum temperature.

Cloud
The type(s) and amount of clouds are assessed visually.

Height of base
Various methods are used. The observer may make a visual estimate of this too but the usual instrument is a 'cloud-base recorder'. This consists of a transmitter, a receiver and a recording unit, which is in continuous unattended operation, day and night. An upwards projected beam of light is scattered and reflected by the cloud base which is detected by a vertically-pointing receiver's photo-electric cell. The base height is measured and automatically recorded on a trace. Other methods are to time the ascent of a pilot-balloon which is rising at a known rate until it disappears into the cloud, and at night to measure the angle of elevation of a patch of the cloud-base illuminated by a vertical searchlight beam based at a known distance from the observer, and to calculate the base height by trigonometry.

Surface wind – measured at 33 feet (10 metres) above ground in an open situation

Direction
Measured by a vane, the large keel-surface at the tail end of which is blown down-wind of the central pivot. Its indication is reproduced on a meter in the meteorological office.

Speed
Although there are some pressure tube anemometers still around (similar in principle to airspeed indicators) most are cup-generator anemometers. Three hemispherical cups mounted radially on a vertical spindle rotate as the wind blows. This rotation is fed to a small electrical generator in a weather-proof housing at the spindle. The generated voltage increases with windspeed and is fed to an indicator calibrated in knots in the meteorological office.

Away from a meteorological observing station, a good knowledge of the Beaufort scale of wind force is invaluable, as is also the angle of dangle of a landing ground's wind-sock relationship to the surface wind speed.

Visibility
Often assessed visually by noting the range at which objects at known distances can still be clearly recognised (fixed lights at night).

Transmissometer
This records the transparency of the atmosphere automatically and continuously by day and by night, keeping a record on a chart. A photocell receiver detects the brightness of the light received from a horizontal searchlight beam, of which the original brightness is known. The poorer the visibility, the greater is the

attenuation, so the chart can be calibrated in terms of meteorological optical range.

Visibility meter

Visibility can also be measured at night by means of a Gold visibility meter (Gold was the inventor's name). The meter is a photometer consisting of a glass slide of increasing opacity through which a light of known brightness at a known range is viewed, and the slide adjusted until the light is just visible. The slide reading is transferred to a table compiled for that observer's eyesight, the light's brightness and range, and the corresponding daytime visibility read off.

Precipitation and thunderstorms

Weather radar

Many stations now have radar heads from which responses are shown on circular time-bases of which the range can be varied. Dense cloud, precipitation and thunderstorms particularly can be tracked in relation to the station, automatically, by night and day.

Other observations that are regularly made, but are not normally passed on to the aviation users, are the amount of precipitation (measured by means of a rain-gauge), the hours of sunshine (from a glass sphere that acts like a burning-blass, the meteorologist's crystal ball), and the state of the earth (from a tended earth plot in an open situation).

The completed observations are put into code, passed on by landline and later redistributed by the same means. In the United Kingdom, the headquarters of the Meteorological Organisation is at Bracknell, Berkshire. It should of course be remembered that aviation is not the only user of the meteorological service. Other forms of transport, e.g. shipping, highway authorities, British Rail, are major users too, as well as other bodies such as the Central Electricity Generating Board and British Gas who have to anticipate demand – not to mention farmers, horticulturalists, builders, major sports promoters and many others.

The procedures are internationally agreed under the auspices of the World Meteorological Organisation (WMO) which is a specialised agency of the United Nations Organisation. The specialised needs of aviation, whether local or international, are catered for by the Meteorological Division of the International Civil Aviation Organisation (ICAO) and in the United Kingdom the Civil Aviation Authority (CAA) devolves this responsibility on to the Meteorological Office. The official ICAO documents to which the United Kingdom conforms are tabulated in the MET section of the Air Pilot.

Depending upon the service supplied, meteorological offices may be:

Meteorological Watch Offices, which are responsible for watching over the meteorological conditions in a Flight Information Region, an Upper Information Region and/or Oceanic Control Area and keeping the responsible Air Traffic Control Centre (ATCC) informed.

Main Meteorological Offices, which are operational on a 24-hour basis serving major aerodromes with forecasting services.

Subsidiary Meteorological Offices, which offer less than a 24-hour, but some forecasting, service.

Observing Offices, which may in fact operate on a 24-hour basis but do not have forecasting facilities.

For a while after World War II, there was period in the UK when the aircraft captain and his crew went to the Met. Office before a flight to collect a Flight Forecast Folder prepared for their particular flight and to receive a personal briefing on the conditions to be expected. The escalation of flights departing in quick succession over the same or nearby routes has led to the present system which is considerably more economical in personnel and time but relies on pilots having a good knowledge of meteorology – self-briefing. In notifying this pre-flight service the UK Air Pilot states that this primary method of briefing does not require prior notification of the flight. However for special forecasts (e.g. for non-scheduled or emergency flights), meteorological offices require prior notification of:

(a) at least two hours for flights up to 500 nm and

(b) at least four hours for flights over 500 nm

before the time of collection, and more time if possible.

Forecasts provided under these special arrangements can include the flight forecast up to the next transit aerodrome that can provide meteorological service together with an aerodrome forecast for the destination (or first transit aerodrome) and for up to three alternates.

When it is necessary to have the personal advice of a forecaster, pilots should contact the nearest forecast office serving civil aviation, as listed in the Air Pilot. The designated forecast office for North Atlantic flights departing from any UK aerodrome is LONDON (Heathrow).

Low level aviation meteorological service in the UK

A service providing low level aviation meteorological forecasts and an aerodrome weather information service is available for the UK by telephone (called AIRMET), Aeronautical Fixed Telecommunication Network (AFTN) and Telex. The introduction of the service in June 1987 led to the withdrawal of the telephone meteorological service to aviation previously available from RAF stations and government aerodromes. Special (route) forecasts are not provided within the coverage of the UK low level service.

The low level service which is an alternative to that provided at the Flight Briefing Units gives three regional forecasts. The regions are:

Southern England (south of a line approximately from South Wales to the Wash)

Northern England and Wales

Scotland and Northern Ireland

and makes use of sub-regions, where applicable, for clarity. The information provided (for an 8-hour period of validity) comprises a general synopsis followed by forecast conditions up to 15000 feet (except *) of:

1. Weather

2. Warnings

*3. Winds and temperatures (2000 ft, 5000 ft, 10 000 ft, 18 000 ft)
4. Clouds
5. Visibility
6. Freezing level
7. Icing
8. Outlook

The format is so arranged that a telephone caller (receiving the information at dictation speed) can quickly determine if the forecast weather conditions are unsuitable for the intended flight and if so, ring off.

Time of issue AFTN/Telex	AIRMET available by telephone	8-hour period of validity	Outlook to
	(All times are local time)		
0500 hrs	0600 hrs	0600–1400	2000 hrs
1100	1200	1200–2000	0200
1700	1800	1800–0200	0800
2300	*	0001–0800	1400

*Not generally available because of the low utilisation and the high cost of night recording. Callers can obtain the information, however, by telephoning Heathrow Airport or Manchester and Glasgow Weather Centres. Similar constraints mean that after 2000 hrs, the 1800–0200 recorded (telephone) forecast is not amended.

The forecasts are issued at every six hours after updating on a routine basis, but can be revised if the need arises between the standard times. The actual process of recording the UK Regional Forecasts for telephone callers has been allowed an hour, so the AFTN and Telex service distributes the data one hour before the forecast's period of validity.

The meteorological offices providing a service to general aviation also operate an 'on-request' telephone service providing available TAFs and METARs for aerodromes in the forecast regions to pilots not having access to teleprinter aerodrome information.

CAA will also, subject to prior request, make arrangements for the supply of specialised meteorological information on:

(a) thermal activity and sea breezes for gliding, balloon, microlight and hang-gliding operations

(b) 1000 ft wind forecast for offshore operations off eastern England

(c) particular needs for special events for which the routine broadcasts may be inadequate.

Documents

For self-briefing pre-flight, the pilot can normally collect all of the documents he will need although they do vary from one area to another.

For a long flight, e.g. trans-Atlantic flights, the documentation available is:
contour-isotach charts for the standard upper pressure levels
significant weather charts

tropopause-maximum wind charts

aerodrome forecasts

For a shorter flight, e.g. to the Mediterranean, the documentation available is:

significant weather charts

spot winds and temperature charts

aerodrome forecasts

The charts all have a period of validity for the data they are forecasting and new editions are issued at regular intervals, particulars of which are given in the Air Pilot. Currently charts are issued every 6 hours. If flights are delayed, new documentation must be collected if the period of validity is going to expire.

Apart from the information in the Air Pilot and similar flight guides, the CAA promulgates any changes to the content, format and coverage of meteorological forecast charts in yellow (operational) Aeronautical Information Circulars. The symbolism used is given in the same documents.

In order that its powerful computers are provided with every item of relevant information, observations collected at the Central Forecasting Office are supplemented by those from:

(a) automatic weather stations located in some of the less hospitable parts of the world.

(b) satellites. These may be geo-stationary in which case their path in space has been so arranged that they look down on the same part of the earth's surface at all times, or they are orbital with carefully planned paths to obtain a particularly required coverage. The pictures obtained and now often shown on domestic television may be direct visual cloud photo-graphs or infra-red.

(c) upper air soundings by radio-sondes or aircraft observations. Radio-sondes are carried upwards by hydrogen-filled balloons and descend at a controlled rate by means of a parachute. The radio-sonde carries a small transmitter, and measuring elements for pressure, temperature and humidity (usually an aneroid capsule, bimetal-strip or electrical resist-ance, and a piece of goldbeater's skin respectively) which are switched into the transmitter in sequence. It may also carry a radar reflector target to enable its position and hence the upper wind to be measured.

The outward distribution of forecast data consists of a facsimile transmission network for meteorological charts (CAMFAX). Typical routine transmissions to major UK aerodromes include charts for Europe, the Mediterranean, North America and the Middle/Far East. On a wider scale, aerodrome meteorological reports (METAR and SPECI), aerodrome forecasts (TAF), and warnings of weather conditions which are significant to flight safety (SIGMET), are broadcast by teleprinter throughout the UK and internationally in text form. Details of the channels are given in the MET section of the Air Pilot. The METARs may be augmented by TRENDs which are short-term landing forecasts valid for two hours. The METAR and TAF codes are explained at the end of this chapter. The Appendix gives particulars and examples of how meteorological observations are plotted around the 'station circle' on a forecaster's working chart. These are also plotted according to internationally agreed practice so a pilot visiting a forecaster at work in his office will see the same presentation wherever he may be world-wide. The plotting may be by hand or computer-generated, in colour or monochrome.

In-flight procedures

Again because of the volume of air traffic, pilots are expected to make use of routine broadcasts when en-route rather than ask for an individual personal service for their particular flights. The sources of information available are VOLMET which issues on a half-hourly cycle METARs for a given list of airports, and Automatic Terminal Information Service (ATIS) for that specific aerodrome.

However, if particular information that is required is not included in the routine broadcasts or if the aircraft is having to divert to a route for which no forecast has been provided, the pilot can obtain the meteorological information he requires on request to the ATS unit which is serving his aircraft.

Aircraft in flight are warned if any of the following SIGMET phenomena are occurring or are expected to occur on the route ahead for up to 500 nm.

active thunderstorms (other than isolated or scattered storms)
tropical revolving storms
severe line squall
heavy hail
severe turbulence
severe airframe icing
marked mountain waves
windspread storm of dust, sand or volcanic ash

For aircraft at transonic and supersonic cruising levels, there are SIGMET SST for:

moderate or severe turbulence
cumulonimbus clouds
hail

Provided prior arrangements are made between the aircraft operator and the forecast office serving the departure aerodrome, in exceptional circumstances an en-route service can be made available for a given route sector between specified flight levels. Other facilities available to aircraft in flight which are applicable only to certain aerodromes in the UK are:

Marked temperature inversion warning
Kirkwall Talk-to-Met
London/Heathrow Windshear Alerting Service (HWAS)

At certain aerodromes, warning of a marked temperature inversion is broadcast on ATIS, or in its absence in the arrival or departure message, when there is a surface inversion of 10°C or more up to any point within 1000 feet of the aerodrome surface. Kirkwall Talk-to-Met service is operated by meteorological office staff outside the aerodrome's published hours 'to enable pilots, particularly those flying at lower altitudes, to obtain meteorological information for a limited number of aerodromes in the area'.

HWAS issues alerts in the arrival and departure ATIS broadcasts, as either:

WINDSHEAR FORECAST or
WINDSHEAR FORECAST AND REPORTED or
WINDSHEAR REPORTED.

The criteria used for potential low level windshear are listed in the Air Pilot.

Whilst in flight, pilots are not required to make routine meteorological observations in the London or Scottish FIR/UIRs. However, AIREPs are required if the aircraft encounters any of:

    severe icing
    severe turbulence
    moderate turbulence, hail or cumulonimbus met during transonic or
        supersonic flight,
    other meteorological conditions likely to endanger or affect the operational
        efficiency of other aircraft (e.g. low-level windshear).

Aerodrome warnings

Provided they have notified the CAA, aerodrome operators are issued with warnings when significant meteorological conditions are forecast. The aerodrome operator then distributes the warnings to aircraft owners and operators using the aerodrome. Warnings are issued for:

    (a) Gales (mean surface wind exceeding 34 kt or gusts over 43 kt)
    (b) Squalls, hail or thunderstorms
    (c) Snow (when, duration, intensity, depth expected, when thaw expected)
    (d) Rising dust or sand
    (e) Frost (ground, air, freezing precipitation, or on parked aircraft)

The METAR and TAF codes

The sets of figures passed to the pilot pre-flight, which have been received over the teleprinter network, are very similar for the two codes as basically they are conveying information on much the same meteorological elements – surface wind, cloud, weather, visibility, etc. They are however prefixed METAR or TAF as applicable. There are also other differences. The time in a METAR is that of the completion of the observation while for a TAF it is the period of validity. METARs sometimes have TRENDs added to them and may include RVR information. Changes form part of TAFs but are no part of a METAR. Non-UK TAFs may include groups giving Forecast Temperature, Airframe Icing and Turbulence.

    To illustrate the decoding process, take the following message:

METAR
            EGKK 0615 33015 9999 80RASH 7CU30 ....
TAF

The prefix is all-important:

METAR   aerodrome report
   TAF   aerodrome forecast

EGKK is the ICAO station location identifier, in this case, Gatwick.

0615 is the time group. For a METAR it means 0615 hrs GMT/UTC.

For a TAF it means that the period of validity is from 0600 to 1500 hrs.
33015 is the surface wind. 330°T/15 kt

If the speed is followed by / and further figures, this is the gust speed.
9999 is the visibility group and indicates 10 km or more.

Otherwise the figures are the visibility in metres with 0000 for less than 100 m.

In a METAR the visibility group may be followed by a Runway Visual Range group and if so, the RVR group starts with R (e.g. R0500/28L) to identify it.
80RASH is the weather. The first two numbers are really for meteorological purposes, giving a more precise interpretation. Pilots should know the de-code of the letters:

FU	smoke	HZ	dust haze	PO	dust devils
BR	mist	FG	fog	TS	thunderstorms
SQ	squall	DZ	drizzle	RA	rain
SN	snow	GR	hail	SG	snow grains
PE	ice pellets	SH	showers	XX	heavy
MI	shallow	RE	recent	DR	low drifting
BL	blowing	BC	patches	FZ	freezing
SA	duststorm, sandstorm, rising dust or sand				
FC	funnel cloud (tornado or waterspout)				

80RASH thus decodes as Rain Showers.

7CU30 is the cloud group and indicates $\frac{7}{8}$ Cumulus base 3000 feet (above aerodrome level). A state of sky obscured is coded as 9// followed by the vertical visibility in hundreds of feet. A group 9//// indicates sky obscured with an indeterminate vertical visibility. Successive groups are used to indicate different cloud layers.

CAVOK   This group is used instead of the visibility, weather and cloud groups when:

visibility is 10 km or more

there is no cloud below 5000 ft or the highest minimum sector altitude, whichever is the greater, and no cumulonimbus

there is no precipitation reaching the ground, thunderstorm, shallow fog or low drifting snow.

(However it should be pointed out that under the tolerances allowed by ICAO, a METAR including CAVOK with also a TREND of NOSIG does not necessarily imply that the above conditions will still prevail. This is because changes in visibility and cloud base height from the above values are only counted as significant changes when the visibility is expected to fall below 5000 metres or the cloud base height of more than 4 oktas of cloud is expected to fall below 1500 feet.)

The subsequent groups differ between METARs and TAFs:

METAR	TAF
Temperature/dewpoint	Probability (as a %)

(in °C, M indicating negative value)
QNH (rounded down to next whole millibar)
TREND

TREND
Valid Time (e.g. 1619 means a sub-period of validity from 1600 to 1900 hours)
Visibility in sub-period
Weather in sub-period

In a METAR the trend group gives a landing forecast for the two hours after the observation time. The abbreviations used under TREND are:

NOSIG	no significant change
GRADU	gradual change
TEMPO	temporary variation(s)
INTER	intermittent variation(s)
RAPID	changing during less than half-an-hour (when it is used instead of GRADU)
TEND	changing, but none of the other change groups applies

The TREND indicator (except in the case of NOSIG) is followed by the forecast changes.

The criteria used in deciding to forecast short period variations as TEMPO or INTER may be summarised as:

TEMPO is used if the change(s) is(are) expected to last for a period of less than one hour and take(s) place sufficiently infrequently for the prevailing conditions to remain those of the METAR report,

INTER is used if the change(s) is(are) expected to occur frequently for short periods of time, with the conditions fluctuating almost constantly between those in the METAR report (or those in the preceding part of the TREND forecast) and those in the forecast itself.

WX NIL means nil weather and SKC means sky clear.

There is also provision for an 8-figure group to be appended to a METAR of which the first two digits designate the runway. Where there are parallel runways (e.g. 28L and 28R) the left runway is given only the runway number (e.g. 28) while 50 is added for the right runway (e.g. 28R = 78). Runway 99 means that the group is repetition of the last message. The subsequent groups cover:

3rd digit – Deposit. In general terms, increasing value indicates worsening state, from 0 = clear and dry to 9 = frozen ruts or ridges.

4th digit – Extent of contamination. Again increasing value indicates great contamination, 1 = less than 10% of runway contaminated, 9 = over 50% covered.

5th/6th digits – Depth. From 01 to 90 inclusive, the code figure is the depth in millimetres, 91 = 10 cm and then increments of 5 cm from 93 = 15 cm to 98 = 40 cm or more. 00 is less than 1 mm and 99 means that the runway(s) is non-operational due to deposits.

7th/8th digits – Friction coefficient, e.g. .35 means a friction coefficient of 0.35. If it is not available, braking action is indicated by a code figure 91 to 95 ranging from 91 = POOR to 95 = GOOD. 99 = Unreliable and // = Runway non-operational, braking action not reported, or aerodrome closed, etc.

Thus an appended group of 58451594 would mean that Runway 08R is covered by dry snow over 26% to 50% of its length to a depth of 15 mm and the braking action is medium to good.

A final reminder. Do not make a request pre-flight, 'I would like to know the weather at xxx' or any similar remark which could be misinterpreted, and certainly do not ask for the 'met. report for xxx' when what you really want is a forecast for the destination and its alternates.

Test questions

Q1.   A Meteorological Watch Office:
      (a) is located at all international airports in the UK
      (b) compiles all the aviation forecasts issued in the UK
      (c) keeps its ATTC informed of meteorological conditions in its FIR/ UIR.

Q2.   Pre-flight a pilot normally collects forecast documents which have been compiled:
      (a) for his particular flight
      (b) for his particular flight and must have them initialled by the duty forecaster in his presence at the end of his crew's briefing
      (c) for self-briefing and if he has any queries, contacts the designated forecast office for the departure aerodrome.

Q3.   When a special forecast is required for a flight of 600 nm direct to the destination, a pilot should give the maximum possible notice and normally should give at least:
      (a) 2 hours before the time of collection
      (b) 4 hours before the time of collection
      (c) 6 hours before the time of collection.

Q4.   Aerodrome warnings of impending bad weather are issued by the authorities to:
      (a) all aircraft owners and operators based at the aerodrome
      (b) aerodrome operators
      (c) all owners hangaring their aircraft at the aerodrome.

Q5.   The United Kingdom uses the Air Pilot to publish that the CAA departs from ICAO in measuring and reporting:
      (a) atmospheric pressure in millibars
      (b) windspeed in knots
      (c) visibility in nautical miles.

Q6.   To make a weather report whilst in flight, a pilot uses:
      (a) VOLMET
      (b) METAR
      (c) AIREP.

Q7.   Flying near Northern Scotland, you decide to use the KIRKWALL Talk-to-Met service. This service is:
      (a) operated by ATC and is available throughout the 24 hours
      (b) operated by Met Office staff outside the aerodrome operating hours

(c) operated by ATC and is available only during the aerodrome operating hours.

Q8. Corrections are made to the reading of a barometer to obtain QFF for:

(a) Position error, difference of temperature from ISA msl temperature, height above msl and instrument error

(b) instrument error and height above msl only

(c) index error, latitude error, temperature error and height above msl.

Q9. Upper wind is measured by means of a radio-sonde by:

(a) an anemometer mounted on its side

(b) an anemometer mounted underneath it

(c) tracking its position.

Q10. To receive the conditions expected at your flight destination at ETA, you should request:

(a) a report, for that aerodrome

(b) a forecast, for that aerodrome

(c) an actual, for that aerodrome.

Appendix
Meteorological Charts

Charts showing surface meteorological information have been drawn on a regular basis in the UK since 1851. The style and format have changed but for many years the chart symbology has followed an agreed international practice. The forecaster's chart seen in the meteorological office may have been hand-drawn locally in black and red or have been received in monochrome by facsimile.

The forecast charts referred to in Chapter 16 that are issued to pilots are also distributed by facsimile for issue at aerodrome self-briefing units. Any changes in content or layout that are initiated by ICAO are promulgated by the CAA through yellow (operational) Aeronautical Information Circulars, the last major changes being introduced in 1984. Taking the individual charts in turn (which do have brief explanatory notes in their margins), points which are worthy of note include:

Significant weather charts: The forecast surface positions of centres of low pressure (e.g. x L956), centres of high pressure (e.g. o H1028) and fronts are shown, together with an arrow indicating the direction of movement with the speed in knots at the arrow head. Areas of significant cloud and flight conditions are shown within scalloped boundaries with base heights and tops expressed as flight levels. Areas of clear air turbulence (CAT) are shown within pecked lines and summarised in a 'box' in the corner of the chart. The maximum winds are also shown as arrows to which pennants (50 kt) and feathers (10 kt) are added to indicate the maximum speed. Tropopause heights are shown in boxes at regular intervals across the chart. It also carries a reminder to pilots that where the symbols $\mathcal{K}$ and CB appear, they imply the existence of moderate or severe turbulence and airframe icing. A section of a fixed time forecast significant weather chart for FL 250–630 with typical symbols is shown in fig. A.1.

Contour-isotach charts: Not all of the contours (shown at 400 feet intervals as solid lines) are annotated, so it may be necessary to interpolate between the values given at the edge of the chart in 100s of feet (e.g. 292 means the contour for 29 200 ft). Centres of low pressure are marked L. Isotachs are shown by pecked lines, annotated in knots, for 20 kt, 60 kt, 100 kt *et seq*. Areas of lowest speeds are annotated MIN and jet streams are shown with their speeds ▶▶▶ 155KT etc. Temperatures are negative °C shown in circles (without the –) at convenient intervals across the chart. The projection of the chart (e.g. Polar Stereographic for the N Atlantic) and a graduated scale line are also given in the margin. A section of such a 300 mb chart showing typical presentation is shown in fig. A.2.

Wind/Temperature charts: Drawn for a given flight level for a grid of selected

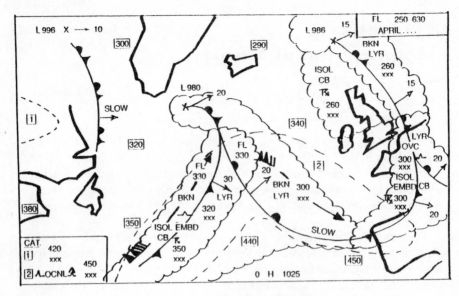

Fig. A.1   Significant weather chart

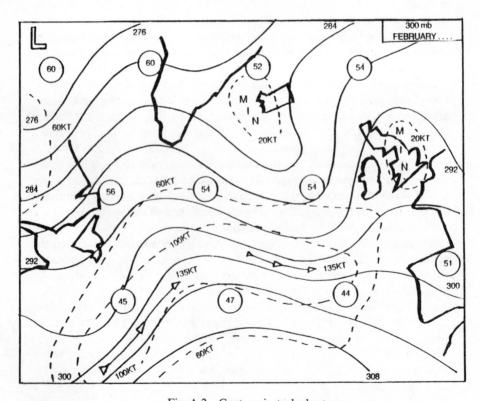

Fig. A.2   Contour-isotach chart

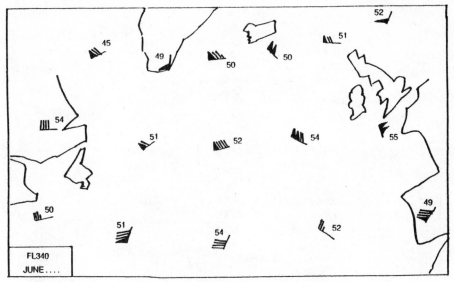

Fig. A.3   Wind/temperature chart

positions quite close together, winds are depicted by arrows flying with the wind on which pennants (50 kt) and feathers (10 kt) or half-feathers indicate the wind speed. Celsius temperatures are printed on the arrow shaft, annotated PS when plus. Figure A.3 shows the form of presentation that is used, the actual chart having the wind arrows much more closely spaced.

Spot wind and temperature charts: Data is provided for various positions across the chart of the winds and temperatures forecast for particular flight levels altitudes (given in 1000s of feet) and of the forecast altitude of the freezing level. A typical 'box' is shown in fig. A.4.

Synoptic charts – the station model
This is the forecaster's working chart and is not issued to pilots. The symbols are arranged to a conventional layout and follow an international code so wherever in the world the office may be, the information shown can be understood whatever the local language. The arrangement of symbols and a typical plotted station are shown in figs A.5 and A.6.

The surface wind direction symbol has a variable position depending upon the

24	27090	– 35
18	27085	– 23
10	28055	– 10
05	28040	– 01
02	29030	+ 06
0°C	04	

Fig. A.4   Spot winds and temperatures

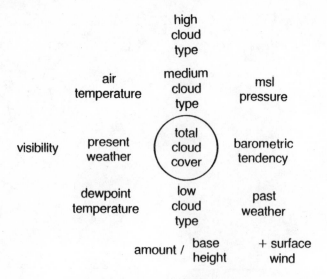

Fig. A.5   Arrangement of information

Fig. A.6   Typical station plot

wind direction, but the other elements are always plotted in the same position relative to the station circle. The decode of the individual elements is as follows. There is no particular significance in the order in which they are considered.
Surface wind. This is shown as an arrow flying with the wind. It is plotted (to the nearest 10°T, e.g. 030, 040 but not 045°T) from the direction from which the wind is blowing and its speed is shown by the 'feathers' on the arrow shaft, as follows:

Speed (kt)	Symbol	Speed (kt)	Symbol
calm	◎	33–37	
1–2	—	38–42	
3–7		43–47	
8–12		48–52	
13–17		53–57	

18–22	�	58–62	
23–27		63–67	
28–32		68–72	

Wind direction given but speed missing ✗——

Wind direction variable ⚙

Total amount of sky covered by cloud. This is shown in the station circle itself, each complete quarter representing 2/8 cloud cover.

Nil	○	³⁄₈	◔	⁶⁄₈	◕
⅛	◐	⁴⁄₈	◑	⁷⁄₈	◖
²⁄₈	◔	⁵⁄₈	◒	⁸⁄₈	●

Sky obscured ⊗

Low cloud type. This is shown immediately to the south of the station circle and the symbol decode may be summarised as:

⌒ small Cu
△ large Cu
▲ Cb without fibrous top or anvil
▆ Cb with fibrous top or anvil
⌣ Sc
⌓ Sc formed by the spreading out of Cu
— St
⋮ Fs – ragged low clouds associated with bad weather and/or precipitation
⌒ Cu and Sc with bases at different levels

Medium cloud type. This is shown immediately to the north of the station circle and the symbol decode may be summarised as:

∠ thin As
⫽ thick As or nimbostratus
ᴡ thin Ac at one level
⋊⋉ Ac formed by the spreading out of Cu
∠ Ac patches, probably lenticular and at more than one level
∠ increasing amounts of Ac
∽ As (or Ns) and Ac, or dense Ac
Ⱶ turreted Ac
∫ Ac at several levels in a chaotic-looking sky

High cloud type. This is shown to the north of the station circle and of any medium cloud symbol plotted. The symbol may be decoded as:

⌐ Ci not increasing in amount
⌐ dense Ci but not from anvil of a Cb
⌐ dense Ci from Cb anvil
╱ increasing amounts of Ci
⌐ Cs increasing

⌒ Cs increasing to high in the sky

⌒ Cs overcast

⌐ Cs not increasing

⌒ Cc

Amount, and height of base, of cloud. This information is given immediately to the south of the cloud type to which it relates. The single figure to the left of the / is the amount of that cloud in oktas (eighths) while the base height figures to the right of the / may be decoded as follows:

Code figure	*Height of base in feet*
00	Less than 100
01	100
02	200 etc

i.e. the code figure is the height in hundreds of feet, up to and including:

50	5000

51 to 55 are not used, then

56	6000
57	7000

i.e. subtract 50 from the code figure to obtain the height in thousands of feet, up to and including:

80	30 000

Height then increases by increments of 5000 feet up to

88	70 000 and
89	is over 70 000

Past weather. This relates to the period since the last synoptic report (six hours at 06, 12, etc., three hours at 03, 09, 15, etc., and one hour at 01, 02, 04, etc.) and is plotted to the south-east of the station circle and the symbol decode may be summarised as:

- ⚡ = duststorm or sandstorm
- ⤲ = storm of drifting snow
- ≡ = fog
- ❟ = drizzle
- • = rain
- ✳ = snow
- ∇ = shower(s)
- ⚡ = thunderstorm(s)

Present weather. This is shown to the west of the station circle. The basis of this code is similar to that of the past weather and it is suggested that the following is the minimum decode for the symbols that should be known by pilots:

- ∞ = Haze
- = = Mist
- ⚡ = Thunderstorm, but no precipitation at the time of observation.
- (≡) = Fog within sight
- ≡≡ = Fog in patches
- ≡⏐ = Fog, sky discernible
- ≡⏐ = Fog, sky not discernible

- ⌇ = Smoke

} Has become thinner during preceding hour

☰ = Fog, sky discernible ⎫ No appreciable change
☰ = Fog, sky not discernible ⎭ during preceding hour

⧉ = Fog, sky discernible ⎫ Has begun, or has become
⧉ = Fog, sky not discernible ⎭ thicker during preceding hour

⩳ = Fog, depositing rime, sky discernible

⩳ = Fog, depositing rime, sky not discernible

, = Drizzle, intermittent ⎫
  ,, = Drizzle, continuous ⎭ Slight

, = Drizzle, intermittent ⎫
  ,', = Drizzle, continuous ⎭ moderate

, = Drizzle, intermittent ⎫
  ,', = Drizzle, continuous ⎭ heavy

∿ = Drizzle, freezing, slight

∿ = Drizzle, freezing, heavy

, = Drizzle and rain, slight

, = Drizzle and rain, heavy

• = Rain, intermittent ⎫
•• = Rain, continuous ⎭ slight

⫶ = Rain, intermittent ⎫
•• = Rain, continuous ⎭ moderate

⫶ = Rain, intermittent ⎫
•• = Rain, continuous ⎭ heavy

∿ = Rain, freezing, slight

∿ = Rain, freezing, heavy

✻ = Rain or drizzle and snow, slight

✻ = Rain or drizzle and snow, heavy

✻ = Intermittent snow ⎫
✻ ✻ = Continuous snow ⎭ slight

✻ = Intermittent snow ⎫
✻ ✻ = Continuous snow ⎭ moderate

✻ = Intermittent snow ⎫
✻ ✻ = Continuous snow ⎭ heavy

    = Rain shower(s), slight

    = Rain shower(s), heavy

    = Rain shower(s), violent

    = Shower(s) of rain and snow, slight

    = Shower(s) of rain and snow, heavy

    = Snow shower(s), slight

    = Snow shower(s), heavy

    = Shower(s) of snow pellets or soft hail, slight

    = Shower(s) of snow pellets or soft hail, heavy

    = Shower(s) of hail, slight

    = Shower(s) of hail, heavy

    = Slight thunderstorm with rain at time of observation

    = Slight thunderstorm with snow at time of observation

    = Slight thunderstorm with hail at time of observation

    = Heavy thunderstorm with rain at time of observation

    = Heavy thunderstorm with snow at time of observation

    = Heavy thunderstorm with hail at time of observation

It will be noted that continuity of precipitation is shown by the horizontal arrangement of the symbols while intensity is given by the vertical arrangement, whether the precipitation is snow, rain or drizzle, i.e.

Intermittent

Continuous

Slight

Moderate

Heavy

Heavy shower symbols have an extra line in the triangle, while heavy thunderstorms have an extra bend in the lightning flash added to the T.

    Sometimes there is no weather occurring at the time of the observation for the meteorological observer to report. Under these conditions, the weather occurring during the last hour but not at the time of observation is shown by a symbol plotted inside a half square bracket in the normal present weather position and may be decoded as:

    = drizzle in the last hour

    = rain in the last hour

    = snow in the last hour

⦶ = rain and snow in the last hour

⦶ = freezing rain or drizzle in the last hour

⦶ = Shower(s) of rain in the last hour

⦶ = Shower(s) of snow in the last hour

⦶ = Shower(s) of hail in the last hour

⦶ = fog in the last hour

⦶ = thunderstorm in the last hour

⦶ = slight rain at the time of observation

⦶ - slight snow at the time of observation

⦶ = slight hail at the time of observation   } thunderstorm in the last hour

⦶ = heavy rain at the time of observation

⦶ = heavy snow at the time of observation

⦶ = heavy hail at the time of observation

Mean sea level pressure (QFF). This is shown to the north-east of the station circle. The value is given directly in millibars to one decimal place, with the initial 9 or 10 omitted, as is also the decimal point. This does not produce any difficulty as usually the QFF lies between 950 and 1050 millibars.

Barometric tendency. This is shown to the east of the station circle and comprises two pieces of information. The amount that the QFF value differs from that three hours earlier is plotted in tenths of a millibar and is accompanied by a symbol to show the nature of the barograph trace during the three-hour period. This is called the characteristic and may be decoded:

∧ = pressure rose but is now falling

⌐ = the rate of rise has decreased   } Pressure now higher than 3 hours ago

∕ = pressure is rising

✓ = the rate of rise has increased

∨ = pressure fell but is now rising, the same or lower than 3 hr ago   } Pressure now lower than 3 hours ago

⌐ = the rate of fall has decreased

∖ = pressure is falling

∧ = the rate of fall has increased

If pressure has fallen very quickly, the amount of the barometric tendency may be in three figures (i.e. in excess of ten millibars in three hours).

For practice, decode the following station plots extracted from an October chart for 0600 hours:

1   2   3   4   5

Test questions

Q1.   The air mass affecting station 1 is probably:
   (a) tropical maritime
   (b) polar maritime
   (c) polar continental.

Q2.   For station 5 above, the present weather and visibility are:
   (a) mist, 19 km
   (b) fog, 190 m
   (c) mist, 1900 m.

Q3.   For station 2 above, the QFF three hours earlier would have been:
   (a) 1009.1 mb
   (b) 1009.9 mb
   (c) 1013.5 mb.

Q4.   A front between stations 1 and 2 which are 100 nautical miles apart in Scotland would be:
   (a) warm front
   (b) warm occlusion
   (c) cold front.

Q5.   If the sequence of reports from station 5, then station 4, and then station 3 were observed, this would indicate the approach of:
   (a) a cold front
   (b) a warm front
   (c) returning polar maritime air.

Q6.   A warm front drawn on the chart between stations 2 and 3 would be justified in that location on the basis that from station 3 to station 2:
   (a) the visibility deteriorates, the broken low cloud becomes continuous and the wind veers
   (b) the temperature rises, the dew point temperature rises and the QFF falls from 1011.7 to 1009.5 millibars
   (c) the wind veers, the dew point temperature rises and the falling barometric pressure becomes steady.

Q7.   The height of the 0°C isotherm at station 1 which is located at an aerodrome at sea level, is:
   (a) 2000 ft
   (b) 3000 ft
   (c) 4000 ft.

Q8.   The cloud at station 4 is:
   (a) 4/8 Sc base 1800 ft amsl, 8/8 Ns base 9000 ft amsl
   (b) 4/8 Sc base 1800 ft agl, 8/8 Ns base 5900 ft agl
   (c) 4/8 Sc base 1800 ft agl, 8/8 thick As base 9000 ft agl.

Q9.   If station 3 is Amsterdam (EHAM) the appropriate METAR at 0600 hours would be:
   (a) EHAM 02025 3000 61RA 6ST05 8NS15 11/10 1012
   (b) EHAM 02025 3000 63RA 6ST005 8NS015 11/10 1011

(c) EHAM 20025 3000 63RA 6ST005 8NS015 11/10 1011.

Q10.   If the TAF for HEATHROW (EGLL) is EGLL 1701 14010 6000 61RA 5SC030 GRADU 1719 15015/25 3ST008 7SC012 TEMPO 1923 3000 62RA 5ST005 8ST010 GRADU 2301 25020 8000 WX NIL 5CU020, then the wind and visibility to be expected for a landing at midnight ($\pm$ 1 hour) are:

   (a) 250°T/20 kt, 8 kilometres
   (b) 150°T/15 kt gusting to 25 kt, 6 kilometres (temporarily 3000 metres), gradually becoming 250°/20 kt and 8 km
   (c) 150°T/15 kt, maximum 25 kt, 6 kilometres gradually becoming 250°T/20 kt, 8 km.

Answers to Multi-choice Test Questions

Chapter 1:
Q1 (c), Q2 (a), Q3 (b), Q4 (c), Q5 (a), Q6 (a), Q7 (b), Q8 (b), Q9 (c), Q10 (c)
Chapter 2:
Q1 (b), Q2 (a), Q3 (a), Q4 (c), Q5 (a), Q6 (b), Q7 (c), Q8 (b), Q9 (c), Q10 (a) 59°F
288K, (b) 32°F 0°C, (c) –5°C 268K, (d) 30°C 303K
Chapter 3:
Q1 (c), Q2 (a), Q3 (a), Q4 (c), Q5 (b), Q6 (b), Q7 (b), Q8 (c), Q9 (b), Q10 (c)
Chapter 4:
Q1 (a), Q2 (b), Q3 (b), Q4 (c), Q5 (a), Q6 (c), Q7 (b), Q8 (b), Q9 (a), Q10 (c)
Chapter 5:
Q1 (b), Q2 (a), Q3 (a), Q4 (c), Q5 (c), Q6 (a), Q7 (c), Q8 (a), Q9 (c), Q10 (c)
Chapter 6:
Q1 (c), Q2 (b), Q3 (c), Q4 (b), Q5 (b), Q6 (a), Q7 (a), Q8 (a), Q9 (c), Q10 (a)
Chapter 7:
Q1 (c), Q2 (b), Q3 (a), Q4 (a), Q5 (a), Q6 (c), Q7 (c), Q8 (c), Q9 (a), Q10 (c)
Chapter 8:
Q1 (b), Q2 (b), Q3 (c), Q4 (a), Q5 (c), Q6 (c), Q7 (c), Q8 (a), Q9 (a), Q10 (c)
Chapter 9:
Q1 (b), Q2 (c), Q3 (b), Q4 (c), Q5 (b), Q6 (b), Q7 (b), Q8 (a), Q9 (c), Q10 (c)
Chapter 10:
Q1 (a), Q2 (a), Q3 (c), Q4 (c), Q5 (b), Q6 (c), Q7 (b), Q8 (a), Q9 (c), Q10 (c)
Chapter 11:
Q1 (c), Q2 (b), Q3 (a), Q4 (a), Q5 (a), Q6 (b), Q7 (c), Q8 (c), Q9 (c), Q10 (b)
Chapter 12:
Q1 (b), Q2 (a), Q3 (c), Q4 (b), Q5 (c), Q6 (c), Q7 (c), Q8 (c), Q9 (c), Q10 (b)
Chapter 13:
Q1 (c), Q2 (c), Q3 (a), Q4 (b), Q5 (a)
Chapter 14:
Q1 (a), Q2 (b), Q3 (c), Q4 (a), Q5 (b), Q6 (a), Q7 (c), Q8 (a), Q9 (b), Q10 (b)
Chapter 15:
Q1 (c), Q2 (c), Q3 (a), Q4 (a), Q5 (a), Q6 (b), Q7 (c), Q8 (a), Q9 (c), Q10 (c)
Chapter 16:
Q1 (c), Q2 (c), Q3 (b), Q4 (b), Q5 (a), Q6 (c), Q7 (b), Q8 (c), Q9 (c), Q10 (b)
Appendix:
Q1 (b), Q2 (c), Q3 (b), Q4 (c), Q5 (b), Q6 (c), Q7 (b), Q8 (c), Q9 (c), Q10 (c)

Glossary of Abbreviations

AIREP	Aircraft report
ASR	Altimeter setting region
ATC	Air traffic control
ATCC	Air traffic control centre
ATIS	Automatic Terminal Information Service
CAA	Civil Aviation Authority
CAT	Clear air turbulence
CAVOK	Cloud and visibility OK (see Chapter 16 for full meaning)
COAT	Corrected outside air temperature
DALR	Dry adiabatic lapse rate
DME	Distance measuring equipment
ELR	Environmental lapse rate
ETA	Estimated time of arival
FIR	Flight information region
ft	feet
GMT	Greenwich mean time
HMR	Humidity mixing ratio
IAS	Indicated airspeed
ICAO	International Civil Aviation Organisation
IFR	Instrument Flight Rules
INS	Inertial navigation system
IRVR	Instrumented Runway Visual Range
ISA	International Standard Atmosphere
ITF	Inter-tropical front
ITCZ	Inter-tropical convergence zone
kt	knot
MATZ	Military aerodrome traffic zone
METAR	Aerodrome routine weather report
msl	mean sea level
NDB	Non-directional beacon
nm	nautical mile
RVR	Runway Visual Range
SALR	Saturated adiabatic lapse rate
SIGMET	Message of occurrence or expected occurrence of certain hazardous meteorological phenomena
TAF	Aerodrome forecast
UIR	Upper information region
UTC	Co-ordinated Universal Time (which replaced GMT)

VFR	Visual Flight Rules
VOLMET	Broadcast of meteorological information for pilots
WMO	World Meteorological Organisation
W/V	Wind velocity

Additionally the following abbreviations are approved by ICAO for use in meteorological reports, forecasts and warnings.

ACT	active
AMD	amended
BKN	broken cloud (5/8 to 7/8)
BLW	below
BTN	between
CIT	near or over conurbations
CLA	clear (glazed) ice formation
CLD	cloud
CNS	continuous
COR	correction
COT	coastal
CUF	cumuliform (cloud)
DENEB	fog dispersal operations
DP	dewpoint temperature
DUC	dense upper cloud
EMBD	embedded in layer cloud or haze
FBL	light (turbulence or icing)
FRQ	frequent (little separation)
GND	ground
GRADU	gradually (at a constant rate)
HURCN	hurricane
IAO	in and out of clouds
ICE	icing
INC	in cloud
ISOL	isolated (individual)
JTST	jet stream
LAN	inland or over land
LOC	locally
LSQ	line squall
LV	light and variable
LYR	layer or layered
MAR	over the sea
MOD	moderate
MON	above mountains
MTW	mountain waves
MWO	Meteorological Watch Office
MX	mixed type of ice formation
NC	no change
OBS	observed or observation
OBSC	obscured

OCNL	occasional (well separated)
OPA	opaque rime ice
OVC	overcast (8/8 cloud)
PROB	probability
RAG	ragged (cloud)
RAPID	rapid (less than one hour)
RTD	delayed (message)
SCT	scattered (1/8 to 4/8 cloud)
SEV	severe (icing or turbulence)
SFC	surface
SKC	sky clear (cloudless)
SLW	slow
STF	stratiform (cloud)
STNR	stationary
TC	tropical cyclone
TCU	towering cumulus
TDO	tornado
TYPH	typhoon
VAL	in valleys
VERVIS	vertical visibility
VRB	variable
VSP	vertical speed
WDSPR	widespread
WKN	weakening
WRNG	warning
WS	windshear
WTSPT	water spout

Index